'THIS FEMALE MAN OF GOD'

'This Female Man of God'* is a study of the controversial part played by women in the early church. In the great patristic age of Augustine, Ambrose, Jerome and Chrysostom, there were comparable women of conspicuous piety, energy and talent; these 'great men' knew women deemed equally 'great' in their own time, who are barely known to us. These women were preachers and teachers; they gave up families, homes and possessions. They took on and confounded secular potentates and religious authorities in their uncompromising pursuit of the path to God; they defied or converted their families and revolutionised their own domestic spheres. Their experiences were incredible, moving, widely inspirational, and inextricably linked to both the temporal and ecclesiastical politics of the time; they were the recipients of the most flattering attentions from the 'Fathers of the Church', yet they have received little attention since.

Gillian Cloke considers numerous examples of these women, and also takes a broad overview of the role of women in the early church. *'This Female Man of God'* is important reading for classicists, historians, theologians and gender studies specialists. Its lively, readable style will make it appeal to all those who take an interest in the changing status of women through the centuries.

Gillian Cloke took her research degree on women in the patristic age at St Andrews University. She is currently working as an administrator in Edinburgh.

* 'This female man of God' is a phrase used by Palladius in his Lausiac History, 9.1.

'THIS FEMALE MAN OF GOD'

Women and spiritual power in the patristic age, AD 350–450

Gillian Cloke

London and New York

270·2

First published 1995
by Routledge
11 New Fetter Lane, London EC4P 4EE

Simultaneously published in the USA and Canada
by Routledge
29 West 35th Street, New York, NY 10001

Typeset in Garamond by
Ponting–Green Publishing Services,
Chesham, Buckinghamshire
Printed and bound in Great Britain by
Clays Ltd, St Ives PLC

British Library Cataloguing in Publication Data
A catalogue record for this book is available from
the British Library

Library of Congress Cataloging in Publication Data
A catalogue record for this book has been requested

ISBN 0–415–09469–0 (hbk)
ISBN 0–415–09470–4 (pbk)

In memorium dilectissimam matris:
'domum suam pie tractaverat'

CONTENTS

vii

PREFACE

This book attempts to convey something of the lives and nature of certain women at a certain period of history; it has used a diversity of odd bed-fellows as its source material in so doing. In apology for occasional translational inconsistencies in presentation, then, I can only say in my own defence that I have found it to be common to this area of work. I have usually translated titles to Latin and Greek works, exceptions being where the original title seemed to me more instantly recognisable and thus affording less confusion; and those (for instance some of John Chrysostom's tracts) where the titles are equally unwieldy in both languages and easier to abbreviate in the original. Periodical titles are abbreviated following the conventions of *l'Année Philologique*.

It is a great pleasure to me to be able to set down in print the debts of gratitude I owe, to colleagues, friends and family. From my former studies which led me finally to this point, my deepest respect and affection go first and foremost to Eda Forbes, without whom I should have fallen at the very first hurdle; and to Miriam Griffin and John Matthews, both of whom have inspired so many besides myself with a desire to 'do something *more*' in this field. In St Andrews, where this book originated in a research degree, I owe more than I can say to the Department of Ancient History with its unique talent for blending scholasticism, support, humour, gossip, and a boot from behind where needed; and particularly to my colleague in the enviable life of a research student, Scottie, who kept me sane and instilled in me a little of each of his humanity, his sense of proportion, and his Gaelic. The greatest debt of gratitude, however, goes to my former supervisor and current mentor, confidante and prop, Jill Harries. Jill's meticulous scholarship lifted my aspirations; her unstinted assistance lifted my spirit at times of crisis and uncertainty.

Without her unremitting care I could have finished neither my research nor this book: I consider myself fortunate beyond words to have been her pupil.

For personal support, there is not space to mention everyone: but deep thanks must go to some in particular. To Christine for her intelligent proof-reading, and to Gillian Clark and Linda McGuire, who read this work in its earlier stages with sympathetic but stringent editorial suggestions (for the faults which remain, I alone am responsible); to Sharon and Marie-Louise, for nurturance and good-neighbourliness; to Julia, Sophie and Katie, for inspiration and affection and for great forbearance with my woes when they had so many of their own; above all to Peter, who has shared few of the joys of this book-making process but *all* of its miseries and whose love and support has been so vital. My family also have borne patiently with me during what must have seemed an interminable time. Thanks go to my adored Big Brothers, Jon and Geoff, who have now been inspired to emulation of that manifestly enviable life of the research student. But 'the eldest have borne most': this work owes its existence to the faith and support of my father and step-mother, Malcolm and Roz. It owes its inspiration to three warmly, inspiringly indomitable sisters: Lindy; Jackie; and, above all, Daphne, for me the very first 'strong woman of the Church'; to whose memory it is lovingly dedicated.

ABBREVIATIONS

AJAH	*American Journal of Ancient History*
Alph.	Alphabetical collection of the *Apophthegmata Patrum*
Apoph.	*Apophthegmata Patrum*
CIL	*Corpus Inscriptionum Latinarum*
CJ	*Codex Justinianus*
Conf.	*Confessions* (Augustine)
CPh	*Classical Philology*
CSCO	*Corpus Scriptorum Christianorum Orientalis* (Louvain 1903–)
D.	*Digest*
EH	*Ecclesiastical History* (various authors)
GCS	*Die griechischen christlichen Schriftsteller der ersten drei Jahrhunderte*
HM	*History of the Monks in Egypt*
JAAR	*Journal of the American Academy of Religion*
JRS	*Journal of Roman Studies*
JTS	*Journal of Theological Studies*
LH	*Lausiac History* (Palladius)
PBSR	*Proceedings of the British Academy*
PG	*Patrologia Graeca* (Migne)
PL	*Patrologia Latina* (Migne)
PJ	*The Verba Seniorum of Pelagius the Deacon and John the Subdeacon*
SC	*Sources Chrétiennes*
SPCK	The Society for Promoting Christian Knowledge
TAPhA	*Transactions and Proceedings of the American Philological Association*

1

INTRODUCTION
'Holy' women?

About this time . . . Danus was accused by his wife, who wished merely to frighten him, of some trivial offences. Somehow or other Rufinus . . . shamelessly seduced this light woman and then cajoled her into a dangerous plot. He persuaded her to accuse her innocent husband of treason by weaving a tissue of lies . . .

(Ammianus Marcellinus *Histories* 16.8)

Many women of high birth were convicted of the disgrace of adultery or fornication and put to death. Among these the most notorious were Claritas and Flaviana; for when the latter was being taken to her death, even the clothing that she wore was ripped off her back, nor was she allowed enough to keep even her private parts covered . . . Esaias, with some others who had been convicted for committing adultery with Rufina, was attempting to have her husband Marcellus tried for treason . . . in the midst of these horrors and others like them a married woman called Hesychia, who was charged with an attempted crime and kept under guard in the house of an official, was in such terror of torture that she pressed her face into the feather bed on which she was lying and killed herself by suffocation.

(Ammianus Marcellinus *Histories* 28.1)

Who can sufficiently praise our dear Lea's mode of living? . . . becoming the head of a convent, she proved a true mother to the virgins in it: she wore harsh sackcloth instead of soft woven fabric, passed sleepless nights in prayer, instructing her companions more by her own example than by instruction. Her humility was so great that she, once the mistress of many, was

1

now the servant of all ... She was heedless of her dress, neglected her hair and only ate the roughest food.

(Jerome *Let.* 23.2)

Shut up in her narrow cell [Asella] wandered in paradise. Her recreation was fasting and her refreshment was hunger... she took her gold necklace made in the lamprey style ... and without the knowledge of her parents, sold it. Then putting on the kind of sombre dress her mother had never wanted her to wear she concluded her pious undertaking by consecrating herself henceforth to the Lord.

(Jerome *Let.* 24.3)

Marcella ... refrained from eating meat, and she knew the scent of wine but not its taste ... She rarely appeared in public and took pains to shun the houses of great ladies so that she would not have to see what she had renounced for all time ... She gave away her ornaments and other possessions to people already rich, content to throw her money away rather than grieve her mother.

(Jerome *Let.* 127.4)

This book examines the kind of women Jerome was writing about; and where and why they chose to part company with the lives of the women of whom Ammianus was writing. It explores the abandonment of many of the classical models for womanhood with the increasing appeal of a life of dedication to an ideal of Christianity amongst women in the world of the later Roman Empire. It examines the rise in popularity of (particularly) ascetic Christianity in the later fourth century and early fifth century, from the grass roots of the movement through to its purchase at the top end of the social scale; and looks at the religious adventures and endeavours of clusters of extremely devout Christian women during the period referred to as the patristic age. It is an attempt to give an overall picture of the form, nature and scope of their activities; of the thinking of their peers, both clerical and lay, about them, set in a context of social background and perceptions.

This is a period and a topic rife with inconsistency and ambiguity: such an exploration is made more complicated by being on the knife-edge of the boundary between the classical and the early mediaeval world. Consider the above excerpts. They were taken from two roughly contemporaneous eyewitness accounts of incidents involving female activities in urban Roman life towards the end of the fourth century. They could scarcely be more different; indeed, they barely seem to represent the same place. The first set are part of an account by a pagan, a historian of Roman times and *moeurs* in the traditional mould, of current society *causes célèbres*: this account is in its form and content entirely the product of classical antiquity. The second set are descriptions by a Christian writer of much venerated colleagues and their ministries, in what was to become a semi-formulaic hagiographical manner: the form and content of this writing is the property of theologians and church historians.

To think of these two accounts as to the same degree historical, and the events they relate as happening almost side by side requires a pause, and a reframing of perceptions. Happening at the same time, they yet demand a completely different set of mental furniture. The one is experienced as classical history and the other as church history – and it is difficult to fit the two into the same frame of reference because these two sorts of history are viewed on such different levels. (From having trained simultaneously with both classical historians and mediaevalists, it is a divide over which I am perhaps particularly sensitive.) It is salutary to think that the same framework of events and personalities were known to both the two men, both writing of the Rome they had lived and worked in at much the same time. It is still more salutary to consider for a moment that the women they are writing about could be the *same women* – except for their fates. They were out of the same social bracket, the senatorial top-drawer élite: however, those written of by Ammianus are the proper and fitting heirs to their classical foremothers such that it could be Dio Chrysostom or Suetonius writing, and the tone is resolutely reminiscent of the golden age of imperial Rome. Jerome's women are already the precursors of Radegund and Hildegard in the twilight world of early mediaeval devotion and they have become most definitely the representatives of the church and church historians; it is the kind of rhetoric which will set the tone for Gregory of Tours, Helgaud and Bede.

This sets a context for the topic I have chosen to write on: just where did the change come about? And, particularly, who were these 'holy' women, and where do they come into it? We know rather a lot about the holy men at this time: of pious males there was something of an embarrassment of riches at this period. These were the men who moulded Christianity as we know it and have been dogging it ever since; just as an example, note how many quotations

3

from Augustine, Ambrose, Jerome and Chrysostom have surfaced in the recent debate on the ordination of women. But: what women? I have found when people have enquired into my topic – even those knowing more than a little about the era – that the almost automatic question has been, '*Were* there any holy women?' – closely followed by, 'you can't have found many . . . (subtext: or we surely would have heard about them)'. Yes; many. There were large numbers of extremely active women of high-profile piety at this time, some of them enormously wealthy, powerful and influential, the stars of their contemporary Christian stage no less than the men. It is more lately that they have come to be overlooked so completely.

The period covered in this book is fairly limited in scope, the boundaries being the last half of the fourth century and the first half of the fifth; limited of necessity because of the enormous amount happening in it. This is the period of settlement and reconsideration following the success of the battle of the Christian movement for legitimacy; of the church coming to terms with the consequences of moving from martyrdom to mainstream in one generation: a sea-change that left church writers floundering as much as secular sources. Take, for instance, the two turning-points highlighted in Peter Brown's influential 1961 study of the effect of Roman women in the process of christianisation in this period: the deaths of Vettius Praetextatus Agorius and Rufius Antonius Agrypnius Volusianus. Between the deaths of these two – similarly high-profile, self-consciously state-oriented pagans with a generation between them – the known world changed in an upsurge of barbarian, Christian and, as I hope to show, female activity. Praetextatus died in 384: two years after Gratian's official disestablishment of pagan cults in Rome, and in the same year as the impassioned debate between pagan and Christian influences on the Emperor over the removal of the Altar of Victory from the senate house, and as the arrival in Rome of Augustine, and probably Ammianus. Volusianus died in 437 – and his not-quite-forcible deathbed conversion, smiling through clenched teeth at the interference of his niece Melania the Younger, was indicative of the writing on the wall. In between the deaths of these two aristocratic old recidivists, *Roma aeterna* was sacked, as were many of the temples representing much that had been most civilised about classical antiquity; Ambrose, Augustine, Jerome, Chrysostom, Basil and their kind were industriously pouring out the stuff that was to change the face of the world; and the larger part of their aristocratic contemporaries adopted Christianity.

4

Some of these contemporaries, aristocratic and otherwise, are to be found amongst the 'holy' women I have studied – but only some. Many women of the later Roman period found assimilating Christianity did not alter their experience or perceptions of life by much; as with today, levels of observance varied with belief. For many men and women, the same diurnal round of life went on as it had; going to church rather than to the temples was simply assimilated as part of life and did not necessarily impinge much on their view of the world around them or their response to it. Amongst such men, attending church became a public relations necessity in the same way that sacrificing to the Gods had been (Ammianus Marcellinus *Histories* 21.2), and assassination was as likely to happen to a general returning from church as from a pagan ritual (*ibid.* 15.5); women would make visits to churches and *martyria* the occasions of assignations in the same way their forebears had used temple-going (Jerome *Let.* 107.9, 147), or were even seduced in church, by church functionaries (Sozomen *EH* 7.16). Many women still lived under the spell of the wealthy, dissipated social world over which Roman writers had moralised for centuries. The women Ammianus wrote of in the scandalous adultery trials did not evidently notice that they were living in a period identifiable specifically by its Christianity; in a time, moreover, when it behoved each soul to behave as if they were to be carried off to heaven on the next cloud.

But this is part of the fascination of this particular area of study. In large part, the women about whom I am writing as heroines of Christian rhetoric and legend were the same kind of women as the *causes célèbres* written of by Ammianus; the same upper-class heroines (and villainesses) who would have attracted note in 'classical' antiquity, for inspiring or betraying their menfolk, or perhaps for contributing to the well-being of their *patria* – but in this generation they employed these qualities rather differently. Ammianus was writing about a world that does not, in his account, seem to be much different from that of previous Roman historians – but it was: and it was changing fast, most notably in the persons and activities of its citizens. The women examined in this book were those for whom a belief in Christianity not only impinged on their view of the world but for whom it necessitated an active change; women emanating from an unexceptional family or social background, who subsequently made a decision to distance themselves from it. Some women at this time thought deeply about the nature of Christianity and the logical conclusions of Christian commandments, and determined to carry them out to the best of their abilities. These women often 'removed' themselves – altogether in a literal and physical sense, or just slightly, within their own homes and minds – from the common course of events, in order to pursue a greater level of concentration on the things of holiness. In doing so, they were perceived by their families and peers as being 'holy'; were thought of as as being 'soldiers of Christ', 'renowned', 'known for virtue'; as overtly playing with different goal-posts from others of their circles. Their 'different' motivations were evident to those around them and they were accordingly identified and described by their 'different' status. I shall examine this phenomenon, how it was believed to happen in women, and how the theologians said it should affect them. However, women following this different motivation were less susceptible of obvious definition than the men following it, who had a clear variety of acceptable, definable paths available to them: reader, deacon, monk, priest, bishop and so on. I shall therefore also examine the routes to a holy lifestyle women did find, both those accepted and those disallowed.

For this has long been the problem with this period and this topic of study: for years, even centuries, the thought, decisions and writings of the churchmen of the patristic age have been influential entirely in self-referential terms; observed and studied rather as if these men, and their ideas, arose out of a vacuum – the ideas in themselves, the pure thought produced, all that need be considered. But no thought arises out of a vacuum. All ideas are the product of an environment: and in this case, the fathers' thought-processes were the product of a female environment – that is to say an environment set up, maintained by and filled with (pious) females – as I shall show. These great men of their age were bought and sold by women. One common and unifying fact about these patristic church writers – of Augustine, John Chrysostom, Gregory of Nazianzus, Gregory of Nyssa, Palladius, Rufinus, and most conspicuous of all, Jerome – is that they were surrounded and supported by women; relays of women. In addition, most of them attest to an early female influence, specifically defined in terms of Christian piety, on their subsequent development.

For this is the crux of what I discovered when I was researching for this study: the absolute ubiquity of these 'holy' women – once one starts to look for them. It is not possible – or it should not be possible – to separate them from a study of the patristic age, for they are everywhere: humble women from the lowest levels of the social strata adopting harsh lives as hermits with such frequency that priests and monks tripped over them at every turn; middle class *Hausfraus* planting ideological trip-wires in the consciences of their children and turning out priests, monks and bishops by the seminary-load; on up to the élite women of the very top-drawer who gave up on secular life and their worldly possessions to such an extent that they precipitated economic crises at the heart of the empire.

This is, of course, partly an attempt to justify what may look like a loose frame of reference for this study: looking only for pious Christian women of the mid-fourth to mid-fifth centuries, there was just so much going on, ranging from the intriguing and enlightening to the simply weird, that I felt there was a great need for a general over-view of how much pious female activity and of what different kinds was taking place; and, particularly, how the different classes of women and styles of activity interwove and cross-fertilised each other. Much ink has been expended in the examination of certain of the upper-class women, mainly by classicists – but not all of them and certainly not all together and as a consideration of the phenom-enon they collectively presented. Further examination has been done into some of the aspects of the female side of monasticism, predominantly by church historians; but again, in a variety of fragmented and discrete studies. This is an attempt to demonstrate how much activity was happening, amongst how many females all within a short space of time, and how great was the cross-referencing between them.

A particular phenomenon taken to denote the presence of 'holi-ness' in individuals of this age was the decision to adopt a sterner than usual version of the Christian life: the undertaking of an 'ascetic' life. After some generations since legitimacy, participation in Christianity, and observing a degree of commitment within it, had normalised and settled down, relatively speaking. The trend that in our period is perceptibly odd and separate and special, and goes some way to filling the gap left by martyrdom as a sign of extra commitment to the faith, is the decision for some kind of ascetic life. And a consideration of the ascetic movement further reinforces the need for looking at aristocratic women of the courts of Rome and Constantinople and peasant women from the deserts of Eygpt, Palestine and Syria in the same volume – and the same breath. The ascetic movement encompassed both and the former learned their asceticism at the instance and example of the latter.

The disparity cannot be overstated between these women who

admired and imitated each other. The women who have traditionally tended to attract the attention of both the fathers and classical historians were out of the very top drawer of society. For a suitable comparison of today one would have to imagine women with the material resources and position in public awareness of, say, Princess Diana and the Duchess of Kent, Ivana Trump and Leona Helmsley, and then imagine them all being swept away by the teachings of the Plymouth Brethren or the Reverend Sun Myung Moon; to such a degree of commitment as to make over all their resources to the movement, doff their power-dressing and executive lifestyles in favour of wearing jeans and tee-shirts, living in shabby communes and handing out tracts on street-corners. The change, for some of the objects of my study, between the environment from which they emanated and that which they chose to adopt was really that extreme: it was not just that they 'got religion', but that some of them took to one of the most excessive and dramatic versions of it, on the far fringe of acceptability. And, further, this was a version that was causing severe angst amongst those in the upper echelons of their own church, who were most acutely aware of the church's need to acquire gentrification. And these blue-blooded women learned their extremism at the instance of the women of the *humiliores*. Some aristocrats fled to the environs and the influence of the peasants and vowed great envy of the simplicity and directness of the latter's route to God – though not infrequently finding the reality rather different from their enthusiasts' imaginings. They then told tales to their own disadvantage of how they had been wrong-footed and edified by these holy peasants; witness the experiences of Melania the Elder, Melania the Younger and Paula. And Marcella and her ladies 'created a desert in the city', trying for the coenobitic life without the wilderness, in their exaggerated admiration for all they could learn of what seemed to be a more direct route to God than the urban and urbane modes of worship they knew already. Then, in their turn becoming spearheads of such tendencies, these ladies became themselves models and mentors to others and attracted many women of all stations around them. Because of the inter-relatedness of these influences it is impossible to examine one without the other; in addition to which the attitudes and problems attendant upon the decision for this life show root similarities which belie the different conditions of the women undertaking them.

But women in particular had to be careful in adopting this kind of extreme tack. From Eve onwards, women were seen by the Christian theorists as the natural first victims of deception, and from the very first condemnation of the very first non-orthodox tendency were regarded peculiarly apt pupils at propagating heresy; 'Do not pay heed to a woman, O Israel. Lift yourself above the evil designs of woman, for it is woman who hunts for the precious souls of men . . . Do not believe a vulgar woman: for every heresy is a vulgar woman' (Epiphanius *Medicine Box* 79.8), a view reinforced by experience of the 'petticoat troubles' of Montanists, Donatists, Pelagians, Circumcellions and so on and so forth. Jerome had a hit-list of such examples:

> It was with the help of the whore Helena that Simon Magus founded his sect; troops of women accompanied Nicholas of Antioch, that inventor of pollutions; it was a woman that Marcion sent as his precursor to Rome, to undermine the souls of men in readiness for his traps; . . . Montanus . . . used two wealthy noblewomen, Prisca and Maximilla first to bribe and then to subvert many churches; . . . when Arius was determined to lead the world into darkness, he commenced by deceiving the Emperor's sister; it was the resources of Lucilla that helped Donatus to pervert many people throughout Africa with his filthy version of baptism.
>
> (Jerome *Let*. 133.4)

Women were ever first with new movements (though few, if any, of their contemporary critics made the link that this was one of the factors responsible for the swifter spread also of mainstream Christianity): but found, all too often, what had seemed firm ground cut from under them with a more or less arbitrary decision by a pope or church council that a previously tolerated movement was in fact heterodox.

This is not a study of women of the heretical movements – it has enough to do to keep up with notable women accepted by the 'legitimate' church: but this thinking underlines the difficulties for many female worshippers of the time. Women were amongst the first and most ardent followers of patristic preaching; and caused great discomfort to the said preachers by at times taking the preaching too literally. Witness the embarrassment of writers who must explain to over-ardent female devotees why their teaching should not in fact be followed: who, for instance, having preached greatly on the virtues of chastity and poverty, were forced to explain to a wife why she must not then desert her husband to pursue these 'preeminent virtues'; or, having lauded the virgin life to the skies, had to explain to a teenage girl who had chained herself to the altar in mid-service in protest at family opposition why, though manifestly the most blessed state, virginity should still not be undertaken in defiance of her family (see p. 130 and 137).

A century before, this kind of vehemence had been perceived by church writers as a positive characteristic, one that provided women with the tenacity to make a martyr like Perpetua or Felicitas, and encouraged other, perhaps weaker, believers. In the later patristic age vehemence meets with an ambivalent attitude; some of these women earned admiration, but some, as those above, were seen as an embarassment to a church that was learning the need to fit itself to the established world rather than stand in opposition to it. This was the expression of the tension between the mainstream tendencies of the more urbane church leaders and the apocalyptic preaching of those embracing the eschatological thinking that taught that the twilight of the world was nigh. While this was a dilemma experienced by the whole church, there was a particular edge to it for women: whether to knuckle under to the more oppressive rhetoric, become quieter and more submissive – particularly given the automatic association of their more extreme activities with suspicions of heresy; or (as some of their supporters seem to have been advocating) to become yet more noisy and notorious in their piety, flaunting the strength of the 'weaker sex' to shame others into better lives.

With this in mind, I shall be highlighting mainly 'orthodox', patristically approved women; with a leavening of 'unorthodox' and vilified women to demonstrate how they became unacceptable. This last verdict, however, can be a delicate distinction to draw when one cleric's meat for debate was another cleric's poison, and women were praised or denounced for comparable actions simply depending on which writer addressed them; even the same woman could be called by the same cleric at different times 'the most noble of the women of Rome' and the new Thecla (Jerome *Chronici Canones*), and 'she whose black name bears witness to the darkness of her treachery' (Jerome *Let.* 133.3). A saint for some, Melania the Elder became 'tainted' for others with her Origenism, to the extent that she was thought too dubious a figure for even a word of her to appear in the account written of the life of her grand-daughter and namesake, Melania the Younger – even though it was the example of her 'dubious' grandmother that had propelled this saintly lady into taking up the life. And this decision by male writers, to vilify or beatify, in itself was largely a matter of luck, dependent on the 'star' cleric to which a devout woman chose to hitch her wagon. Melania had simply supported and served Rufinus and followed him into his intellectual dilemmas as Paula did Jerome; it was very much the luck of the draw that Melania and Rufinus became suspected 'heretics' rather than Jerome and Paula (and given how many more people Jerome upset, to many of their contemporaries it seemed a close-run contest). Following the 'wrong' cleric was all part of the dangers of being devout for women, whether aristocrat or peasant – as witness the circumcellion women or those 'deceived' by Donatist priests (see p. 76).

As far as the actual writing on women goes, the 'celebrities' are certainly useful for detailed information and analysis, and the possibility of some kind of account of their entire life being un-covered to us; their problems are those attendant on their fame, i.e. a tendency of writers on them to tidy up loose ends. (Not uniformly, though; some of the *Vitae* from this period are all too evidently just in the middle of the divide mentioned earlier in this chapter; they hover fascinatingly, if uncomfortably, between representing the tail-end of the Roman tradition of warts-and-all portraiture and the beginning of the mediaeval style of spotless hagiography.) The achievements of the humbler women tend to be told of more in anecdotal cameos, or in the context of an account of a community. Their problems must have been more typical to the general ex-perience of women in this age and life and we do know a reasonable amount from them; their problems or enlightenments are told us, though often without much of a background to the life of the woman or community from whom it comes – but, on the other hand, without the sanitising that dogs the accounts of the saints.

So the juxtaposition of individuals and communities, highborn and humble, East and West: the kind of testimony that has attracted some unfavourable opinions as being 'the anecdotal evidence of stray items from diverse sources' (cf. Saller and Garnsey 1987) I have used extensively. This is because it serves to illustrate, not least, how very extensive is such evidence, how widely divergent and yet how similar; and because at the other end of the spectrum lie dangers of being too narrow, too skewed towards the doings of the aristocracy and urban dwellers. But in the period I am observing, the élite and those writing the tale of their times became suddenly, over-whelmingly interested in the doings of those who previously would barely have merited an inch of expensive writing-space. So I have

11

taken in both ends of the spectrum in my overview, using whatever it can uncover: juxtaposing literary and anecdotal evidence with whatever can be gleaned from medical notes, legal asides, epigrams, letters, tombstones and inscriptions; above all, attempting to set the patristic sources aside for the moment from their almost intrinsic permeation with the odour of sanctity and legality attendant on a theological text, and subjecting them to the godless scrutiny of the social historian. This approach is the more necessary because, unlike in other areas of study, one of the outstanding and most frequently stressed problems with the study of women in the early church is the lack of an authentic voice from those most nearly concerned; as I shall deal with in the next chapter.

2

PATRISTIC PERCEPTIONS
The sources and the problems

The women in this study, inspired by the ascetic Christian tendencies of their age, will be observed mainly from the viewpoint of the patristic authors. It is through these male commentators we must look at the women: from them learn the kind of rhetoric addressed to women and their condition, the models held up for imitation, exemplary females adduced from personal experience; and from them receive assessments of whether and how women lived up to the ideals projected for them. All of this has to be received through the medium of the church Fathers of necessity. The first and most obvious problem in studying women of the early church is that what these women thought of themselves and their devotions has not survived in their own writings – though some of the writers purport to be using their words.

The only writings indisputably by women from this period are fairly peripheral in their usefulness: the *Pilgrimage of Egeria*, the *Cento* of Faltonia Betitia Proba, and the *Martyrdom of St Cyprian* by the Empress Eudocia. Of these three, *Egeria* is the only factual, personalised account and provides a partial portrait of one well-to-do devotee in action at an isolated point in her life: but it has all the limitations of a travel diary, and a fragmentary and problematic one at that. Its provenance and even the identity of its heroine are dubious; she is profoundly unhelpful with names and details of the personalities she meets *en route*; and this is a circumspection that even extends to information about herself. The work tells us very little of her and her sisters' more normal surroundings, activities and thoughts, and thus deprives us of a first-hand participant's account of a community of nuns of the time.[1] Proba's *Cento* is a devotional epic poem on the life of Christ composed entirely (in the commonly-used cento format of the day) from lines and half-lines of Virgil. On a literary level it argues a massive knowledge of Virgil as well as of theology, and the work, despite Jerome's harsh comments[2] achieved a certain success as a popular school text into the middle ages (and that despite Gelasius' decree of 496 relegating it to be included in the 'apocalyptic' writings, to be used only for private reading). Nonetheless, its interest is primarily literary, and for the fact of a much read best-seller of the day having been written by a woman. Eudocia's *Life of St Cyprian* was the only one to survive of a reputed six works by her, including poetic paraphrases of the Octateuch and of the prophets Daniel and Zacharias, a paean to her husband Theodosius' victory over the Persians in 422 and a Homeric cento on the life of Christ. Evidently a widely-read lady of some energy, she is perhaps not best represented by her sole surviving work, which is gullible, fantastical and full of the metaphysical preoccupations of the time. By intention at least of historical/hagiographical purport, *Cyprian* is for the purposes of any kind of serious investigation or critique of its author's times about as helpful as *Hello!* magazine would be for future social historians of this era.

This being so, we are left with mainly the copious but tendentious writings of the male authors in order to try and gain an understanding of the lot of women; the limitations of this are self-evident. We can examine what we are told by the patristic sources of these women's motivations and their practical pursuit of their vocations, set them in the context of their social milieu, and consider the various pressures on them from church and social background. But while attempts can be made to discern the real, as opposed to the attributed, motives of the women concerned, it must always be borne in mind that all of what we can deduce is filtered through the outlook of the male writers and what they wish to highlight, or fail to tell us. Any direct question of what women really thought of what they did is self-frustrating. Even when considering what can be learned inadvertently, from the ways in which women made achievements that surprised the patristic writers, or how they were reckoned to have failed, we are still faced in that telling with a mass of patristic presuppositions that render any sense of objectivity largely spurious. The best effects can be achieved by juxtaposing social evidence with the clerical rhetoric to come up with a more overall picture; evidence to be found in legal documentation and epigraphic material. The legal sources, though equally from the male perspective, are perhaps more representative of the overall social picture and give more insight into factors such as the pressure on the more unorthodox to conform. But for the actual written detail of the lives of pious women of these centuries we should remember at all times that we are in the invidious position of interpreting what the Fathers reported women as doing in response to what the Fathers advised them to do.

The absence of written evidence by women is not to say that they did not contribute to the intellectual life of the period; the foremost Christian women of the day were obviously greatly aware of the importance of scholastic and literary skills in disseminating Christianity. Literarily admired women studied and argued on theology and biblical commentaries and studies, or assisted established male authorities, as did Melania the Elder, Melania the Younger, Marcella, Paula, Eustochium and Olympias. Their scholarly capacities seem frequently so prodigious as to astound the men who wrote of them; Melania the Elder,[3] for instance, evidently could have taught some of her male colleagues a thing or two in this respect according to Palladius:

> being very industrious and loving literature, she turned night into day, perusing every writing of the ancient commentators including 3,000,000 lines of Origen and 250,000 of Gregory, Stephen, Pierius, Basil and other standard writers. Nor did she read them through only once and casually, but laboriously went through each book seven or eight times.
>
> (*LH* 60)

Jerome's distinguished follower Marcella,[4] he says, asked questions he found hard to answer and corrected priests – giving her pronouncement as Jerome's in order not to offend,

For she knew that the apostle had said: "I suffer not a woman to teach" (1 Tim. 2:12), and she did not wish to seem to inflict a wrong upon the male sex, many of whom questioned her (including priests sometimes) concerning obscure and doubtful points.

(Jerome *Let.* 127.7)

She also worked with him against Origenism, writing a succession of letters challenging the heretics and helping to get them condemned. Jerome himself complained of the exactions of her detailed theological queries and the demands she made on his writing due to her never-satisfied intellectual curiosity. Paula and her daughter Eustochium[5] learned Greek and Hebrew, until they were more proficient in it than Jerome, to assist him in his studies; indeed, he recommend to another Christian lady, Laeta, that her small daughter be educated in Greek,

15

just as boys were, with small bribes to expedite her learning.[6] This kind of learning was, it seems, what devout women were understood to excel in: the literacy which might be of use in support of men, translating, copying, disseminating what they themselves might not write. Melania the Younger[7] won fame for her community's industrious copying and dissemination of texts known for their elegance and correctness.[8]

But women of this period, however literate and literary, did not, it seems, comment on what they found around them, and did not write history. Nor do their undoubted contributions to the epistolary rounds survive.[9] Jerome, Augustine and Chrysostom preserved copies of their outgoing letters to these women, but none of the letters that provoked their replies. The judgements on the times and the participants were made by the Fathers; trained rhetors, lawyers, philosophers turned Christian theorists, or sometimes sincere, undistinguished men justified by inspiration.

The only outstanding exception to this general rule is in the *Apophthegmata Patrum*, the anonymously written collections of the *Sayings* of the desert Fathers, which, amongst the collected wisdom of a myriad, frequently anonymous, coenobites and eremites, include what purport to be the teachings of three women, in their own reported speech. While making it clear at least that there were women of renown in the desert communities, with sayings attributed to them which were thought worthy of inclusion in the collections, this evidence needs its own caveat: as oral tradition transmitted to written memorials of Coptic, Syriac, Aramaic, Greek and (later) Latin origins by copyists who 'did not regard themselves as bound to transfer any written material that they had without change' (Ward 1975a: xiii), and with a premium placed on spiritual edification over historical authenticity – 'written to answer the question in the mind of the reader, "Why am I told this?" not the question "How did this come about?"' (Ward 1987: 91) – the *Sayings of the Fathers* are frustrating as often as they are illuminating and to be used with care. The voices of the women reported by them are sufficiently different and have enough incidental personal detail to seem to be reasonably representative; but 'authenticity' is a will-o'-the-wisp quality when applied to writings emanating from the desert.

Bearing these reservations in mind, however, holy women were a frequent enough source of inspiration to Christian writers of the fourth and fifth centuries to be extremely well observed, from the centrally influential ascetics of Rome and Constantinople in their aristocratic 'cells' to the extreme eremitic tendencies of the desert mothers. Individually eminent women particularly attracted wide documentation. When Olympias turned her back on secular glory and combated the establishment on behalf of Chrysostom (see p. 181), we hear of it from two ecclesiastical historians, Sozomen and Palladius of Helenopolis, as well as from her anonymous hagiographer, and from Chrysostom's own letters.[10] When Melania the Elder left family, friends, and the centre of the civilised world in favour of self-immolation in Palestine (see p. 94), we have the voices of Palladius, Jerome and Paulinus of Nola as witness[11]; on Proba, Anicia Juliana and Demetrias we have Jerome, Augustine and Pelagius. The presence of these women generated sermons and homilies, on them and to them, inspirational works, commentaries and exegesis, histories, *Vitae*, and, often most revealing, letters.

The first obvious categorisation to make of male writers on women is that of the many who can offer observations derived from close personal relations with women of conspicuous piety; many of the eminent writers and male saints of the period seem to have their own devoutness inspired, reflected, or actually directed by a sister, a mother, an aunt of particularly devotional disposition. Piety seems to beget piety in certain families in this field of survey; the writers so studied all too frequently acknowledge the benign influence of a devout female relative.

Certainly Augustine, one of the most prolific and influential writers of the fourth century, found his progress towards catholicism (and his attempted evasion of it) dogged by feminine influence. His mother Monica was a strong-minded woman of deep and unwavering devotion to her faith and the provincial African church traditions she had always known, [12] and she upheld these for her son against the indifference of his pagan father, Patricius. Hers was the more resonant presence in his upbringing in small-town Thagaste, a presence that after he was grown he could not escape: she continued to pursue him, first in person when he rebelled against her beliefs, and after her death by still occupying a deep-rooted place within his conscience. His treatment of Monica's life in his *Confessions*, and his further references to her influence in more general works of theology such as *De Beata Vita* and *De Ordine* are unique for the clear light in which they show his piety as relative to hers and her influence as the deciding factor in his capitulation to his vocation. Gregory of Nazianzus was another cleric created by the ambition of a formidable mother. His mother Nonna, herself from an impeccably Christian family, also ensured her talented son was brought up austerely in her own beliefs during his early upbringing in and around the family estates at Nazianzus in south-west Cappadocia. In all Gregory's writings on the personal, Nonna has a prominent place, cast as responsible for the ordination of his father and himself, and the main influence on his sister's devout lifestyle also, by his account. In the case of Gregory of Nyssa, his elder sister Macrina was the strong influence on their mother Emmelia along with the rest of the family: he related of his sister in his *Life of Macrina* how she bore the responsibility for his ordination and that of his brothers, Basil of Caesarea and Peter, having practically brought them up and completed their education herself. Besides this she trained her mother in the religious life, the two women finally co-instituting a convent at the family estates at Annesi. Gregory's manner in the *Life of Macrina* when treating of her intellectual and spiritual apparatus verges on the awe-struck; and in his account of her counselling to his vocation are telling echoes of the 'big sister' whom he still seems to consider very much his intellectual superior.

Other sources with female relatives eminently suitable for similar eulogisation are less helpful. John Chrysostom was possessed of a mother, Anthusa, who, widowed early and left in sole charge of the upbringing of her brilliant son, was a woman able to draw encomia on the superior quality of Christian motherhood out of even notably misogynistic pagans; as well as an aunt who was a deaconess noted by Palladius.[13] But he writes only incidentally and reprovingly of his mother and emphasises how in certain respects her maternal concern overcame her devoutness: she tried to prevent him becoming a priest. Ambrose's few extant letters to his sister Marcellina, the superior of a convent, tell us almost nothing about her, serving only to enlighten us as to Ambrose's situation; though in this connection it is worth observing that the otherwise more helpful Augustine has a similarly unregarded and barely attested sister (and according to some traditions two); we know that he constructed a rule for a convent run by her but from him we do not even know her name.

Paulinus of Nola is very nearly as frustrating: usefully related as he was to the famous Melania the Elder and possessed of a wife, Therasia, who was noted for her own devotion, still he was a writer more concerned with literary style, theological niceties and his patron saint than with preserving a factual account of his life and times. His usefulness as a historical witness is thus limited, except occasionally: for instance, in a letter to Sulpicius Severus, he gives one particularly vivid cameo of Melania in action, when recounting a visit she made to him – though this is subject to the limitations of his treating the occasion in a consciously traditional style calculated to do justice to the *dignitas* bestowed on his family by this old-style visitation from an illustrious connection. On the pious women more intimately connected with him, he is unfortunately more reticent; denying us, for instance, the opportunity of any insights into his (latterly) continent marriage with 'the Tanaquil of our times', Therasia, a consort who aroused much admiration in their Christian aquaintances. Small items and phrases only from his letters and poems make this reticent aristocrat still a useful, though tantalising, witness.

Other men wrote on women from the standpoint of being an admirer or follower of a notable holy female. Some wrote from the position of advisor to devout female satellites, to counsel, admonish and praise them, to their further renown. Augustine, for instance, courted notable Christian women such as Proba, her daughter Anicia Juliana and grand-daughter Demetrias, and used them as sounding-boards for various of his improving addresses. He attempted to do the same thing with Melania Junior and her mother Albina, and his failure to do so provoked some of the more interesting and revealing letters about his relations with his congregation as well as with the aristocracy. John Chrysostom was similarly in the centre of a network of pious aristocratic females, and might have been as illuminating a source as Augustine, but he largely fails to fulfil promise here as in the family sphere. Surrounded and supported by ladies eminent in birth as in spirituality while he was as Patriarch in Constantinople, we yet get no systematic account from him of his relations with them; again, with one partial exception. This was that of Olympias, his friend, provider and disciple, who was so influential and instrumental to him and many other bishops of the Eastern church. That she was important to him we may deduce from the witness of other writers who testify to his spiritual and material dependence on her; but his letters to her, though certainly indicative of a high and even affectionate regard are not a reasoned account of their relationship, such as we gain from other writers in close proximity to outstanding women.

One of the most helpful and informative of the Fathers with regard to names, narrative details and statuses of pious women of his day was, ironically enough, one who most often and stridently doubted their capacity for spirituality (and that despite being surrounded by some of the most ferociously ascetic females of the age): the problematic Jerome. Around Jerome we find a large circle of women to whom he writes and makes reference and his relationships with whom he is forced to defend against the scandalous tongues of Roman society gossip-lovers. The majority of information about these comes from the more workaday letters of which Marcella received so many, and those of a more rhetorical nature, of exhortation or consolation or admonition. *Letter* 22 to Eustochium on the Virgin's profession, and *Letter* 54 to Furia on the duty of remaining a widow, are each really a broadsheet, advertising his stance respectively on virginity and widowhood; *Letter* 77, to Oceanus about the death of Fabiola, a kind of text exercise in consolation on bereavement, in Christian imitation of the stoic Roman set pieces in such an eventuality.

In his letters, more illuminating in their passionate rhetoric of vituperation and self-justification than those of any of the other Fathers, we have Jerome's account of Paula's severance with her family and her commencement of a life of asceticism alongside him: a contemporary eyewitness (albeit one with an axe to grind) to a noblewoman's experience of the road to *ascesis* through adverse peer and family pressure, and through personal tragedies such as the death of her eldest daughter Blesilla – arguably a victim of her own ascetic fervour. Jerome is simply interested in women, possibly in response to their interest in him; the number of female admirers and followers attested is not coincidental. It is difficult to find parallels in other writers with such items as his long and detailed letter to Laeta about the proper Christian upbringing for her small daughter (who eventually ended up at Bethlehem as Eustochium's successor as the head of the women's convent Paula and Jerome had instituted) or his letter to Pacatula on feminine training for her small child, or his whimsically graceful note of thanks to the youthful Eustochium for a gift of bracelets, doves and cherries.

Nor is Jerome alone in using his letters partly as the excuse for a general airing of dogma; the letters of these great men received often as widespread an airing as their theological treatises. They were part of the Christian expression of the *ratio bene vivendi*, the Roman preoccupation with the good life translated into terms of Christian duty. The letters are intensely conscious of obligation and of literary merit: witness Ambrose, Augustine, Jerome, John Chrysostom, Paulinus of Nola, Basil of Caesarea, following Symmachus, Praetextatus, Macrobius and Libanius in writing to their large circle of acquaintances who eagerly copy the letters and pass them on.

But besides great men writing to satellite holy women, we have the witnesses of more humble men who were themselves the satellites of female luminaries, writing of their close acquaintance with these saintly ladies. Such a one wrote the anonymous *Life of Olympias, Deaconess*; in similar case was Gerontius, the successor of Melania the Younger as head of her community, who wrote her *Life*. These have the disadvantages of being written more in arrears and at a greater distance than, for instance, Gregory of Nyssa's *Life of Macrina* or Gregory of Nazianzus' biographical works on his family, in addition to which, as hagiography rather than biography, they are subject to a certain amount of historical revisionism. Nonetheless, leaving on one side the increasingly formulaic attitudes depicted for their subjects, their background is helpful.

Other writers were enthusiasts or hangers-on of less close acquaintance, collecting scrap-books of sanctity which include useful information on workaday female piety along with occasionally piquant cameos of some of the celebrities. The *Apophthegmata Patrum* noted above comes into this category; Palladius is another prime example. While knowing personally many of the most eminent holy men and women around during his sojourn in the desert he is content to give a spectator's account rather than entering the dogmatic lists. Palladius is a particularly enthusiastic and gallant witness where women are concerned, and actually addresses himself to balancing out some of the more misogynistic claims of the male writers of his period; he proclaims that he is positively concerned

> to mention in my book certain women with manly qualities, to whom God apportioned labours equal to those of men; lest any should pretend that women are too feeble to practise virtue perfectly. Now I have seen many such and met many distinguished virgins and widows. . .
>
> (*LH* 41)

– and he is at pains to relate what he can of all those he has met and heard of through others, even of isolated, 'little' folk for whom he has no name; he is very useful in his little vignettes of some of the more obscurely devout desert women who practised extreme forms of self-denial in isolation. His accounts of notable holy women on the other hand, such as Melania the Elder (with whom he travelled) and Olympias in his *Lausiac History* and *Dialogues*, are no less invaluable for being less closely bound up with them than some of our witnesses.

All the above, and many others besides also contributed to the great body of exhortatory literature which provides us with yet more material for consideration. For instance, virtually every Christian thinker of any note felt constrained to add his voice in the debate over continence. Most galloped into prose over avowed virginity: following Tertullian's strident lead of the preceding century, Ambrose, Augustine, John Chrysostom, Jerome, Gregories of Nyssa and Nazianzus, Basils of Caesarea and Ancyra, Clement of Alexandria and Methodius are just the most notable writers on this topic. But there are also enough treatises from different voices on widowhood and marriage to make a useful synthesis of their common points. Some writers were particularly alert to women's problems: Augustine, for instance, besides his valuable personal witness on a close female relative, shows a predisposition towards a positive estimate of the value of female piety, which makes him a valuable contributor of more indirect textual material assessing women's contribution to ascetic spirituality in his time. His exhortations to women's lot are not empty homilies imparted to the intellectual air, but concerned directives written to real women of his acquaintance seeking help in these regions of theological dispute. In the case of *On the Good of Widowhood* and *On Virginity* the women concerned are a mother and daughter we hear of (used again as the prop for inspirational homilies) from other church Fathers: Anicia Juliana and her daughter Demetrias, originating from the very topmost rank of Roman society but showing the familial tendency towards asceticism that is a feature of the age. Gregory of Nyssa similarly shows himself in possession of an understanding of women's issues gained from a closer perspective, in his *On Virginity*; a gentler work than many on this topic. In exhortatory areas, John Chrysostom is unexpectedly helpful: in a series of homilies addressing the theology of 'women's problems' – *On Not Marrying Again, On the Kind of Women who Ought to be Taken as Wives, On Virginity, On the Necessity of Guarding Virginity* – he takes a perhaps surprisingly perceptive line on the difficulties encountered by his female adherents, as he considers the issues of the powers of women within the church and their troubles over celibacy. Incidentally this tendency also crops up in others of his works not addressed to the generality of women, in his more personal *Letter to a Young Widow* and in portions of *On the Priesthood* and various of his exegetical homilies.

In addition to the highly personalised contributions of these men, we have much anonymous, more generic evidence about the issues raised by female devotions in the variety of teaching documents abounding from this period: the *Teaching of the Apostles*, *Church Order*, the *Apostolic Constitutions* and *Canons*, to say nothing of the canons of the various church councils. As with the law of the land, these are more eloquent about what the recipients were doing amiss, particularly where there is reinforcement and repetition: and are sometimes a useful index to cases of the Fathers being over-enthusiastic about the capacity of their female protégés for ministry.

The treatment of women's concerns by men could be handled with great sympathy and discretion, depending on the author. Augustine's predispositions, for instance, give him a slightly hectoring tone when writing general discourses on subjects in the abstract – on Christian concepts of marriage, widowhood and so on – but also have the effect that in the particular, when writing of individuals, he is much more pliable and warm with his female subjects. Monica, painted in lively colours wherever she appears, is made to express surprise in *De Ordine* that a woman's words should be recorded in such a discourse; but in the Socratic atmosphere of *De Beata Vita* she serves as a useful foil for Augustine when, with characteristic bluntness and determination, she compels him to explain fully anything she (and by implication the untrained mind in the audience) does not understand.[14] Contrast this, however, with Gregory of Nyssa humbly according Macrina the central, philosopher's role in their Socratic dialogue on the origin and final home of the soul at her deathbed. Endowed with a great capacity for hero-worship of his formidable family, Gregory's treatment of them is also informative in its differences: 'Macrina is brought near by a biography, Basil is made distant by a panegyric' (Momigliano 1985: 449). The difference may reflect family dynamics; it is more likely to represent the difference between what was proper in the treatment to a pious male, who represented the priesthood, and a pious female, however devout and awe-inspiring a sister.

What is illuminating from all of this is that however fierce the degree with which views on women, often derived from the more nugatory pronouncements of the apostle Paul (see Chapter 3) were held, a great and constant double-think is in evidence in our sources. All, even the sternest of the Fathers, while embracing apostolic teaching on women as sinful in nature so subject in worship, nonetheless know and approve as 'superior' certain female exemplars to their sex. Every single writer knows of some female paragon or paragons (though each must of course be 'unique' in their virtue), astonishing in devotion, sufficiently pious to be examples even to their male contemporaries. Even Jerome the hard-liner, while fully subscribing to the point of view that 'women are burdened by sins, carried about by every wind of doctrine, always learning and never reaching knowledge of the truth' (Jerome *Let.* 133.4) yet found so many women to admire and counsel that his name became a byword amongst the scandal-seekers in Rome, as he bitterly complained; [15] the monk who was so tormented by she-demons seems to have been equally beset by she-saints. If knowledge of female involvement is rather lacking from our picture of this time, it is not necessarily for want of such involvement; nor necessarily from a want of reportage in the male sources of the time.

3

MODELS FOR PIETY IN A SOCIAL CONTEXT

WOMANHOOD AND THE FATHERS: THE *IMAGO DEI* ARGUMENT

He for God only, she for God in him.

(Milton *Paradise Lost* 4.299)

If, then, our main eyewitnesses for the period are the group of patristic authors – the Fathers – the first objective must be to see from their writings how unified was the thinking of this group: whether we can identify any homogeneous theological thinking applied to women wishing to further their devotions – even a roughly coherent theological line on the female route to salvation. This necessitates examining the kind of criteria that they thought women must meet to be accounted 'virtuous', and the routes they approved for its most suitable expression; also the grounds on which a reputation for piety was disqualified or disputed.

Patristic attitudes take their root, though adopted in varying degrees, in the writings of the Apostle Paul; for them the first and greatest Christian writer. The ambiguities in Paul, however, complicated further innate divisions in patristic attitudes. In the centuries immediately following the legitimisation of the church, the church authorities were seeking more and more to define and regulate; hence the importance of the distinctions in Paul between what was and what was not a commandment. Women in particular were subject to a great lack of definition with regard to what positions in the hierarchy, if any, they could occupy; and as to acceptable modes of expression of their piety. In the sub-apostolic period the effect of Christian teaching was to seem to make women less heedful of the restrictions of family, upbringing and state; in the fourth and fifth centuries we see the same authorities used as part of

25

an attempt to 'place' women within the established environs of the church. It was a period of reinforcement and shoring up of the embryonic existing organisations, of church councils and canons and the troubled attempts to establish a dominant and accepted orthodoxy in the aftermath of divisive persecution, which left wayward strands such as the Montanists, the Arians and the Donatists unaccounted for.

In this process, the dicta of Paul on such irregular situations as women ministering for the church were somewhat less than clear. 'I do not permit a woman to teach or have authority over a man' (I Tim. 2:12) sounds unequivocal; were it not for the way that he also accords the woman Phoebe the appellation 'diakonos' (uncertain of application in his time, but full of resonance in the later period), commends Tryphaena and Tryphosa as 'fellow-workers' and even accords Priscilla precedence over Aquilla as leaders of a house-church (Rom. 16:1, 16:2, 16:12). Nonetheless, after Paul's time, appeals to scripture were mainly made in efforts to define the role of women in a more restricted capacity in the vexed process of defining the church as a whole. This is not due to anything so simple as 'misogyny', mistrust of women, or a desire to restrict their activities on grounds of prejudice. The process is much more complex and subject to many levels of thought about women; arising out of social expectations of their 'place', it was influenced by what scriptures said of women's subjection by original sin, confirmed or contradicted by clerical experience of women as the temptation or the example. This is further complicated by the ways in which degrees of female status had developed independently, influencing clerical thought. Some of our most interesting material comes from the not infrequent clashes between the theoretical views postulated by the church writers and the practicalities of what folk were actually doing – and often continued to do, church writing notwithstanding.

The starting position of most patristic application of the scriptures to women is from the theory of the naturally abject condition of women, advanced to back up exhortations to women to be appropriately silent and submissive in their behaviour. Much of the Fathers' consciousness of women as inferior members of the church centres around the notion of the imperfect participation of women in the *imago dei*: the idea that man alone had been made in the image of God and woman derived only from man (cf. Gen. 1:26, 2:7, 2:21) – an imitation of an imitation. This was then further expounded by Paul in I Corinthians 11; texts such as 'the head of every man is

Christ, and the head of every women is man' (I Cor. 11:3) and 'a man has no need to cover his head, because he reflects the image and glory of God. But woman reflects the glory of man' (I Cor. 11:7) were hailed as authoritative statements and formed the backbone of the position that because of their more tenuous link with the divine, women lacked some essential quality that men shared with the Godhead.

Patristic advice to female vocations was then informed by patristic notions of what was wrong with women – and what was right with them – largely based on Paul; hence their advice to their vocations. The ideal properties of women were seen in modesty, silence, faithfulness and purity; but to judge from the constant reiteration of these goals as necessities, this was often perceived as not being the case. For the Fathers also saw womankind as being essentially sinful; vain, inconstant, deceitful – more liable to temptation. An integral scriptural authority for this stance was the alleged First Letter of Paul to Timothy. This has some of the most unequivocal sections in the New Testament, such as the often-quoted 'I do not permit a woman to teach or have authority over a man: she must be silent', and 'Adam was not the one deceived; it was the woman who was deceived and became the sinner' (I Tim. 2:12, 2:14). Modern biblical scholars are now inclined to reject the authorship of I Timothy as being attributable to Paul (Clark 1983:16) but to the early church authors it was an indisputable guideline from one of the most incontrovertible sources available to them on the position of women with regard to the church.

John Chrysostom's commentary on this letter (with which he does seem to have been naturally in sympathy) is a case in point; he finds nothing to balk at in the severity of the supposed pronouncements of the apostle in this case. Women should be silent, the Apostle rightly says, for 'the sex is in a certain way loquacious' and 'the mind of woman is somewhat infantile' (*Hom.* 9 on I Tim. 1). Arising out of this, because she was deceived 'the women taught once and for all and upset everything . . . for the female sex is weak and vain, and here this is said of the whole sex' (*On the Epistle to the Ephesians*, *PG* 42.148). Paulinus of Nola, a gentler voice, still explains the prohibition in terms of woman's innate pride and weakness: 'Women are forbidden to teach in church, so that their spirits may not be puffed up and so that they may not dare to gaze on the decrees of wisdom and then secede through becoming haughty with pride.' The exemplary woman should 'prefer fear to depth of knowledge'

(Paulinus of Nola *Let.* 23.24). As Ambrose simply states: 'By a woman, care entered the world' (ibid. 42.3).

Others of the Fathers, such as Augustine, did differentiate between the woman and the lifestyle, the most notable qualifying criterion being the sexual attitude. But for many, following Paul, women fundamentally represented the downfall of rationality through sexuality and were seen as being so tied to their sexual nature that to renounce it was to go completely against that nature; a phenomenal achievement representing a completely altered, as it were sexless, state like that in which the angels were said to live. Choosing celibacy broke the bond of their subjection to original sin; but those not able to encompass this, or those attempting it and failing were represented as an actual danger to the Christian life; therefore any woman was inherently dangerous, following Tertullian: 'you have been made the sword that destroys' who 'although you are free from the actual crime, you are not free from the odium attaching to it'; for 'that other, as soon as he has felt desire for your beauty and has mentally already committed the deed to which his desire pointed, perishes' (*On Female Dress* 2.2).

On women, then, is particularly laid the burden of avoiding being the occasion of leading others to sin. The Fathers were emphatic that if a man lusted, the woman at the very least shared the blame for his lust. The prostitutes who converted to asceticism that we will examine in Chapter 8 turned to penitence invariably through the agency of a strong holy man who confronts each with the danger she represents to the souls of others. 'Why are you causing the loss of so many souls so that you will be condemned to render an account not only of your own sins but of theirs as well?' is the formulaic question; the penitence of Thaïs, Paësia and Pelagia is for being the agent of those others' downfall more than their own.[1] This is also the attitude accepted by the anchoress Alexandra, formerly a maid-servant, who told Melania the Elder: 'A man was distressed in mind because of me and, in case I should seem to afflict or disparage him, I chose to take myself alive into the tomb, rather than cause a soul made in the image of God to stumble' (*LH* 5). To prevent this, she 'left the city and shut herself up in a tomb, receiving the necessities of life through an opening, seeing neither men nor women face to face for ten years' (*ibid.*).

Even those living under vows do not escape the responsibility of guarding against precipitating the fall of others: the nuns at Hippo are told by Augustine, 'you are not forbidden to see men, but you must neither let your desire go out to them, nor wish to be objects of desire on their part' (Augustine *Let.* 211.10). Similar but even more stringent advice is given by the hermit Hilarion after his cure of a Christian virgin from sickness reputedly caused by possession put upon her by the spells of a youth whose advances she had determinedly and repeatedly resisted. Her resistance avails her little in his eyes: 'he reproved the girl when her health returned, for having by her imprudent conduct permitted the devil to gain control over her' (Jerome *Life of St Hilarion* 21). Despite the steadfastness in resistance which led the young man to try these desperate measures, hers is still the responsibility for his temptation in Hilarion's eyes. Likewise, a devout and God-fearing virgin of senatorial rank, was reviled by the eremitic Abba Arsenius, from whom she had sought edification while on pilgrimage from Rome, in essence for coming to him, as a woman: 'How dare you make such a journey? Do you not know that you are a woman and cannot go just anywhere?' (*Alph.* Arsenius 8). The archbishop Theophilus, who had been their unsuccessful go-between, reinforced this: 'Do you not realise that you are a woman and it is through women that the enemy wars against the saints?' She evidently had known of his reasons for refusing to see her, but had insisted on going anyway because her motives were pure: 'I trust in God to see him: men we have in our town and I have come to see not a man but a prophet' (*ibid.*). But Abba Arsenius' caution was well-founded: even when 'a God-fearing virgin' visits an 'old man' 'dead to the flesh' for spiritual edification, examples of such rediscovering, to their chagrin, the persistent vitality of their flesh and succumbing to carnal desires were well enough known to justify his attitude; and the woman must bear the responsibility of obviating this risk and hold herself in isolation.[2]

This attitude activated much of the animus against those living as *agapetae* or *virgines subintroductae* and the monks with whom they lived. These were unmarried couples living together in what they advertised as an entirely spiritual union (considered in more detail in Chapter 4), beneficial to the religious life of both. More realistically, perhaps, Chrysostom says that if scripture says that men who lust after women with their eyes have already committed adultery with them in their hearts (Matt. 5: 27–28), then he estimates these monks must be guilty of a thousand adulteries daily; and though both partners in the union are guilty in this regard, he assigns the greater blame to the women, who he asserts, like prostitutes or adulteresses, were responsible for the man's madness (*Hom.* 17 on

Matt. 2; *Quod reg.* 1). Jerome further reinforces this when writing to a mother and daughter in Gaul who were living apart, each under the protection of a 'spiritual advisor'. He sternly admonished the daughter for placing herself and him in constant temptation; 'Why must you live in a house where you must daily struggle for life and death?' (Jerome *Let.* 117.3). She is to mend her behaviour and if she will not part from her mentor, live obviously decently in the company of her mother. He too advises her not even to walk abroad lest she be the occasion of lustful speculations in others; our sources are adamant that the very contemplation is as sinful as the deed (Jerome *Let.* 117.7).

Thus the need for exaggerated modesty, the apostle again providing the pattern: 'if a woman has long hair, it is her glory; for long hair is given her as a covering' (I Cor. 11:15); a text frequently resorted to by the Fathers, the need for covering as visible proof of feminine modesty. 'Salvation consists in the exhibition principally of modesty' (Tertullian *On Female Dress* 2.13). 'Modesty everywhere accompanies the virgin's unique virtues: without it virginity cannot exist; it must be the inseparable companion of virginity' (Ambrose *On Virginity* 2.14). Modest dress is to underline the difference between women of God and the rest, personal adornment is to be shunned: 'Let your dress be neither too neat nor too slovenly; in neither let it be so remarkable as to draw the attention of passersby' (Jerome *Let.* 22.27). This modesty should extend to the virtuous woman's entourage as well as herself; 'sometimes the tone of the mistress in inferred from the dress of the maid' (*Let.* 54.12). Hence in the models offered for women to admire and imitate, 'She whom we are praising was unadorned, and the absence of ornament was beauty to her' (Gregory of Nazianzus (*Or.* 8.3)

Modesty should also be manifest in internal qualities as in outward appearance: pious women should guard their tongues as their beauty. Gregory of Nazianzus' female relatives were offered as exemplary in this: his mother, Nonna, 'was the kind who would sooner conceal something quite public than boast about private matters for vainglory' (*On his Own Life* 65); and similarly his sister Gorgonia, though the men around her according to Gregory 'regarded her counsels and advice as a law not to be broken', still 'who was less ready to speak, confining herself within the due limits of a woman?' (*Or.* 8.11). Not only how they appeared to others but when and where must be scrutinised: 'Christian women should not have the same cause to appear in public as gentile women ... all Christian occasions to go abroad are businesses of sobriety and sanctity' (Tertullian *On Female Dress* 2.13) and it is not enough that God should know them to be chaste: 'let your probity appear before men'. Jerome goes further in his advice to Laeta about the rearing of Paula; she should never go in public at all (Jerome *Let.* 107.7). Thus also the exemplary Gorgonia: 'who was more deserving of renown, and yet who avoided it so much and made herself inaccessible to the eyes of men?' (*Or.* 8.9). A nun named Taor from the austere desert disciplines took extreme measures to compel her own observance of this: she steadfastly refused a change of clothes or footwear during her thirty years of convent life 'lest I be forced to go out' (*LH* 59); her intention being that the condition of her appearance in rags should make it impossible for her to be able to venture abroad even if so tempted.

This care over not submitting oneself to the public gaze might quite laudably be taken to the extremes of risking one's health to preserve bodily modesty. Gregories of Nyssa and Nazianzus both give accounts of such situations as proof that their respective sisters, Macrina and Gorgonia, were examples to good Christian women. Macrina was stricken with a deadly tumour on her breast, so that

> her mother implored her often and begged her to receive the attention of a doctor, since the medical art, she said, was sent from God for the saving of men. But [Macrina] judged it worse than the pain to uncover any part of her body to a stranger's eyes.
>
> (Gregory of Nyssa *Life of Macrina* 992)

Gorgonia was 'seriously injured' when her carriage overturned in an accident; but 'all crushed and bruised as she was in bones and limbs ... she would have no physician ... because she shrank from the observation and hands of men, preserving, even in suffering, her modesty' (*Or.* 8.15). Both women subsequently prayed themselves back to good health. Gregory of Nazianzus, however, is guilty of some inconsistency on this point: two passages later, Gorgonia seems to have quite forgotten, or been persuaded out of, this modest aversion to physicians as Gregory tells us that she was stricken with 'an extraordinary and malign disease' of such virulence that 'the skill of physicians who carefully examined the case, both singly and in consultation, was of no avail' (*ibid.* 8.17).

There were echoes of this notion of women providing the occasion and carrying the burden of sins committed about them in the furore over the Roman lady Fabiola's second marriage. She was judged to be sinful in her second union with Jerome's follower Oceanus (both she and he were Christians) after divorcing her first husband, even though he was 'an adulterer and a sodomite' (Jerome *Let*. 55) and she was forbidden the church until, obeying 'Christ's laws, not Papinian's', she did extravagant penance and sold off her property for the poor and 'heroically undertook the blame of separation rather than the same of the union' (*Let*. 77.3). Jerome was writing to Oceanus himself but there is no word of any penances or debarring on his part; though he had joined in her sin in the regard of Christian teaching, the blame rests with the woman. The Christian carefulness over the single marriage was given its most extreme expression by Macrina, sister of Gregory of Nyssa, who took this thinking to its logical conclusion when she refused to consider a second betrothal after the death of the boy to whom she had been betrothed, 'since in the nature of things there was but one marriage, as there is one birth and one death': and, taking the stance that she was as bound 'as if the intention had been accomplished in fact' (Gregory of Nyssa, *Life of Macrina* 964) she achieved the fame of being *univira* (having known only one man in her life) to add to her lustre of virginity. This may in fact have been opportunistic reasoning on her part, advanced as special pleading to back up her strong desire for a nun's vows; but equally it expresses a very real potential ground for concern amongst women of the Christian communities. Given the oppobrium endured by Fabiola, and the highly elastic nature of Roman marriage conventions (cf. pp. 101–2) which were such as to lend themselves to much uncertainty, Macrina might not unreasonably argue the wish for the deed to avoid any possibility of confusion on Judgement Day.

But if too often seen as merely the instigators of sin, women were seen also as capable of making a significant contribution to the spiritual reserves of the church; within certain preconditions. If these preconditions for piety were met, women could fulfil the highest spiritual destiny: 'It would be shameful for every woman to think merely that she is a woman', wrote Clement of Alexandria (*The Instructor*, PG 8.429); so 'Women must seek wisdom, like men, even if men are superior and have first place in every field, at least if they are not effeminate' (*Miscellanies*, PG 8.1275). For after all, after care has entered the world through a woman, salvation came through a virgin woman. From certain approved stances of informed purity, women were allowable in patristic thinking as fulfilling roles within the church.

SEXUALITY, ALIENATION AND SPIRITUAL CONDITION

If women were essentially sinful because essentially sexual, the first and most obvious need was to negate that aspect of their nature – or to stand it on its head. If 'woman represents the flesh and the passions' (Origen *In Exod.*, PG 12.305), then 'he is truly male who ignores sin, which is to say female fragility' (Origen *In Levit.*, PG 12.188). With this in mind, Paulinus of Nola's advice was to completely reverse the way of nature: 'Let us kiss him whose embrace is chastity. Let us have intercourse with him with whom marriage is virginity' (Paulinus of Nola *Let.* 23.42). In the fourth century, abstinence from the flesh in the thinking of many of the patristic authors became the equivalent to martyrdom; it equated with a willingness to suffer for God in the manner of Paul's testimony that he crucified himself to the world and the world to himself (Gal. 6:14). In the more puritanical, eschatologically obsessed cultural climate of the later Empire, writers such as John Chrysostom may be found regretting that martyrdom, the ultimate in self-denial, was no longer an option for Christians and hinting that those who from their love of God struggle to overcome carnal lust and the world can expect the martyrs' reward.

First, then, for the faithful there was an obvious need to liberate themselves from the distractions of the life of everyday, of the temporal world; not just thoughts of material things, but even the bonds of family life, and as far as possible in each individual case, from the flesh altogether. If at all possible, continence and chastity were to be embraced as a liberation from the subjection to sin, which then placed one in a state of more immediate availability to the agency of the Holy Spirit: of necessity in most cases this entailed the loosening of the bonds of duty and affection to family. There are repeated echoes in all the sources of this central theme of family as against spiritual life, constantly reiterating and paraphrasing the text from 1 Corinthians 7 which said that 'the unmarried woman thinks on the things of the Lord that both in body and spirit she may be holy; the married is careful only as to pleasing her husband' (Tertullian *To his Wife* 1.3). She is not alone with this problem; similarly 'the man in the married state is anxious for the things of this world': 'the married man is frequently forced against his will to err and sin' (John Chrysostom *On Virginity* 14.6 and 43). This being so,

It is necessary that whoever wishes to aim here and now for that Kingdom must hate, not the people themselves, but those temporal relationships through which this life of ours is propped up, this life which will pass away from us, which comprises merely being born and dying. For he who does not hate them does not yet love that life where there will be no condition of being born and dying.

(Augustine *On the Sermon on the Mount* 1.15.40)

To further this end of divorcing men and women from the distraction of married life, its pains and trials are laboured by most of the patristic authors: fear for one's husband if the marriage is happy, fear of him if it is not; anxiety and grief if the marriage is childless, but anxiety, pain and hardship if children are produced; the struggle for dominance, sexual jealousy and constant fear for the future (John Chrysostom *On Virginity* 52–5, Ambrose *On Virginity* 1.25). In particular it was stressed how much worse were the evils of marriage for women.

A marriageable girl is in a kind of market, offered, as it were, at auction, for the purchase of the highest bidder. More tolerable are the conditions under which slaves are sold, for they may often choose their masters; but if the girl chooses for herself it is an outrage.

(Ambrose *On Virginity* 1.25)

John Chrysostom also likened marriage to slavery for women, and set to work also to weaken their natural inclination towards children. He challenged the traditional view that even with all its evils marriage must be in order to repopulate the world:

Marriage was not ordered just in order to produce children . . . chastity is the foremost reason for marriage, and now above all since our race has come to fill the whole world . . . If you long for descendants . . . we are summoned to the pains of spiritual birth, and offshoots of real worth which will be of far more use to us in our old age.

(John Chrysostom *Hom.* 19 on I Cor. 7:2,3)

One outcome of this dismantling of social bonds was, of course, that the women who chose to implement this preaching became more available as a resource at the disposal of the bishops and their clergy; the proper protectors of avowed women, they would channel their energies and time newly available for the service of God (and attempt to channel their wealth, if any) to the services of the church, as we will examine in a later chapter.

This thinking puts in context the congratulatory tone with which the actions of Paula, Melania the Elder and Melania the Younger were greeted in our sources. Martyr tales from the previous centuries are filled with women who set their families at nought in their dedication; women such as Thecla, Perpetua, Felicitas, Agathonice. Their attitude is summed up in the almost formulaic answer uttered by Agathonice when she was about to be executed in Pergamum in the time of Marcus Aurelius: when the assembled crowd beseech her to give up her faith and 'have pity on yourself and your children', she replies 'My children have God who watches over them' (Musurillo 1972:35). Agape, Irene and Chione in Saloniki in Macedonia, in 304 fled from their families for 'we think them worse than our enemies in fear they would denounce us' (Musurillo 1972:289) and this attitude is presented by the text as reasonable and indeed praiseworthy.

So when Jerome's acolyte Paula in 385 deserted her family in Rome to follow him to the Holy Land, leaving her relatives weeping on the quayside, the appropriate Christian reaction is held to be admiration. Paula was a wealthy aristocratic widow (her family claimed descent from the Scipios and the Gracchi) who had been drawn into the dedicated circle of Marcella and Jerome at Rome; she had come to experience the same need as Marcella to throw off the yoke of the world the better to express her devotion, but unlike Marcella, who remained within familiar environs to fulfil her commitment to Christ, Paula felt it incumbent on her to relocate to more inspirational surroundings, in the wake of her mentor. Hence the situation in which she is depicted on the point of permanent departure from Italy, surrounded by a family unwilling to let her go – her son, Toxotius, was possibly still only a child whom Jerome describes as 'extending supplicating hands on the shore' while one of her three elder daughters, Rufina, 'now a young woman, implored her mother with silent tears that she wait [to depart] until her marriage' (Jerome *Let.* 108.6). Paula, like Agathonice 'raised dry eyes to heaven, overcoming her devotion to her children by her devotion to God . . . she did not know herself as a mother that she might prove herself worthy as a handmaid of God'. Despite 'battling with grief as if she were being torn limb from limb . . . she sought this with a rejoicing spirit, making little of the love of her children by her greater love for God' (*ibid.*). And subsequently, when sent word of the serious illnesses of her children, and 'particularly of Toxotius, whom she loved dearly', Jerome says she simply thought of Christ's words: '"He that loveth son or daughter more than me is not worthy of me"' (*ibid*. 108.19) – though as a sign that something of the fondness of maternity prevailed through ascetic integrity, one should contrast this with his reports that at their subsequent deaths 'on each occasion the shock of their loss endangered her life' (*ibid*. 108.21).

The same tone is evident in the accounts of Melania the Elder's departure from Rome ten or so years previously. Another wealthy aristocratic lady, and like Marcella widowed young (at the age of 22), she further lost two of her three children, leaving only one surviving son. Then, becoming influenced by the ascetic movement, she made the decision to abandon Rome and her family for an ascetic life in Egypt; again a matter that is treated in our sources as being worthy of the highest praise. According to her relative Paulinus, she 'joyfully threw off the burdens of human love along with the ropes of the ship, while all wept' (Paulinus of Nola, *Let*. 29.10) when she made her departure. She is made to echo the female martyrs when she is described as having 'loved her child by neglecting him and kept him by relinquishing him' (*ibid*. 29.9), further that 'once Melania had torn her only son from her breast and set him in Christ's bosom so that he might be nourished by the Lord himself, she herself gave him no further personal care, thinking it a sinful lack of faith to still devote attention to one whom she had entrusted to Christ' (*ibid*.). Melania had to leave Rome less publicly than Paula, for she it seems was defying family and state; Paulinus, presumably privy to what must have been a rancorous family dispute, says 'the devil attempted to thwart her plan, through the fiercest pressure from her noble relatives, whom he armed to restrain her and prevent her departure' (*ibid* 29.10); and Palladius of Helenopolis who travelled with her adds 'She told no-one her plan, because she would have been prohibited at the time since Valens had rule in the empire' (*LH* 46). Melania had also been less blessed than Paula with her family; but Jerome endeavours to convince that in any case in the best ascetic manner she smiled and thanked God for her liberation. Paulinus however attests to his relative's tears, and says that at best 'she was taught by this experience not to remain bound up with this fragile world and to rest her hopes in God alone, the only one whom we cannot lose without wishing it'. Jerome is probably further misleading in the cause of ascetic propaganda when he implies that Publicola was the same sort of age as the infant Toxotius when Paula left: other evidence indicates that he was in fact of an age to be already on the path to his later public career (Harries, in Craik 1984:58–9).

Melania's example then inspired her grand-daughter, Melania the Younger, the daughter of Publicola, to her own extreme manifestations of piety; though (see p. 146) her wish for poverty and abnegation were only set in opposition to the previous generation of her family, since she was, to all intents, childless – one of the counts her family held against her. All this lends point to Jerome's statement that the woman dedicated to the Eternal Life needs 'neither mother nor sister nor kinswoman nor brother'. John Chrysostom stressed that particularly in this later age, more was demanded of the committed Christian; to be right in the eyes of God was to abandon all trammels: 'Today it is not possible to achieve perfection without selling and renouncing everything; not only your possessions and your house, but even your life' (*On Virginity* 83.1). Detachment from the family was advocated as right and necessary for the woman pursuing the ascetic life, very much as earlier female martyrs were 'in noticeable isolation from their families, in defiance of rather than in loyalty to, their husbands and fathers, and demonstrating a surprising eagerness to abandon young infants' (Lefkowitz 1976:418–9).

In fact, we may discern in some of the Fathers the onset of uneasiness at the fervour with which some women were embracing this particular aspect of the devotional lifestyle. Separation from the trammels of the family was an admirable goal, but in the cases of ascetically inspired women eager to make a unilateral declaration of their intentions to pursue it, difficulties could arise. Ambrose was put in an awkward position when a girl from his congregation attempted to pre-empt family opposition by running up to the altar in mid-service and wrapping the altar-cloth round her as if it were a veil, pleading for consecration as a virgin. When a relative protested: 'do you think your father would allow you to remain unmarried if he were alive?' the girl replied 'Perhaps he died so that no-one could hinder me.' This is so similar to the sentiments of the female martyrs that it could be almost a paraphrase; but it met with a cooler reception. Ambrose, uneasily acquiescing that natural parents should not try and keep one from the heavenly birthright, nevertheless advises virgins in like case with some fervour: 'Conquer family feeling first; if you overcome your household, you overcome the world' (Ambrose *On Virginity* 1.11.63–5).

Similarly one-sided decisions in the case of married women created a dilemma which puts the authorities who had inspired them to some uncomfortable shuffling. Continence in marriage was admirable; but those who seized on the exhortations to practise it without first making certain that their husbands concurred were obeying the apostle in one respect only to disobey him in another. 'Wives, respect your husbands' (Col 3:18; Eph 5:22) was the commandment applied to: for 'it is evident that she is subjected to the man and that the subjection is because of sin' (John Chrysostom, *Discourse* 4 on Gen. 2). Thus the pious married woman was caught in a double bind; she was under subjection because of sin and the bonds of subjection to sin are broken by choosing continence, if not celibacy; but by making this choice, she was brought up against that very subjection she was attempting to escape. Augustine heavily rebuked the matron Ecdicia, who had adopted an ascetic life with more enthusiasm than judgement, for unilaterally making the decision that her marriage was henceforth to be a continent one and then talking her reluctant husband into acquiescing (along with some fairly extreme displays of largesse and self-abasement); he subsequently fell into the sin of fornication, which Augustine is adamant is Ecdicia's fault (see p. 130). Even the personal adornment that negates modesty was subject to this obedience; elsewhere, Augustine wrote 'only for their husbands ought women to be permitted to adorn themselves' even if only at the behest of 'the tolerance, not the injuncture of scripture' (Augustine *Let*. 245). Thus the woman again shoulders the responsibility for sin; attempting to avoid her own sin of carnality she once more becomes 'the sword that destroys' and the occasion for another's sin.

THE DEBATE OVER CELIBACY

Abstinence from carnality was a vexed issue, but one of such importance that these questions of volition, and discretion in its application, are stressed in all our sources as being of primary importance. Time and time again in the middle of an exhortation on the beauties of chastity, as if drawing back from the treacherous ground, the authorities will add that of course this is not to be lightly undertaken, nor attempted at all if there is thought the possibility of failure. They are all emphatic that chastity is a grace, 'a gift from God' (Augustine *On the Good of Widowhood* 5): not all can or should consider continence. Clement of Alexandria maintained 'there is no other way to receive continence except by the grace of God'

(*Concerning Righteousness* 3.5.57); likewise that Christians should 'bless sexual abstinence in those to whom this condition has been given by God', but also 'marvel at monogamy and the majesty of a single marriage, for we think that we should suffer with each other and "bear one another's burdens" (Gal. 6:2) lest anyone who believes he is standing firm all by himself should fall (I Cor. 10:12)'. Thus the difference between marriage and virginity, that 'the one is under law, the other under grace' (Ambrose *Let.* 42.3).

Even Jerome, who blesses marriage only 'because it brings me virgins' also says that 'only those to whom it is given should be virgins' (Jerome *Let.* 22.20). He himself is 'a eunuch by choice' and the volition sanctifies it still further; it is 'better if it is freely offered' – though he mourns that not more choose to offer it. Chrysostom avers that this is what makes the state so especially honourable, in being a matter of choice, not compulsion; it must only come from willing agreement (*On Virginity* 2.2). Jerome further warns, in one of his most extreme statements for virginity and against marriage, the *Against Jovinian*:

> if all were able to be virgins, the Lord would never have said, "He who can receive this, let him receive it" [Matt. 19:12] and the Apostle would not have wavered in his recommendation, "About virgins, however, I have no commandment from the Lord" [I Cor. 7:25].
>
> (Jerome *Against Jovinian* 1.36)

and laments 'Do not fear that all will become virgins: virginity is a difficult business and is rare just because it is hard'. Even in this qualification, however, Jerome subtly increases the pressure for the choice. In the New Testament Greek, Jesus' advice is 'o dunameino chorein, choreito': 'chorein' signifying 'receive' or 'accept with the intellect'. Jerome in the Vulgate translated this by using the blunt 'qui potest capere, capiat', turning a rather metaphysical quality into a more direct appeal. Jerome may in this caveat have been exercising caution as to the welfare of his flock and the realities of the situation, as were Augustine and Clement; alternatively he was bearing in mind the finite limits to the numbers of souls that were capable of being practicably saved by this means – 'it is better to submit to marriage with a man than strain for the heights and fall to the depths of hell' (Jerome *Let.* 22.6).

This offers little consolation for those earnestly wishing for continence and refraining for reasons other than personal weakness.

The mother of Gregory of Nyssa and Macrina, Emmelia, is alleged by her son to have very much wished for the life embraced by her daughter but feared abduction or forcible marriage, being very beautiful and left an heiress completely without family; and so she practised discretion in marrying a known and safe young man, and perhaps transmitted her urgings for piety to the next generation.[3] But for those in a fortunate enough situation to be able to heed the call, and disposed to do so, the volitional aspect of the choice for continence looms large in the Fathers' consciousness with regard to the justification of celibacy – 'a trap is not to be set for women, nor a burden of continence which is beyond their strength to carry; it must be left to each to weigh the matter for herself' (Ambrose *On Widows* 71) – although they may, like Jerome, tend to the attitude that all could, if they but would.

This caution in the inspirational writings of the fourth century suggests a need to defend the course being promoted against critics within and without the main body of the church; Jerome's work mentioned above, the *Against Jovinian* highlights typical accusations from such critics. One of the dangers of advocating too close a devotion to celibacy was to risk running into accusations of dangerous doctrine. Such attacks as Jovinian's, imputing near-heresy to Jerome's works, cut very close to the bone – and so provoked an extreme and pungently *ad hominem* reply. Jovinian had written a popular book defending marriage in which he argued that virgins, widows and married women were all equal if they once passed through Christian baptism: superior merit was not to be accorded to celibacy. From Jovinian's imputations, Jerome had to protect himself from the accusation of heresy, and from hints that he colluded with unsound theological teaching: 'Indeed, we do not follow the teachings of Marcion and Mani; we do not disparage marriage, nor do we judge all sexual intercourse foul. We have not been deceived by the error of Tatian, the head of the Encratites' (*Against Jovinian* 1.3). The last-named was an extremely ascetic sect of Christians that flourished in the late second century, which, along with the equally reviled Severians and Naasenes, practised a particularly rigorous asceticism and regarded women and marriage as the works of Satan. Chrysostom also singled out Marcion and Mani for obloquy, for abhorring marriage and making virginity virtually compulsory for their followers (*On Virginity* 3). But Jerome's ascetic advice sometimes seemed to come very close to these in spirit, if not in detail; despite these disclaimers, the *Against Jovinian* contains matter so derogatory of marriage that his friends attempted to remove the book from circulation.

Jerome also highlights another often-repeated criticism: 'But you will say, "If all people were virgins, how would the human race continue?" ... on this line of reasoning, there will be nothing at all lest something else cease to be.' (*Against Jovinian* 36). This is a problem also dealt with in Augustine's *On the Good of Marriage*, which is a more moderate answer to the same treatise. Augustine's answer is that marriage is to prevent sin, but that if all the world did become celibate and the race did cease, it would be no bad thing: 'Would to heaven that everybody might wish this ... the City of God would be more quickly filled and the end of the world hastened' (*On the Good of Marriage* 9). John Chrysostom also uses the 'Last Days' argument to counter this objection: earlier races desired children to leave a remnant of themselves 'because they had no hope of the resurrection', but 'since the resurrection that will be is almost upon us now ... and we will be going to another life that is better than this present one, fretting over such matters is unnecessary for us' (*Hom.* 19 on 1 Cor. 7:2).

The defensiveness felt over these positions, and the criticism levelled at the advocates of celibacy, not just from the fringes of the church but from some of the established mainstream is a fair indication of the hold these writers were gaining, such as to cause consternation amongst more comfortable clerics. Witness Jerome's difficulties with the church in Rome while resident there (Jerome *Apologia* 3.22; *Let.* 45.3–5); and the coldness displayed by Pope Siricius to Paulinus of Nola during the latter's visit to Rome in 395, fairly certainly because of his stance on asceticism. Jerome was right to worry about his status with regard to orthodoxy, given his unpopularity; Pelagius, an advocate of fairly extreme asceticism who was far more personally popular (certainly at Rome), achieved in 415 the status of a heretic (due in no small measure to the attacks on him by Augustine) despite his previous high standing in the regard of the Roman upper classes. His message to the times had the virtue of simplicity, but was terrifying in its implications: perfection is possible for men and therefore it is obligatory. Nor was Pelagius without supporters in this extremism – Augustine's epistolary friend Paulinus of Nola amongst them. And Augustine was particularly alarmed when Pelagius had the temerity to address his views to Proba, Juliana and Demetrias, and Albina, Melania the Younger and Pinianus; the strong-minded aristocratic women whom Augustine regarded as to some extent protégés were fertile ground for Pelagius' invitation to a central role in such an influential movement. The popularity of his views must have been particularly galling to those like Jerome, who had been made so much the victim of the counter-currents elevating normal marital conditions that drove Jovinian and Helvidius into writing against him; by the standards of Pelagius, his position, regarded as sensitive by so many, was moderate indeed. But after a prolonged campaign by the African bishops, Pelagianism was condemned by the Emperor and the Pope, and such fanaticism gradually lost its purchase on upper-class piety.[4]

Allowing for both sides of the debate over celibacy, however, a pattern is evident. For Christian women of this era, justification was not achieved by faith, or even by deeds, on their own; it was achieved by observing a hierarchy of degrees of sanctity ordered in a logical progression. This system was related directly to their sexual and marital status. 'We are taught that the virtue of chastity is threefold; one kind is that of married life, the second that of widowhood, the third that of virginity' (Ambrose On Widows 23); logically, then 'for different degrees of virtue a different reward is set forth. The one is not scorned so that the other may be praised; but all are set out in order that what is best may be preferred' (ibid. 71). Further, according to some writers the status thus acquired could be affected by the attitude of mind in which women observed their sexual condition: a virgin could be brought low by improper thoughts, but a woman of a less abstemious physical condition could be devotionally enhanced merely by a yearning for a higher life. We see this underpinning the rhetoric applied to Paula and Ecdicia: Paula being attributed with the glory pertaining to a continent marriage without in reality adopting it, because it was said she sincerely wished for such a condition, while Ecdicia was strongly recommended to follow the route of 'the wish for the deed' in preference to undertaking real continence against her husband's wishes.

The issues centre round the marital bond. One of the greatest controversies of this period was based on the ascetic dilemma of whether or not to recommend marriage to the many. Given that 'she that is married is careful for the things of the world, how she may please her husband', yet still, 'it is better to marry than to burn'. This is the crux of the difficulty for the ascetics. Paul expressed a wish – but not a command – that 'all were as I am', i.e. celibate (I Cor. 7:7–8, 32–33). This path is, then, to be recommended; but as not all are capable, how strongly? After all, marriage was not without its own rewards for asceticism: 'I praise marriage because it gets me virgins' (Jerome *Let.* 22.20), 'virginity itself cannot exist unless it has some means of coming into existence' (Ambrose *On Virginity* 1.35) and Proba and Juliana were told that they had gained more glory 'in giving to Christ women consecrated to his service than in giving to the world men called to the honours of the consulship' (Augustine *Let.* 150) – namely Juliana's consecrated virgin daughter, Demetrias. 'The virgin is an offering for her mother, and by her daily sacrifice the divine power is appeased' (Ambrose *On Virginity* 1.32). Marriage for the purpose of incubating piety was seen as eminently praise-worthy.

The patristic authors were demonstrably torn between conflicting needs: whether to exhort their flocks to more exacting efforts leading to greater rewards, or whether to soft-pedal this course since it was fraught with difficulties and greater penalties for failure. In that celibacy was a higher path to virtue, it could not be recommended strongly enough; but in that some might try it and fail, thus being worse off spiritually than before, great caution was needed. As we have seen, being the cause of another's downfall was as culpable as backsliding oneself; hence the collective neurosis about being too extreme and so tempting weaker vessels to failure. Such 'dangerous' extremism resulted in the proscription of formerly respected clerics such as Pelagius and fostered the suspicion that anyone strongly recommending the higher path must, *ergo*, of necessity be con-demning marriage; a suspicion all the great proponents of celibacy must counter time and again.[5]

To be taken for a fanatic in advocating celibacy to women was not to be lightly laughed off. The lunatic fringe of extreme practitioners of asceticism was bringing the whole movement into disrepute; and reserved for especial scorn were the women drawn to these suspect tendencies, often led into 'unbecoming' modes of behaviour. 'Come now, servants of God, let us assume a manly mind and banish the madness of these women. This whole deception is female; the disease comes from Eve, who was deceived long ago' was Epiphanius' judgement on the Montanists (Epiphanius *Medicine Box* 79.2). Held up as a model for scorn and derision were females such as those who were with the *circumcelliones*, the itinerant and violent zealots who were the most extreme and active tendency of the Donatist move-ment and roamed the African hinterlands performing alternate acts of worship and violence. These fanatics had in their train numerous female camp-followers who attracted particular condemnation; 'those troops of homeless women who have declined matrimony that they may avoid restraint' was a typical view (Augustine *Let.* 35.2). The Synod of Gangra of 340 saw a need to forbid women to cut their hair and dress like a man; also condemning Eustathius of Sebaste, an ascetic rejecting marriage (Rousselle 1988:186). The Marcionites from whom we saw Jerome and Chrysostom needing to dissociate themselves, while disparaging marriage, advocated complete sexual freedom for men and women alike (including homosexuality and paedophilia), as compatible with Christian faith. Subject to prurient finger-pointing also were the female religious dedicatees around Hierakas, a revered ascetic leader in Egypt. He was taken to task by Athanasius for doubting that married persons had any place in Paradise, and expecting his followers to be ministered to by virgin female companions without mishap (Athanasius *On the Synods of Ariminum and Seleucia* Brown 1987 : 298).

Ambrose was the target of another group of uncontrolled women, this time Arians, promoting their religious differences as a justification of disorderly behaviour on the occasion of his consecration of Anemius in the disputed see of Sirmium. One of them 'more impudent than the rest' mounted the tribunal and seized him by his clothing, attempting to drag him to her companions 'so that they might beat him and drive him from the church'. Ambrose's response was to warn her of God's judgement (afterwards seen to be wreaked on her in her premature death), for 'even if I am unworthy of so great a bishopric, it is not fitting that you or your kind lay hands on any bishop of whatever sort' (Paulinus of Milan *Life of Ambrose* 11) – 'your kind' referring whether to Arians or to women is less than clear.

These women were attached to heretical movements, and could therefore safely be lambasted for their violent behaviour; but much of the fervour of patristic authors such as Augustine on the circumcellion women arose out of their need to dissociate their own approved female ascetics from inclusion in the criticism they attracted. It expresses an anxiety about the ends to which their own preaching can be put; thus the need to draw distinctions between such hoydens and devout Catholic women and to assert their faith in the orthodoxy of the motives of their own side, that they might not be accused of fostering such tendencies.

Such anxieties set the Jerome–Jovinian controversy in context. Not just another of the interminable wrangles in which Jerome became embroiled because of his confrontational theology and his acerbic pen, it expresses the tremors of a school of thought frightened by its own logical conclusion. There existed a genuine confusion about the relative merit of chastity as set against the married state; and when some clerics maintained the equity of these conditions, their works were gratefully received by many. Jovinian, and before him, Helvidius, against whom Jerome's treatise on *The Perpetual Virginity of Blessed Mary* was written, had tempered the party line on chastity to suit those less inclined to ascetic endeavour: 'You compelled me [to write], Helvidius; for, brightly as the Gospel shines at the present day, you will have it that equal glory attaches to virginity and to the marriage state' (*Against Helvidius; the Perpetual Virginity of Blessed Mary* 24). Helvidius in fact concluded that virginity was ranked below matrimony, appealing to the mention in the Gospels of 'sisters' and 'brethren' of Christ, and supporting his opinion with the writings of Tertullian and Victorinus. Jovinian asserted that 'virgins, widows and married women, who have once gone through Christian baptism, if they are on a par in other respects, are of equal merit' (*Against Jovinian* 1.3). Jovinian, however, also held that the birth of Christ had been by a 'true parturition' and so contravened the orthodoxy of the time, according to which the infant Jesus passed through the walls of the womb as His resurrected body did afterwards out of the tomb or through the closed doors. Thus Jovinian was not just controversial but adjudged to be heretical, and his book was condemned in synods at Rome and Milan at around 390, after Jerome's friend and patron Pammachius had brought it to the notice of Pope Siricius.

Notwithstanding his lack of orthodoxy, Jovinian's views were expressive of the unease felt by many at the time; Jerome attested to his success in influencing those who had already vowed virginity to marry (*ibid.* 2.36–7). The rancorous tone of Jerome's treatise might have been scarcely expected for a treatise defending accepted orthodoxy, and reflects his fury at having his own letter-of-the-law orthodoxy recast as unpopular extremism. 'They affirm that to preach up chastity till no comparison is left between a wife and a virgin is equivalent to a condemnation of matrimony' (Jerome *Let.* 48.2), and Jerome must defend himself at length to Pammachius that to prefer virginity is not to condemn marriage, reiterating his comparison of gold with silver, of the 100-fold with the 30-fold. His faults as they have been judged, he asseverates bitterly, are not his faults at all, he is merely expounding the apostle who is the first to make the distinction; further that 'whilst he applauds those who lead the van, he does not despise those who bring up the rear' (*ibid*. 14). The issue as Jerome sees it is clear: of two paths one is preferable but both are lawful; one brings great rewards, the other moderate rewards. He quotes the more conciliatory Ambrose to back himself up: 'The nuptial tie is not to be avoided as a crime but to be refused as a hard burden' (*ibid*.; Ambrose *On Widows* 13).

As one who had previously defended a twice-married bishop as being within the bounds of lawfulness, and advised against the individual in question being pilloried – if only because of his cynical rider that, after all, 'the whole world is filled with persons ordained in similar circumstances' (Jerome *Let*. 69.2) – Jerome's outrage at the charges levelled at him with regard to his orthodoxy is understandable; 'I have said that there are diversities of gifts within the church, and that virginity is one gift and wedlock another . . . Can it be said that I condemn that which in the clearest terms I declare to be the gift of God?' (*Against Jovinian* 1.5). 'From all considerations it is clear that I have said nothing at all new concerning virginity and marriage but have followed in all respects the judgement of . . . Ambrose and others who have discussed the doctrines of the church' (*ibid*. 15). But the furore was equally understandable, given the pungency with which Jerome expressed his preference: '[The Apostle] did not say, it is good not to have a wife: but it is good not to touch a woman, as though there were danger even in the touch: as though he who touched her would not escape from her who "hunts for the precious life", who causes the young man's understanding to fly away' (*ibid*. 1.7). While not actually condemning marriage – 'Do I condemn marriage if I enumerate its troubles, such as the crying of infants, the death of children, the chance of abortion, domestic losses and so forth?' (Jerome *Let*. 48.18) – Jerome has been quite justly charged with attempting to bring it into disrepute. He is carefully within the law also on his position on marrying more than once: 'I do not condemn digamists or trigamists, or even, to put an extreme case, octagamists' (*ibid*.) – with statements such as 'it is more tolerable for a woman to prostitute herself to one man than to many', (*Against Jovinian* 1.14–15) who could fail to be reassured? To say 'Marriage is like a plank offered to a man who has been shipwrecked; by its means you may remedy what you have done amiss' (*ibid*. 1.7) is not to pronounce it condemned, by the letter of the law; but it is small wonder that Pammachius and his friends were so anxious to withhold the treatise from publication, however unsuccessfully.[6] The most literal orthodoxy did not save Jerome from once again provoking a hornet's nest; indicating the strength of feeling the ascetic movement awoke in those afraid or unwilling to regard the Apostle's dictates on marriage in their strictest sense.

PRACTICAL CONSIDERATIONS: ASCETICISM AND THE AGE OF CONSENT

Devout Christian women of the time had thus to make a choice. Marriage, or more specifically, marriage in its full sexual capacity was the great dividing standard by which one's devoutness was judged; the choice was between the acquisition of merit through abnegation of one's sexual capacity, or encompassment of one's devotions within it. Having said this, however, women of these centuries often found external factors pre-empted any decision-making process. For some, the idea of the choice dictated by religious scruple offered them in church writings was purely notional – the decision as to their future was thrust upon them. In considering women in the presentation of patristic ideology it is important not to ignore the backdrop of the social and peer pressure in favour of marriage in late Roman society, and particularly for early marriage – by our standards – in the circles most accessible to our view, the aristocracy and minor nobility.

That girls could be married 'too early' was not a concept that had much currency in Roman thinking, a fact that was deplored by Roman writers and doctors. While the Codex Justinianus renews a law stating the legal minimum age for girls was twelve (fourteen for boys), it seems to have been one of the *leges imperfectae* that were a not uncommon occurrence in the Roman statute books; that is, laws that while prohibiting something neither threatened their violators with penalties nor invalidated their transgression – thus effectively removing any incentive to obey them. This may have been due to what would now be termed a 'lack of political will' concerning the 'crime'; certainly it implied a lack of serious concern for its consequences. As a result, cases of girls married before their twelfth year were not uncommon.[7] There was nothing out of the way in pre-pubescent marriages in a society which thought puberty took place in the fourteenth year[8] but legalised marriages for girls in the twelfth year; nor did Christianity necessarily differ from this, as witness the epitaphs penned by two Christian writers, Agathias and Paulus Silentarius to girls who died aged 12 and 14 describing them as ripe for marriage.[9]

In opposition to the theory of a predominantly young age at marriage it has been suggested that the evidence is of a very specific nature in being skewed towards the upper classes and city-dwellers (Shaw 1987a:44ff) but against this one should set the medical writings and beliefs of the time. It is clear that Roman doctors made, and went on making over several centuries, some fundamental anatomical errors about female reproduction. They believed, for instance, that the vagina was sealed completely by an internal membrane between the womb and the hymen; and that intercourse induced menstruation. These misconceptions were the result partly of their seclusion from the centre of operations at childbirth and all examinations prior to it, for reasons of modesty; but more specifically because of the prevalent custom of marriage for girls while still pre-pubescent – as was repeatedly, and vainly, pointed out to them by such Greek-trained doctors as Soranus of Ephesus, who directed his writings particularly at the fathers of girls in an effort to persuade them not to have their daughters married before menstruation (Soranus *Gynaecology* 1.20). Plutarch gives the reason why this largely fell on deaf ears when, writing of what he has seen, he says 'the Romans . . . give their maidens in marriage when they are twelve years or even younger. In this way more than any other it was thought both their beds and their disposition would be pure and undefiled when their husbands took control of them' (Plutarch *Lycurgus and Numa* 4.1–3). The epigraphic and medical evidence show that girls did marry at ages earlier even than those allowed for in the law, given that the law may have provided for what it considered to be the lowest likely age of marriage rather than the most typical.

In addition, there was a factor increasing the pressure towards marriage for girls which needs particular underlining for today's historian; that the Romans in any age seem to have had no concept, as no instances, of 'surplus women'. There were fewer women in the Roman population than men; Dio comments on this in the freeborn population of 18 BC. Since this is 'demographically surprising' (Gardner 1986: 156) it may be attributable to the custom of exposure of unwanted infants (not prohibited until 374), though evidence on the prevalence of this is hard to come by. Whatever the cause, the imbalance of the sexes would have increased the incidence of marriage for girls at an early age. There is no word in Latin for 'spinster'; it is revealing that on the rare occurrences when Latin writers are called upon to describe the condition, they use the word *vidua*. 'Before Christianity consecrated celibacy, unmarried adult women must have been rare' (*ibid.*) In the upper classes, daughters marry, and re-marry, until in the fourth century they begin to opt out; a norm difficult to grasp properly for those with our long sociological and literary history of 'surplus' and 'redundant' women, and with marriage seen as a desirable goal and frequently unattainable.

For many girls, even had they been decided on such a course at an early enough age, the possibility of declining marriage did not lie in their hands in any case. A woman *sui iuris* or independent in the eyes of the law, like Jerome's aristocratic disciple Marcella (who had been married young and been widowed after only seven months, at an early enough age to make remarriage an automatic assumption for her mother Albina) might exercise choice against marrying; for prospective marriage partners still *in potestate* (under the control of the *paterfamilias* of the household), the relevant parties whose consent was required to legally validate the marriage were their *patres*. The consent of the betrothed parties was a bonus, but by no means a legal necessity to a marriage. Paul the jurist says that marriages of minors should not take place without their consent; but in the case of it happening, the marriage should not be dissolved (*D.* 23.1.12). This applied to males as well as females; for the *Digest*, having asserted that 'a son *in potestas* cannot be forced to take a wife' (*ibid.*) then pulls its own teeth with the circular argument that if, however, he *was* so forced, 'then he has nevertheless entered into matrimony, which cannot exist between those who are unwilling' (*D.* 23.2.21). In the case of girls, Ulpian was of the opinion that the daughter's consent can only be withheld in the event of the *pater* selecting someone morally undesirable (*D.* 23.1.22).[10] Even the austere church Fathers might be seen fostering this custom; John Chrysostom is to be found advocating early marriage for sons, in case the youth be tempted into impurity by prolonging the period between puberty and marriage – 'or do you think it a matter of minor importance to the marriage whether the bride and her young man are virgins?' (*On Vainglory* 81.2).

In the post-Constantinian period then, a girl wishing to dedicate herself to a religious life would need to have escaped the more peremptory manifestations of *patria potestas* and struggle against a social expectation tantamount to coercion into marriage; and that at an age which if not considered premature for matrimony was too soon to expect in the girl a realistic faculty for making such a momentous decision against expectations (except in the case of a Eustochium or Asella with a strong familial counter-influence). From the standpoint of traditionalists, no doubt this was one of the advantages of the system. Not, as previously stated, that this exclusively affected girls; we have plenty of examples of young men who yearned for the dedicated life coerced into matrimony by family expectation. Pachomius, the great monastic founder, was faced when a young man with an enforced marriage by his pagan family; as was another desert monastic, Abba Amoun, compelled into marriage either by 'rich parents who forced him to marry against his will' (*HM* 22.1), or, in Palladius' more detailed version 'being unable to resist the pressure of his uncle' who was his *paterfamilias* (*LH* 8). However, the young men demonstrate more capacity to alter the state thus forced upon them than do the girls. Pachomius fled before his marriage could take place; Amoun 'when they had compelled him to [marry] ... persuaded the girl in the bridal chamber that they should preserve their virginity in secret' (*HM* 22.1) which they did for some eighteen years, by Palladius' account, until he departed for Nitria, leaving her to convert her household and turn her house into a monastery.

In the case of girls, with little choice but to submit, there are indications that in some cases an unfulfilled choice for abnegation was, as it were, carried over a generation by being passed on to one of the children (Brown in Veyne 1987:302–3); Martha the mother of Simeon the Younger of Antioch, the stylite, raised her son from the start with the intention that he should become a dedicated monk, since her own yearning for dedication had been cut short by an arranged marriage against her will. This is another consequence of an early marriageable age; it is interesting to speculate on how many of our notable ascetics were the product of maternal repinings over a thwarted longing for 'the desert'. It is probable that for this reason treatises on virginity were directed more towards the mothers of promising daughters than at the girls themselves, who would in all likelihood be too young to act upon them, even if they did understand them (Rousselle 1988:188). There are many obvious examples of such an idea of family training-up: Paula with Eustochium, Juliana with Demetrias, Avita with Eunomia.

It has been argued however that Christianity did have a tangential effect on Roman society in respect of marital age for girls. Not all girls were married at the earliest viable age; Keith Hopkins observed from a collation of funerary inscriptions from which the age of the dead girls could be ascertained that in these inscriptions, while the modal[11] age at marriage of pagan girls was twelve to fifteen (43.41%), for Christian girls it was fifteen to eighteen (41.67%) (Hopkins

1965:319). This may be a social phenomenon rather than a religious one, however; Brent Shaw has pointed out the disparity between the quality of the pagan inscriptions ('reasonably elaborate') and the Christian ones ('exceedingly poor') from which he argues that the 'Christian' inscriptions merely provide us with an insight into the free poor and poor of distant servile origins of Rome, to whom the habit of funerary commemoration was spreading after the beginning of the fourth century, rather than being peculiarly 'Christian' (Shaw 1987a:41–2). But as Shaw indicated, the definably 'pagan' evidence is predominantly from the more well-off classes; so given the lack of any real evidence from the point of view of the 'pagan' free and servile poor, this assumption is surely only as reliable as that of Hopkins and those who follow him. All that can be inferred realistically from these samples, backed up by our literary sources, is the strong upper-class bias, Christian and pagan, towards early marriage. This brings additional sociological implications. While girls may have first married in their mid to late teens, similar evidence indicates that men tended to begin marrying in their mid to late twenties with modes in the range of twenty-seven to thirty, and hence an age-gap of ten or more years between husband and wife was fairly typical. Upper-class patterns of marriage would exaggerate this tendency towards an age-gap, since modes of marriage for girls were significantly lower, but for men probably much the same, as in the lower classes; and this wider gap between husband and wife would have significant implications for reproduction, conjugal relations, widowhood and re-marriage and the devolution of property.[12]

This provides the backdrop for much of our literary evidence. Our writers show us Melania the Elder married at fourteen by parental precept and widowed by her twenty-second year (Murphy 1947:64); Marcella, a youthful widow after only seven months of marriage resisting a remarriage with the elderly Neriatius Cerialis (Jerome *Let.* 127.2), Melania the Younger married in her thirteenth year (*Life of Melania the Younger* 1), and Macrina provided with a husband-to-be and then deprived of him by his sudden death in her twelfth year (Gregory of Nyssa *Life of Macrina* 964).

This is to say, in fact, that of our most prominent female exponents of asceticism, both of virginity and widowhood, those out of the top-drawer are particularly marked in their precociousness and determination in their decisions; since they were likely to be subject to heavier familial pressure towards an early marriage or swift remarriage. This sheds new light on the 'problem' of the over-reported struggle of the over-represented aristocratic women; as it is disproportionately represented, so it would seem to have been disproportionately difficult. Those who had, like Melania the Younger and Eustochium, to 'take on' their family to adopt asceticism fought not only the social norm towards marriage for girls as inevitable, but also their class tendency towards the earlier end of the marriageable age scale – which, as the inscriptions to two girls married at six and seven respectively[13] indicate, could start early indeed. This kind of evidence puts Eustochium's decision for virginity at around the age of ten in a relatively mature light, and Demetrias' decision just before her projected marriage at fourteen is towards the upper end of the aristocratic curve; by the standards of the Christian Agathius and Paulus Silentarius, let alone the pagan writers, she would have been regarded as highly nubile. Girls of this age, furthermore were regarded (legally, if not practically) as responsible for their own actions within marriage; legal advice existed for husbands – and concubines – wanting to bring charges of adultery against partners of younger than twelve (*D.* 48.5.14.8).

Christian eschatological ideas set in opposition to this kind of conditioning can be observed causing a certain amount of double-thinking on the parts of concerned parents. Melania the Elder's mother Albina, so anxious to marry and re-marry her youthful daughter, was a devout Christian; and Melania the Younger's parents, horrified at her decision for asceticism, had brought their daughter up to be proud of the fame of her illustrious grandmother. There are also evident examples of familial anxiety resulting in attempts by other relatives to regulate the 'deviant' behaviour and re-impose the norm. Little else could explain an attempt made by Eustochium's aunt and uncle, Praetextata and Hymettius, to interfere with the pre-pubescent girl's upbringing and expectations; by fairly crude means, given the pervasive nature of her conditioning from her mother. Her aunt and uncle offered her the temptations of personal adornment, an elaborate coiffure, jewels, rich dresses and so on, presumably imagining that any 'right-minded' girl of her age could not fail to be thus won over. Jerome exults over their failure, and attributed Praetextata's premature death soon after to divine retribution for this attempt to subvert one of God's chosen virgins (Jerome *Let.* 107.5). However, this fortuitous explanation may have been less than convincing in an age where the comparatively youthful death of a wife was a sufficiently regular occurrence, as witness the instances of all three of Eustochium's sisters. Though only one of them had died before she left Rome, the probabilities of surviving many years of marriage and child-birth were never better than evens – a consideration which must have weighed with the pre-pubescent child.

But Praetextata was not just representing social pressure or the opinion of an anti-Christian older generation: she might also have been very properly worried about her niece's health if she followed this odd scheme. The gaps in the gynaecological knowledge of Roman doctors led them to make dire prognostications as to the active dangers inherent in delayed defloration. Praetextata would conceivably have been influenced by the opinions of doctors such as Rufus (who was used and quoted by Oribasius, a court doctor in the fourth century) that illness such as *plethora* – overabundance of humours – and attendant problems threatened girls who stayed virgins too long (Oribasius *Medical Collections* 18). Perhaps she would have met with more success had she waited a little for the onset of the 'hasty desires' in girls that Macrobius considered the explanation for marriage at twelve, accounting for it by the greater degree of heat in girls (Macrobius *Saturnalia*. 7.7.6). Perhaps this might be one of the reasons for the epigraphic evidence of later marriages for Christian girls: the length of time unwilling parents had to wait for them to be 'warmed' by the onset of puberty out of a yearning to be a nun. However, to back up her position, Eustochium – and the others like her – might have read and, given her sisters' experience, believed opposing medical opinion, such as Soranus, that 'among women we see that those who, for reasons of rules of service to the Gods have forsworn intercourse and those who have been kept virgins as ordained by law are less susceptible to disease' while married women did not enjoy good health (Soranus *Gynaecology*. 1.32–3). A further scarifying factor in Roman medical advice might have been the advice to men seeking heirs that it mattered little whether their wives actually wanted sexual intercourse or not; Soranus ruled out the need for conscious desire in women (favoured by the Greek doctors) as an aid for conception. This lack of consent in the act could extend to its consequences; Galen talks of women who refused to admit that they were going to be wives and Soranus offered advice to midwives tending women who would not cooperate in the delivery (*ibid.* 4.2).[14]

Another incident demonstrating attempts at external regulation of unacceptable behaviour is that of the behaviour of the crowd at Eustochium's sister Blesilla's funeral and their interpretation of her mother Paula's grieving behaviour: 'Isn't this what we've said? She weeps for her daughter, killed with fasting; she wanted her to marry again, that she might have grandchildren ... They've misled this unhappy lady; that she's not a nun from choice is clear.' Blesilla, previously a light-minded girl of carefree habits even in her premature widowhood, had become a convert to asceticism after a serious illness and had then died only three months into her new lifestyle; Paula's grief at her funeral had been extreme (Jerome *Let.* 39.6). The crowd reaction is significant as a protest at the current ascetic drift of opinion in a century notable for more frequent decisions against marriage and a higher rate of continent widowhood (supported by the law; from the fourth century the legal minimum interval between the death of a husband and re-marriage became one year; as opposed to the previous ten months, with legal penalties for those not swift to re-marry (*CJ* 5.9.3 (381)). Jerome used the crowd's normative attitude as a stick with which to beat Paula; all very well for an ignorant rabble, her attitudes were 'unfitting', even 'detestable' in a Christian mother and served only to provide further ammunition for the unwashed masses. Blesilla (whose feverish convert's asceticism may well have hastened her own end) would say 'she is not my mother who displeases my Lord' (Jerome *Let.* 39.6). Nonetheless we have only Jerome's word that Paula, though a fervent ascetic personally, did not in fact expect and look forward to the prospect of the continuation of her (earthly) family through grand-children; it is entirely possible that she felt in fact that two ascetic women in the family would be enough for heavenly prominence, leaving the earthly branch to carry on with the temporal notability.

The most notable example of a familial attempt to impose conformity, and by Christian parents, was that of Publicola and Albina taking legal action against their daughter Melania the Younger and her husband Pinianus to thwart their ascetic endeavours, on the grounds that they were *in potestate*; more overtly motivated by the dangers to the family property that Melania and Pinianus were disposing of so blithely. Nonetheless, Melania had married in the first instance despite a strong wish to follow the example of Publicola's own mother (Melania the Elder) and even twice attempted to produce an heir, in obedience to familial expectations (Gerontius *Life of Melania the Younger* 1).

The church writers of the fourth century were galvanising new family dynamics (examined in more detail in Chapter 6), with the increasing dissemination of monastic ideals through a wider section of society. More and more felt the pull of such a life, as is possible to observe in these girls defying families and social norms to follow it. While in the East the tendency was still for the World and the Desert to be geographically distinct from each other (though the World could call upon the metaphysical resources of the Desert for arbitration and protection), Western writers such as Jerome and Augustine were introducing elements of the Desert into the life of the World, attempting to make these values a relevant part of the life of every believer – a shared and heavy responsibility. And for the women, a prominent part of their commitment to the Desert in their lives was perceived in a heightened awareness of their sexual status; their dedication to God seen directly in terms of their sexual condition, ranked in order by their commitment whether to celibacy, continence or a chaste observance of the status quo. They need not go the lengths of taking to the wilds of the Holy Land, or any other wilderness; any woman could quietly become a dedicatee at home, by simply forswearing the physicality which was looked on as her inescapable lot.

This is the basis of the stratification into which the treatment of the pious woman settles in the writings of the later church Fathers. Abstinence was by no means the only commitment incumbent on the devout woman but it signalled the degree by which her commitment might be known: her sexual condition dictated her rung on the ladder of the church hierarchy. With this precondition comes the formulaic reiteration of a phrase adopted from the Parable of the sower to fit women into categories of almost mathematical progressions of acquired virtue: the often-repeated idea of 'the thirty-fold, the sixty-fold, the one hundred-fold' harvest – 'the thirty-fold refers to marriage ... the sixty-fold to widows ... the hundred-fold expresses the crown of virginity' (Jerome *Against Jovinian* 1.3); a formula which signals a need to find an expression of the legitimacy of marriage and conjugal relations within a wider context of other, arguably preferable, conditions. The patristic authors were not merely relegating women to a more confined, categorised condition; they were also the victims of their own ascetic conditioning, and the heirs to the dilemma of whether to counsel the lawful or the laudable, a dilemma given first expression and no solution by the Apostle Paul.

Sexual abstinence was not particularly a Christian contribution to late antique society but marched alongside pagan experiments with continence for religious reasons (such as in the worship of Cybele); but adopted by the Christians it acquired a new regularity and prominence. This represents the popular impact of the early Christian belief in 'the doctrine of sexuality as a "privileged" symptom of personal transformation', in Peter Brown's resounding phrase (Veyne 1987:257); that the avoidance of physical relations was the sign of a greater commitment, possession of which rendered one in a condition of unhesitating availability to God and one's community. This state was also a signpost to outsiders; and hence the obsessive worrying about preserving all the outward appurtenances of modesty, and the constantly reiterated frets in advice to women 'that you might not give scandal to unbelievers'. It is also, perhaps, the victory of the 'morality of the socially vulnerable' (ibid. p. 300) over the perceived morals of the aristocracy, spearheaded by the aristocratic women who adopted preaching on asceticism with such alarming alacrity. What, then, to advise to those swelling the groups living under vows, the orders of widows and virgins – representing all that more house-bound and earth-bound women should aspire to – was a source of worry to not only the moderates but even to those proselytes of ascesis whose counsel they were obeying. These orders, in their purest forms, represented in the fourth century the logical end of the preaching of the Fathers as directed to women; but their establishment and the care and charge over them caused infinite difficulties to those same preachers.

4

'EUNUCHS FOR THE LOVE OF HEAVEN'

Avowed virginity

VIRGINITY IN PATRISTIC THEORY

> You know yourselves how slippery is the path of youth . . . she
> must have the advice and encouragement of all, she must be
> aided by letters from you. As you know, a girl's courage is
> strengthened when she knows that persons in high places are
> interested in her.
>
> (Jerome *Let.* 7.4)

The regard in which consecrated virginity was held equated with the
standing of martyrdom in preceding centuries as the sign of a
superior commitment to Christianity. For all that 'we do not
disparage marriage' (Jerome *Against Jovinian* 1.3) and 'the first
natural bond of society is that of man and his wife' (Augustine *On
the Good of Marriage* 1) nonetheless 'in the resurrection there will
be no marrying nor giving in marriage' (Augustine *On the Sermon
on the Mount* 1.15.40); 'the fruitfulness of the flesh is not equal to
holy virginity' (Gregory of Nyssa *On Virginity* 8), 'for this is a richer
and more fruitful condition of blessedness, not to have a pregnant
womb but to develop the soul's lofty capacities' (*ibid.* 9). To abstain
from the usual patterns of life, to refrain from the temptations of a
relationship and a family, was to be at least peculiar, at best
outstanding, and in a highly visible and controversial way; if successfully pursued, such a route must surely be a visible sign of greater
commitment and power; and greater gifts from God.

Virginity is a grace but also 'a helpmate' to greater efforts,
according to Gregory of Nyssa (*ibid.* 4, 9); it is incumbent on those
practising it to be still more pure in other respects also, as they are
the vanguard of the church. Thus the great difference between
fleshly and spiritual virginity is underlined: 'virginity is only holy

57

because it is dedicated to God, not in itself; it is fleshly but of the spirit' (*ibid*. 8) and 'Virginity of the body is devised to further such a disposition of the soul' (*ibid*. 5). Similarly John Chrysostom stressed 'virginity is defined not just by the one point of never having had sex: she who is careful for things of the world cannot be a virgin' and 'evil is not in cohabitation but in impediments to the strictness of life' (*Hom*. 19 on I Cor VII:7); 'she is not pure who is compelled [to virginity] by fear, nor honourable who does this for gain' (Ambrose *On Virginity* 1.15). By that same token, 'virginity can be lost even by a thought'; and those possessed of such thoughts 'are evil virgins, virgins in flesh, not in spirit' (Jerome *Let*. 22.5).

All this is to the end that virgins should properly be the first rank in heaven, the vanguard of the church, the earthly counterpart of the Angels for whom there is no giving in marriage. 'Those who decide to marry ... must of necessity confess that they are inferior to virgins' (Ambrose *On Virginity* 1.36). So Demetrias, a Roman girl of distinguished family who came under the spotlight of some of the patristic writers when she made the decision to embrace the life of a dedicated virgin, is lauded as superior to her devout and *univira* mother, Juliana, who is told

> [she], coming after you in birth, has gone before you in conduct; descended from you in lineage has risen above you in honour; following you in age has gone before you in holiness ... spiritually enriched in a higher degree than yourself, since, even with this augmentation, you are inferior to her.
>
> (Augustine *On the Good of Widowhood* 11)

Augustine sets out this idea again in introducing to bishop Quintilianus another widow and virgin daughter, 'Galla, a widow who has undertaken holy vows, and her daughter Simplicia, who is subordinate to her mother because of her age, but superior to her because of her holiness' (Jerome *Let*. 212). Similarly Paula's virgin daughter Julia Eustochium is represented by Jerome as superior to her widowed elder sister Blesilla: 'Your sister Blesilla is superior in age, but inferior in firmness of will' (*Let*. 22.15). John Chrysostom sums up of the virgins: 'this group is a more honourable and princely possession than the others' (*On the Priesthood* 314). This pronouncement comes in a passage where the behaviour of the virgins is in direct contrast to that of the widows:

> As it is not the same thing for a maiden who is free, and for her serving woman to sin, so it is not for a virgin and a widow;

because it has become a matter of indifference for widows to talk foolishly, and to revile one another, and to flatter, and to be shameless, and to appear everywhere, and to parade in the public places; but the virgin has prepared herself for greater things, and entered on the pursuit of the wisdom which is above ... while she is in this body it is her purpose to display the qualities of incorporeal powers.

(John Chrysostom *On the Priesthood* 315)

Thus the Fathers manifested a much greater concern for the fitness of behaviour in virgins; they have far more to lose, and their status is more precious to the church. 'It is as if virginity were a kind of bond in humans' relationship with God', even 'an actual representation of the blessedness of the world to come' (Gregory of Nyssa *On Virginity* 2, 13) and by being modelled on the chaste relations of the Father, Son and Holy Spirit, adoption of virginity on earth allows one to participate in the heavenly quality of 'incorruptibility', of defeating death itself. Gregory argues in his treatise:

The virginal life, since it is stronger than the power of death must be to those who think the preferred one ... the process of generation starts off the process of corruption; because from the moment of birth the process of dying commences. But those who by virginity desist from procreation set a limit within themselves for death and by their own action have checked death's progress; they have made themselves a frontier between life and death and a barrier which thwarts him ... a body is justly called 'incorruptible' that does not render service in a dying world nor become the instrument of corruptible creatures.

(Gregory of Nyssa *On Virginity* 13)

These arguments are symptomatic of the increasing rarification of the order of virgins within the fourth century church. Their specialness was manifested in their apartness, which should most fitly express itself in strictly contemplative and prayerful activities: 'A virgin is not ordained, for we do not have a commandment from the Lord. For the advantage of virginity is not so that marriage is slandered, but in order to provide time for piety' (*Apostolic Constitutions* 8.24.2).

In the light of this continual linking of virginity with superior virtue, and seclusion and chastity with superior worship, it is interesting that virginity seems to have been regarded as especially the property of women in this period. Though Gregory of Nyssa considered it clear that when the apostle said 'women' he actually meant both sexes (*On Virginity* 20), more writers thought like Jerome, the sceptic about women's capacity for virtue: 'For this reason virginity is more abundantly poured on women, because it began with a woman' (Jerome *Let.* 22.21). Most treatises on virginity from this period, whether addressed to men or women, are about women's virginity (Gregory of Nyssa is the only exception), starting with Methodius' *Symposium*, depicting ten virgin women discussing the relative merits of marriage and virginity. The successful virgin becomes the archetype of all that the church aspires to and by being in this set-apart, better-than-human position can acquire merit for the church on earth; more than this, is the living symbol of the church on earth. This thinking dovetails with the imagery of the Virgin Church that The Bridegroom, Christ, will take in chaste marriage; 'Let us kiss him whose embrace is chastity: let us have intercourse with him with whom marriage is virginity' (Paulinus of Nola *Let.* 23.42). The virgins on earth were to represent the church's highest expression of piety against apocalyptic expectations.

Yet this increasingly rarified elevation of virginity carried with it its own difficulties. The mystic quality of virginity, as we have seen, could be lost merely by a thought, not just of carnality but of the theologically dubious variety also. This being so, it behoved the wise virgin to examine closely even the fulsome praises to her own address. For instance when Pelagius said, via a dedication to Demetrias, to all consecrated virgins:

> You have here, then, those properties on the account of which you are deservedly, and more, especially to be given preference over others; for your earthly rank and wealth are known to be derived from your relatives, not from yourself, but your spiritual riches no-one can have conferred on you but yourself; for these, then, you are rightly to be praised, for those you are deservedly to be preferred to others, for they can exist only from yourself and in yourself.
>
> (Pelagius *Epistle to Demetrias* 11)

– this might have been thought by its addressee to be just another of the eulogisations of virginity already observed in their excesses in other writers. But on this occasion, if a virgin listened and believed, she would be lost. These sentiments horrified Augustine, who hastened to write to Demetrias reminding her that her condition was through grace; while spiritual riches were the peculiar property of the dedicated virgin, they came not from herself, but from God.

> Far be it from any virgin of Christ willingly to listen to statements like these. Every virgin of Christ understands the innate poverty of the human heart and . . . refuses to have it adorned otherwise than by the gifts of her spouse. For her possession of this great and excellent gift of chastity, she ought to give thanks to our God and Lord rather than to listen to the words of anyone who tells her that she possessed it from herself.
>
> (Augustine Let. 188.4–5)

Apotheosised on one side, threatened with hell-fire on the other, in addition to all her other preternatural qualities the conscientious virgin would need the theological delicacy and insight of an Aquinas to thus distinguish amongst all the rhetoric so industriously poured out addressing her state. And amongst this effluence of theology, she had little really practical advice to her condition. Basil of Ancyra is noteworthy for being the only theologian to talk realistically to women about the practical problems of celibacy, by virtue of being a doctor as well as a bishop. He described the state with accuracy and in a way addressed to female needs, teaching women that all their senses are potential media through which they may expect desire; how sight can be more seductive than touch and last longer in the memory; and accurately describes female masturbation, the better to fight it.[1] Such pragmatic help was rare for avowed virgins.

VIRGINITY IN PRACTICE – WISE VIRGINS

What, then, was the experience of these girls? What was the practice of virginity in this age like? What can we learn of the qualities needed, the recruiting methods, the practical details of their day-to-day existence? This will be told in the first instance from the point of view of those who were deemed to have 'succeeded' in the life; this is the experience of those whose tales would be told as exemplars.

A lifestyle of abstinence gave superior standing in the Christian community; and without question, the highest status, as we have seen, came from abstinence total, from vowed, lifelong virginity. But the irony of this senior position is that its incumbents were subject to the most vigorous restraints of any of the categories; seniority here did not carry responsibility. These maidens may have been the 100-fold, as Jerome asserts; each may have had the ability to make 'a noble family yet more noble by her virginity' and even 'to lessen the calamity of the ruin of Rome' (Jerome *Let.* 130.6), and take precedence over other devout relatives in heaven but their everyday existence was drastically curtailed in consequence.

Large numbers of the virgins observed their vows from home, supervised by their parents. 'A virgin is the inseparable pledge of her parents, and neither troubles them for a dowry, nor abandons them, nor harms them by word or deed' (Ambrose *On Virginity* 1.32) – a seeming continuance of the Roman recognition of the separate identity and authority of the family and the daughter's subjection to her *pater*. 'Be subject to your parents ... Rarely go abroad, and if you wish to seek the company of martyrs, seek it in your own chamber' (Jerome *Let.* 22.17). 'Let your companions be women pale and thin with fasting, and approved by their years and conduct' (*ibid.*); 'Be subject to your grandmother and your mother. Never look upon a man ... except in their company' (*ibid.* 130.12). Virgins should entirely 'avoid the company of married women who are devoted to their husbands' because of the risk of hearing unfitting talk – 'such conversations are filled with deadly venom' (*Let.* 18). The ever-practical Basil of Ancyra saw the need to advise virgins particularly not to fraternise with what they might be tempted to see as a no-risk category, eunuchs: 'It is said that those who, having reached virility and the age when the genital member is capable of copulation, have cut off only their testicles, burn with greater and less restrained desire for sexual union and that not only do they feel this ardour, but they think that they can defile any woman they meet without risk' (Basil of Ancyra *On Virginity PG* 30.718). Even if within the confines of home and parental super- vision, virgins must be carefully supervised by the priest, said Chrysostom, more so than any other group; for their fall will result not in divorce, but in hell-fire. Therefore they must not be suffered to go abroad unnecessarily or often, or talk idly, or abuse or flatter; they should even be forbidden to attend funerals and vigils as these are often occasions of misbehaviour (*On the Priesthood* 314–5). Melania the Younger as abbess further attempted to police the very minds of the virgins within her community, 'carefully scrutinising their thoughts, not to let the smallest impure reflection live in them' (Gerontius *Life of Melania the Younger* 23).

As the rewards were higher, so were the lines between right and wrong more finely drawn. The rule for virgins, whether in their parents' house or in a community with others was 'fasts, holy vigils, meekness, obedience, poverty, courage, humility, patience' (John Chrysostom *On Virginity* 63.1): in practical terms this meant seclusion almost total, emerging only for worship; as little company as possible, preferably only that of like-minded women, family and spiritual directors (and those last only when with the protection of others present); and a regime of frequent prayer, study and some physical work, combined with fasting and deprivation. The testimonies of Jerome to the hardihood of Asella and Eustochium and Gregory of Nyssa to that of Macrina bear eloquent witness to this.

As regards qualifications, for the virgins, unlike the widows as we shall discover, their fitness for the job in terms of their virtue and purity of life prior to making their vows seems to have been taken very much on trust; but since age was not one of the qualifications and, as examined in the previous chapter, the decision would have had to be made before puberty to be reliably in time to forestall marriage (as with Eustochium), or might be made for the girl in infancy by her family (as with Paula's grand-daughter Paula the Younger), this was not altogether unreasonable. Little proof of a 'godly life' would have been necessary – or forthcoming – in the case of girls vowing virginity at ten like Eustochium, or Marcella's sister Asella: who, as devout as her sister and inspired to the same ascetic life, was able to make her decision early enough to forestall the marriage her sister chose to avoid a second time around, and so adopted a vocation when 'a mere babe', 'still wrapped in swaddling bands' according to Jerome (*Let.* 24.2) – actually at about ten years old. Accepting them at this age was to ignore Tertullian's admonition that virgins should not be accepted before puberty, which symbolised Eve's 'intelligence of her sex' (*On the Veiling of Virgins* 11), which chimed with the view of certain secular authorities. Actual practice seems to have varied considerably. Augustine certainly believed in this guideline, as is evident in his deliberations over the future of an orphan girl left in his care. Writing to his colleague Benenatus he takes a realistic view:

> The maiden . . . is at present disposed to think that if she were of full age, she would refuse every proposal of marriage. She is, however, so young, that even if she were disposed to marry, she ought not yet to be either given or betrothed to anyone . . . If she were disposed and prepared to marry, your proposal [of

a suitable husband] would not displease me; but whether she will marry anyone – although for my own part I would much prefer that she carried out what she now talks of – I do not know, for she is at an age in which her declaration that she wishes to be a nun is to be received rather as the flippant utterance of one talking heedlessly rather than as the deliberate promise of one making a solemn vow.

(Augustine Let. 254)

Interestingly, the girl's mother seems to have been still around, though 'she does not make herself known', but Augustine expresses his intention of taking her wishes into consideration 'unless the maiden herself be already old enough to have legitimately a stronger claim to choose for herself' (*ibid.*) – it would be interesting to know more concretely what age Augustine would have considered 'old enough'. In any event, he makes no reference to her wishes and acted seemingly on his own cognisance (though it lay within his province as *tutor minoris*) in bluntly refusing to entertain the suit of one Rusticus, a pagan; an interesting reflection on his opinion of 'mixed' marriages, after his own upbringing. It would be tempting to see this as another expression of his great emphasis (examined in more detail in Chapters 3 and 6) on each believer's capacity to make their own decision in the mortally important sphere of sexual abnegation, and possibly as an indication of a belief in more equity in decision-making for women; probably more significant, however, is his roundly rebuking Benenatus for proposing for the girl a marriage which would not strengthen the church (*Let.* 253).

Basil of Caesarea is also to be found advocating a choice in later teens, at sixteen or seventeen, and only then after much testing of the vocation (Basil of Caesarea *Let.* 199.18). Ambrose, on the other hand, accepted the dedication of girls by their parents at birth, from as far away as Bononia and Mauritania, in his order of virgins at Milan, though they did not take their vows until puberty (Ambrose *On Virginity* 1.57); this was done in a public ceremony, after which they would continue live with their parents, but under the control of the bishop. Melania the Younger had similarly dedicated her short-lived daughter at birth. By Ambrose's route, some element of choice, along with a nod to Tertullian's school of thought, was at least theoretically preserved; but resistance to these lifelong expectations must have been equally as hard as for those girls who were brought up to expect marriage.

As regards actual duties, the rules of this period were still embryonic beyond a general emphasis on regular routines of prayer, study, hard work and self-denial. For those who took to the life on a wholly serious basis the important factors were the isolation and the time; their duties were not those of the average women of the church, since 'the advantage of virginity is . . . in order to provide time for piety' (see p. 59). There is a great emphasis in the sources on the importance of self-denial and austerity as necessary preconditions for the right attitude of mind for this contemplative ideal. In this, many followed the wisdom of experience garnered by the isolated desert monastics: 'When one wants to take a town, one cuts off the supply of water and food. The same applies to the passions of the flesh. If a man lives a life of fasting and hunger, the enemies of his soul are weakened' (*Apoph. PJ* 4.19). So for virgins, 'let fasts put a halter on tender age, and a sparse diet put a curb on unsubdued appetites' (Ambrose *On Virginity* 3.5). However, in the kind of extreme lifestyle practised by some devotees, it was necessary for the virgin to exercise some native caution. Ambrose found it necessary to admonish his sister Marcellina against excessive fasting: 'you pass untold periods without food . . . a veteran of virginity, you should sow the field of your devotion with differing crops, at one time with moderate nourishment, at another with sparing fasts' (*ibid.* 5.15–16). Melania the Younger, though over-keen in her own personal fasting and mortification, is also related to have warned her virgins about overdoing it, and 'left fasting to each one's own decision' (Gerontius *Life of Melania the Younger* 43, 45) and we find even Jerome warning Demetrias – in milder old age – 'I do not, however, lay on you as an obligation any extreme fasting or abnormal abstention from food. Such practices soon break down weak constitutions and cause bodily sickness before they lay the foundations of a holy life' (Jerome *Let.* 130.11). The consequences could be as detrimental to one's vocation as to one's health: 'I am myself acquainted with anchorites of both sexes who by excessive fasting have so impaired their faculties that they do not know what to do or where to turn, when to speak and when to be silent' (*ibid.* 17).

Actual regulations for observance were not as yet very systematically laid down, and owed more to personal inclination and situation than would be the case a century or two hence. Asella, for instance, as an example of a virgin enclosed in her own home, followed a regimen of fasting 'for two or three days at a time' all the year round and 'from week's end to week's end' in Lent, taking only 'bread and salt and cold water' when she did eat; combining this with mean clothes and harsh living conditions, visits to *martyria*, long prayer, till her knees were 'hardened like a camel', and strict isolation, rarely seeing even her sister Marcella, 'much as she loved her': and thus 'found for herself a monkish hermitage in the centre of busy Rome' (*Let.* 24.3–4).

A factor frequently decisive in the lifestyle of many of these candidates for enclosed virginity was the proximity and advice of well-meaning relatives. Marcella, mentioned in Asella's case above, was probably not the less influential for being infrequently seen; older than Asella, she had gathered round her and strongly influenced many other ladies and even priests in Rome. Jerome also directed advice on the upbringing of Paula the Younger, Paula's granddaughter and intended successor, to her mother Laeta, the wife of Toxotius; vowed to virginity in infancy, she was to be trained in the virgin's life by her family, drawing on Jerome's precepts. She was to be enclosed even more straitly than Asella, barely to go abroad at all – 'let her never visit a church or a *martyrium* unless with her mother' – and even her contact with the rest of her family was to be strictly supervised: 'let her not take her food with others, that is, at her parents' table' to avoid the dual temptations of company and 'dishes she may long for' (*Let.* 107.7–8). She was to forego cultural improvement and the pastimes of leisure in favour of a practice of manual labour and study of the scriptures. For Demetrias, of whose actual practices we know little, again Jerome is profuse with advice as to conduct, and again this is proffered more for the information and assistance of the female relatives who will be expected to safeguard her: he recommends a regimen of regular prayer, allotted times for study and manual work, overt poverty, self-denial and isolation from company (*Let.* 130.12–15). Eunomia, another product of this élite circle living with her parents Avita and Apronianus, was trained by her mother while still 'a little girl', and also 'schooled by the guiding voice of Melania' – the Elder, her overpowering cousin (Paulinus of Nola *Let.* 13.60).

Eustochium's lifestyle – if not her decision – was similarly regulated for her by those who knew the virgin's business better than she did herself. Jerome gave extensive advice addressed to her, implying that hers were the decisions over her conduct; but then also revealed that from taking her vows at the age of ten until Paula's death some twenty years later, Eustochium

always kept close to her mother's side, obeyed all her commands, never slept apart from her, never walked abroad or took
a meal without her, never had a penny that she could call her
own, rejoiced when her mother gave to the poor her little
patrimony

(Jerome *Let.* 108.27)

– and by Jerome's account, Paula was possessed of a formidable
sureness and strength of will.

Macrina's story is superficially similar: she also provided herself
with a safety net when 'as a safeguard she resolved not to be separated
from her mother even for a moment' (Gregory of Nyssa *Life of
Macrina* 964). But in her case there is a very different flavour to this
process, since Macrina at all times is represented by her brother and
biographer as being very much responsible for her own decisions; to
the extent that she seems to impose them on her mother Emmelia –
who made the potentially ironic comment that 'she carried the rest
of her children in her womb for a definite time, but Macrina she bore
always since in a sense she carried her about' (*ibid.*). Further, while
Eustochium only appears to us during Paula's lifetime as a vague,
shadowy appendage to her extremely high-profile mother, Macrina
seems to have occupied a much more central and positive role in
proceedings:

she helped her mother to bear her burden of responsibilities,
for she had four sons and three daughters and paid taxes to
three different governors, since her property was scattered in
as many districts . . . In all these matters she shared her mother's
toils . . . also by her own life she instructed her mother greatly,
leading her to that same mark of philosophy [as her own].

(Gregory of Nyssa *Life of Macrina* 966)

And Macrina's was the responsibility for their change of lifestyle: she
it was who 'persuaded her mother to give up her ordinary life . . .
and bring her point of view down to that of the masses and share the
life of the maids' (*ibid.* 966). Further, when her favourite brother,
Naucratius, died prematurely in an accident, Macrina in Gregory's
account is considerably more in evidence and influential than was
Eustochium during Paula's grief over Blesilla or subsequent bereave-
ments – Macrina assumes the role of a Jerome, in fact, for

facing the calamity in a rational spirit, she both preserved
herself from collapse, and becoming the support of her

mother's weakness, raised her from the depths of grief, and by her own steadfastness and imperturbability taught her mother's soul to be brave. In consequence, her mother was not overwhelmed by the affliction, nor did she behave in any ignoble or womanish way, so as to cry out at the disaster, or tear her dress, or lament over the trouble, or strike up funeral chants with mournful melodies.

(Gregory of Nyssa Life of Macrina 970)

The respect which Gregory held for Macrina is evident here, in that the idea of Emmelia being tutored out of her 'womanish' inclinations by one who was after all also a woman does not seem to strike him as at all contradictory. Macrina may have been a woman; she was not, in his view, 'womanish'. But in these qualities Macrina stands out as somewhat exceptional amongst the avowed virgins available to us for study.

But in other respects the virgins were held to have positive and important powers. Their distance from the world and their 'freedom' from sexuality was held to imply their extra availability to God – and, at secondhand, to their church. A primary expectation of such successfully practising virgins is of their functioning as a kind of natural resource to be channelled into their community: to in some sort improve their environs, by lending sanctity and the lustre of their dedication to those around them.

The most obvious and immediate beneficiaries of this common glory were the families who were seen as such an integral part of the process. The girls' observances, besides more obvious benefits, reputedly had the power to 'ennoble' their mostly noble families still further. Demetrias' mother and grandmother, of a family 'second to none in Rome' must have 'congratulated each other that now a virgin was to make a noble house still more noble by her virginity. She had found, they said, a way to benefit her family and to lessen the calamity of the fall of Rome' (Jerome *Let*. 130.6). Augustine, indeed, advised them to consider 'how incomparably greater is the glory and advantage gained by your family in giving to Christ women consecrated to his service than in giving to the world men called to the honours of the consulship' (*Let*. 150); Demetrias 'has acted the more magnanimous part in choosing to bring a blessing on that noble family by forbearing from marriage than to increase the number of its descendants' (*ibid*.).

However, this process of bringing down Christian lustre might not always have been a joyful or a welcome experience for the family concerned – particularly for those with a history of resisting the pietistic impulses of their females. Eustochium's power in this respect is written of in singularly combative and vengeful terms. She, it was said, 'by resolving to be a virgin had breached the gates of nobility and broken down the pride of a consular house. The first of Roman ladies, she has brought under the yoke the first of Roman families' (*Let.* 66.3). This is rather different language to the mild fulsomeness addressed to Demetrias' relatives, and of exactly the tenor that would dent an aristocratic Roman *gens* in its *amour propre*. Paula the Younger's ability in this respect is similarly ambiguous in import: she was attributed the power to add sanctity, the one thing lacking, to the venerable and distinguished consular Albinus, 'the one unbeliever' in her family – and she has a duty to impose this on him willy-nilly. 'When she sees her grandfather, she must leap upon his breast, put her arms around his neck and, whether he likes it or not, sing Alleluia in his ears' (*Let.* 107.4). And in the case of such an example to normal women, what was blood to the point anyway? Paula 'through the virtues of her grandmother and aunt is nobler in holiness than she is in lineage' (*ibid.* 13).

The virgin in action then should not just be a prop to an already believing family; she must be prepared to do battle even in her withdrawn circumstance. The theoretical ability Jerome proposes for Paula the Younger in this respect was practised in fact by Macrina, who is given the credit by her brother Gregory for the conversions of two other brothers, Basil and Peter. Basil, already a noted rhetor and heading for local power as a civic potentate, she 'drew towards the mark of philosophy with such speed that he forsook the glories of this world' (Gregory of Nyssa *Life of Macrina* 966); Peter, the youngest, she conquered even sooner; she 'took him soon after birth from the nurse's breast and reared him herself and educated him on a lofty system of training' becoming all things to him, 'father, teacher, tutor, mother, giver of all good advice' (*ibid.* 972).

Other virgins, if not the chief prop of a familial predisposition to piety, still acted as support groups to relatives in the same line of work. Augustine's sister, though we do not know for certain of her history, sounds like a case in point, capably conducting the convent under his jurisdiction at Hippo, which reputedly fell into disorder only after her demise; and Augustine wrote to a consecrated virgin named Sapida who evidently lived with her brother Timotheus, a deacon of the church of Carthage, tending to his need. On the occasion of the death of her brother, Augustine accepted from her (against his own rule in the matter of gifts) a tunic which she had prepared for her brother shortly before his death (Augustine *Let.* 263).

Outside of the family environs, though understandably more curtailed than the devout matrons and widows of the time, the virgins were called sometimes to exert more power than could be expressed in contemplation. Largesse to the local church was one very acceptable activity: Demetrias was persuaded by Pope Leo to build a church dedicated to St Stephen on her Via Latina estate.[2] Macrina was active in the setting up of the convent from family resources at Annesi; companioned by her mother and the double house co-headed by her brother, the initiative still seems to have been very much Macrina's, and the rest followed her lead.

Service to humbler communities of a more readily useful kind was also in evidence. The peasantry of the Eastern villages, believing wholeheartedly in the mystique and concomitant power of virginity, took it in fact as an emblem of a more material and practical relationship with the Almighty; and considered that a household virgin's solitude and scruples need not preclude her serving her community, even if not so materially endowed as a Demetrias or Macrina. Palladius tells us of Piamoun, 'a virgin who lived the years of her life with her mother, eating every other day in the evening and spinning flax.' Even more usefully, 'she was accounted worthy of the gift of prophecy' (*LH* 31), which she bent to the service of her neighbourhood – a handy advantage in a village threatened by Nile floodings and hostile neighbouring villagers in competition for the distribution of water. Nor was this all that she was called upon to perform: on one occasion, having received intelligence through an angelic envoy, she was able to warn the elders of her village of an imminent attack by a neighbouring village; but they, being too terrified to go and intercept the marauders, 'fell at her feet, beseeching her . . . "have pity on the village and your own house, go out yourself and meet them"' (*ibid.*). Piamoun would not agree to this, implicitly because this would seriously compromise her seclusion; but instead she bent her formidable powers of piety to a more signal display of the greatness of God and prayed that the marauders' feet be nailed to the spot. Sure enough,

> when they were about three miles away, they were nailed to the ground and could not move. And it was revealed to them also that their hindrance had come about through her petitions,

and they sent to the village and asked for peace, saying "Give thanks to God and the prayers of Piamoun, for they hindered us."

(*LH* 31)

VIRGINITY IN PRACTICE – WEAKER VESSELS

The virgin ... is of necessity in the middle of the ocean, and sails a sea with no harbour. If a very severe storm should arise, she has no right to drop anchor and rest.
(John Chrysostom *On Virginity* 34.1)

That many women fulfilled the blueprint for piety outlined by the Fathers beyond their expectations is evident in the witnesses to those like Eustochium, Asella, Macrina, Demetrias, and the many virtuous virgins found in the tales of Palladius and the desert Fathers; that many women similarly found it extremely hard to live up to or live with the increasing rarification of the lifestyle is equally evident. The Fathers frequently highlighted particularly luminous examples of individuals as we have seen; but we hear of not a few communities in difficulties with the life. In this context, Palladius' description of the nuns of the famous foundation of Pachomius at Tabennisi in the Thebaid, and their problems with attempting to maintain the higher standards required, is illuminating. So rigid was their guardianship of their purity of mind as of body that one of their number was driven to suicide by the rumours of impropriety against her; these had sprung up because she had a chance encounter with a man who accidentally landed on their enclosed side of the river. The unhappy corollary of this was, however, that the nun responsible for originating the scandalous stories against her unfortunate sister was judged equally harshly for lacking in charity and ultimately also killed herself (*LH* 33).

This was a problem with which the desert Fathers were only too familiar; from their experience, they concluded that denunciation was of no help to the denounced and of great harm to the denunciator. Many Abbas such as Ammonas and John the Dwarf were noted for rebuking those who informed on their brethren.[3] By this reluctance to encourage accusations, we can find a case directly analogous to that of the Tabennesiot nuns nipped in the bud before reaching such a damaging conclusion; that of a monk denouncing

71

two brothers for being lovers. The anonymous 'old man' to whom the brother made his report evidently had a clear understanding of the psychological concept of 'projection' – of attributing to others one's own guilty desires – and ordered the accuser to be isolated, 'for he himself has the passion he attaches to them' (*Apoph. PJ* 5.29).

The nuns at Hippo evidently had the same problem: but either Augustine was not familiar with this thinking, or he did not consider it safe advice for women; he encouraged them to police one another. Addressing the same issue, he advised that whoever noticed immodesty in a sister should first personally warn her that this has been observed, to give her a chance to check herself; and only if she persisted, 'whoever may have had the opportunity of seeing this must now report her as one who has been injured and needs healing', in which case he stresses

> do not think that in informing upon one another like this you
> are guilty of malice; for it is rather the case that you are guilty
> if you allow your sisters to fall by keeping silent when you
> could correct them by giving information as to their faults.
>
> (Augustine *Let*. 211.11)

If the sister concerned denies the charge, however, she cannot be disciplined for it until other witnesses to the offence have been secured, 'so that before the whole sisterhood she may not be accused by one witness but convicted by two or three' (*ibid*.) – advice intended to provide against the kind of scenario reported of the Tabennesiot nuns. However, while covering the aspects of the official consequences of denunciation, and the danger to the offender and the community from a real offence, it rather fails to face up to the kind of prurient whispering campaign that was more probably the cause of those two deaths, a problem addressed head-on by the more prosaic Abbas of the desert mentioned above.

This advice was given in the context of problems at the convent in Hippo necessitating several sharp letters from Augustine, following the death of his sister, who seems to have maintained the foundation with admirable stability. Professing dissatisfaction with her successor, however, after several years of her rule, the nuns 'riotously demanded her replacement' (*ibid*. 211.4) and agitated for 'concessions involving ... some most dangerous precedents, subversive of sound discipline' (*ibid*. 211.1). This dissatisfaction seems to have coincided with the arrival of a new prior, with whom, however, they asserted themselves to be well content – perhaps their dissatisfaction was brought to a head by finding him in fact more sympathetic than their ill-regarded prioress. Even so, Augustine refuses to put in a personal appearance at their request, observing sapiently that 'perhaps your rising against authority would have been even more violent in my presence' and stating that he would in any case have felt compelled to refuse what they demanded in such an unfitting fashion, with the warning that had he been faced with such a tumult in person, he would have had to take a more severely punitive stance. In sum, he had no intention of removing the prioress, and they should reconsider their duty and learn not to quarrel. Similar was the experience of Elias, reported by Palladius, who built a great monas-tery for some 300 virgins of different walks of life at Athribe in Egypt, only to find himself having to live with them – to the detriment of his own spiritual well-being – to keep the peace because they 'continually had fights' (*LH* 29).

Some nuns, however, were misled by the very clerics on whom they depended. Jerome castigated a subdeacon called Sabinianus for subverting a virgin in Jerome's own Bethlehem convent, which was ironical given Jerome's especial preoccupation with foolish virgins who encouraged bogus spiritual advisors. Sabinianus had conducted an unsuspected dalliance with the virgin right under Jerome's nose and by the time it came to his attention, had arranged to abscond with 'your unhappy victim' (Jerome *Let* 147.4) – after promising to marry her, revealingly. She had exchanged pledges of devotion with him and seems to have been quite prepared to elope with him, and he was reputed to have served 'many virgins' after the same fashion; which suggests that not all the girls in this life were as anti-marriage as the high-profile models offered for example. Some of them probably had not made the choice to be a virgin willingly, and the opposition to marriage was not theirs but their family's, whether out of excess of zeal or in an attempt to save on a dowry – and some, doubtless, having initially made their own decision, had had leisure to repent of it.

Another example we have in more detail of a virgin thus betrayed is one of those whose life was imposed on her by family expectation, and whose dramatic fall came after more than 20 years of an exemplary life in vows. This was Maria who came to be known by the cognomen 'the Harlot', the niece of the hermit Abraham; she fell into her harlotry when she failed to maintain the standards he had set up for her. She was not accorded the virtue of her own choice in the life; an heiress, she did not have the 'glory' of beggaring herself, like Paula or the Melanias. When her father, Abraham's brother, died when she was seven, and 'left her untold riches', Abraham decided her future for her: 'so that her mind might not be entangled in the affairs of this world . . . at once the servant of Christ ordered it all to be given away to the needy and the orphans' (Ephraim *Life of Maria the Harlot, passim*).[4] He then built her a cell adjoining his, and simply incorporated the small girl into his own lifestyle.

> He taught her the Psalter and other Scriptures; she kept vigil there with him, singing the praises of the Lord; she sang psalms without number and strove to emulate her uncle in all his ascetic practices . . . So she held constantly to the rules he taught her.

Maria 'held constantly' to this regime well into adulthood; then, after twenty years of 'living like an unspotted lamb or untouched dove', she succumbed to the blandishments of a visiting monk of somewhat less than Abraham's perfection of life, 'climbed down to him' and was seduced. She was overcome with remorse 'when she had put on her clothes again', and unsurprisingly, after her upbringing, she assumed herself to be destined for damnation. In an environment where the coveting of an extra vegetable or the addition of water to one's bread was regarded as a betrayal of the way of life, with such a 'pollution' on her conscience, Maria despaired completely:

> I feel as if I am dead already; I have lost all that I had before by the hard work of asceticism; all my prayers, tears and vigils have come to nothing. I have angered God and destroyed myself . . . how can I, a sinner, covered with filth, ever speak again to my uncle? If I were to dare to do so, fire would come out of that window and consume me . . . there is now no hope of salvation for me.

Feeling thus completely unable to confess to her uncle and his colleagues (who included Ephraim, who wrote the story), she 'fled away to another city, changed her appearance and began to ply her trade in a brothel'.

Abraham took three days to notice her disappearance and then two years to actually set enquiries in train, according to the *Life*; however, he did ultimately ascertain her whereabouts. He then, in an unusually improbable story even by the standards of the medium, disguised himself as a soldier, went in search of her, hid from her his identity throughout an evening's roistering in her company ('Forty years of abstinence when he tasted nothing but bread,' marvels

Ephraim, 'and now, without hesitation he chewed meat to save a soul from hell! The choir of angels rejoiced and was amazed at his discretion, for without hesitation he ate and drank in order that he might draw a soul from out of the mire!') and retired with her to the inner chamber. ('What' enquires Ephraim 'shall I say of you, athlete of Christ? Shall I speak of continence or incontinence, wisdom or foolishness, discretion or indiscretion? After forty years of conversion, you lie down on a prostitute's bed and wait for her to come to you!' But 'all this' he concludes firmly 'you did for the praise and glory of Christ'.) After this, the story follows a pattern common to desert tales of harlots turning to penitence: he reveals himself and exhorts her; she is overcome with guilt and grief and pleads for a chance to repent; leaves for the desert with him and performs her penance with such extremes of grief and asceticism that all beholders marvel. After three years of this wonderful observance, Ephraim asserts that she was granted the power of healing as a visible sign of the acceptability of her penitence by a merciful God.

Virgins under obedience nursing sick clerics seem to have been equally at risk from them. Many virgins playing Martha fell victim to their charges; particularly those nursing normally desert-dwelling patients overcome by their first contact with a woman in many years. One such, a bishop so ill that 'all had given him up as lost' was still overcome by lust at a visiting nun merely touching his foot. He obtained her services as a nurse, since all thought him at death's door, ate a revivifying meal she had cooked and propositioned her: 'lie down with me and conceive sin' (*Anon. Apoph*. 32). A severely ill 'old man' from the isolated community at Scetis, who went to convalesce in the nearby town because he did not wish to burden his brethren with his care, fell into the trap of assuming 'my body is dead' only to discover otherwise when allocated 'a devout virgin' to tend to him (*ibid*. 188). Both virgins subsequently became pregnant and both clerics had to assume the responsibility – these kind of incidents lending credence to the many false accusations of clerics impregnating hapless girls. Another devout virgin came to temptation when she got into the habit of ordering items from a coenobite working as a linen-maker to feed the poor; she ended up living with him for six months before he was overcome with guilt and fled (*ibid*. 63).

Other virgins were potentially more seriously lured away; not just from bodily purity (for which penance was possible) but from the body of the church. One Primus, mentioned by Augustine, entered into 'intercourse unsanctioned by the church' (Augustine *Let*. 35.2) with the nuns at Spana, and when disciplined by the church authorities, in pique went off to join the Donatists, taking two nuns with him. Augustine wrote also a sympathetic but warning letter to Felicia, the virgin concerned in what seems to have been another such case, admonishing her against 'disturbances' of her mind because of 'bad shepherds'. She also seems to have been drawn towards the Donatists (who were particularly active in the region around Hippo) by such bad priests, since she is advised to

> love with all your heart Him and His Church who did not permit you, by joining yourself with those who are lost, to lose the reward of your virginity or to perish with them. For if you should depart from this world separated from the body of Christ, it will avail you nothing to have preserved your virginity inviolate.
>
> (Augustine *Let*. 108.7)

She should rather give 'sincerest affection to those good servants of his through whose agency you were compelled to come in [to the feast]' (*ibid*.); but how an isolated and confused virgin was to know whether it was the good shepherds rather than the bad who were influencing her, in the event of two strong but contradictory persuasions such as those of Augustine and Primus, was not enlarged upon.

The desert chroniclers are thoroughly illuminating about the problems of the consecrated life, with many unhappy little stories of lone female ascetics who either genuinely fell into error, or who endured obloquy from their colleagues as if they had because their actions were misunderstood. Palladius tells of an immensely ascetic virgin who fell, after six years of enclosure in a cell wearing sackcloth and 'taking no pleasure'; in the end she sinned with the man who waited on her. Palladius attributed this to her spiritual pride; she practised *ascesis*, he says austerely, for human ostentation and vainglory, and thus the 'guardian spirit' of her chastity left her (*LH* 28). Six years of abstinence, it would seem, left her no credit balance of virtue; the judgement still awaited the ultimate outcome of her struggle. Others must similarly have tired after a firm initial purpose and received as little credit for the struggle they had gone through and the period of abnegation already achieved; a daunting consideration for those some years into an ascetic vocation with strength flagging.

It was particularly discouraging if even resistance of temptation might gain one no credit in the eyes of male judges. Hilarion the hermit, having achieved the cure of a virgin driven to madness by possession, 'reproved the girl when her health returned, for having, by her imprudent conduct, permitted the devil to get hold of her' (Jerome *Life of St Hilarion* 21). The interesting aspect of this case, particularly since the author is the censorious Jerome, is that absolutely no instances of the girl's alleged 'imprudence', such as would give the tale a clearer moral, are given; on the contrary, she seems to have been quite firm in her vocation. We are told that her possession was caused by the spells of a youth enamoured of her, made desperate because he had repeatedly made advances to her which she had been steadfast in resisting. But the virgin, like Caesar's wife, must be above the very suspicion of reproach and by attracting misfortunes she is rebuked as the author of them. It was a fine-drawn line, however, and exactly how fine tended to depend on which cleric was consulted: Abba Serapion, by contrast, found a virgin blame-worthy in her lifestyle for being too careful. A household virgin in Rome who had made a virtue out of not appearing in public for 25 years, she broke this rule when Serapion pointed out to her that if she were truly dead to the world 'it is all the same to you whether you are seen or not, so appear in public' (*LH* 37.14). It availed her nothing: subsequently she balked at a command to walk through the city naked, on the same rationale (Serapion seems not to have been as leery as some of his contemporaries at the prospect of one of God's virgins 'giving scandal to unbelievers') – thus earning his criticism that the motives for her seclusion were not religious but prideful.

VIRGINS 'WITHOUT LICENCE' – THE 'SUBINTRODUCTAE'

Some took steps to make the daunting path easier to follow. The virgin who sinned with her 'attendant' may well have been one of a breed that aroused much ire and contention in the more severe Fathers: that of the *virgines subintroductae* or *agapetae*. These women set up a virginal lifestyle, lived in conjunction and cohab-itation with a member of the opposite sex in what amounted to a partnership: 'the cohabitation of the sexes under the condition of strict continence, a couple sharing the same house, often the same room, and sometimes the same bed, yet conducting themselves as brother and sister' (Bailey 1959:33) – a situation understandably open to suspicion. These virgins have been accredited by historians of their phenomenon with 'the earnest desire to keep [the vow of continence]' (Achelis 1926:177) – but were all too frequently not so accredited at the time.

The advantages of such a system, if sincerely practised, are evident. Lone women shrinking from the rigours of fending for themselves could have, as well as a companion, an agent to carry out their business, thereby avoiding the need for the going abroad so much complained of in virgins. Frequently one of the pair would be better off and provide for the less fortunate partner, thus acquiring merit and making life easier for a fellow Christian. They could assist each other in material ways, inspire each other and, ideally, avoid the pitfalls open to those who became tired or deceived or lonely through isolation in their struggle. This system must have proved vastly more attractive to many than more orthodox methods of asceticism. Mentions of this practice are frequent in our period: in the three Cappadocian Fathers, in Jerome, in the canons of various church councils banning the practice, including the famous Council of Nicaea in 325, in John Chrysostom – who devoted two homilies to attacking it; even the desert Fathers have sayings citing cases of 'old men' needing to prove their purity because they were 'served by a holy virgin'.[5]

The suspicions to which these partnerships laid themselves open are obvious; Chrysostom, though conceding that many of them were sincere in their beliefs and had retained their bodily purity, nonetheless was convinced that only sexual desire, however unacknowledged, could so permanently bind a man to a woman, for 'why else would a man put up with the faults of a woman? He would find her despicable' (*That women under vows should not cohabit with men* 5–6). Jerome too cavalierly dismissed the practical plea of necessity on the part of the women: 'How many virgins and widows there are who have looked after their property for themselves without thereby incurring any scandal!' (Jerome *Let.* 123.14) and he 'gleefully noted the frequency with which the supposed virgins were betrayed by their "swelling wombs"' (Clark, 1977:176). He also sarcastically indicated the thinness of some of the excuses preferred for close cohabitation, in a letter concerning a monk accused of this (who happened, coincidentally, to be a critic of Jerome's *Against Jovinian*): 'I should like everyone to take a wife who, because they might get frightened in the night, cannot sleep alone' (Jerome *Let.* 50.4).

A further irritation to Chrysostom it seems was the claim of many of these couples that their arrangement gave them tougher moral fibre to withstand temptation; a contradiction to Chrysostom, since in his eyes they were living in a constant state of temptation and opportunity for thoughts of lust which, as indicated above, were as fatal as the deed to those embarked on the ascetic lifestyle. But in any case, even if he had been willing to countenance this plea, Chrysostom advances against them the argument of Paul (Rom.14; I Cor. 8) that those capable of strength must help those less capable: these couples are providing the occasion for sin in others by giving rise to unchristian suspicion and offence; therefore if truly strong as they claim, they should be willing to suffer for God by giving up that which only arguably profits them and which definitely leads others astray. In addition to the harm to other Christians is added the harm to the church through the ill-repute attached to it by these irregular couples.[6]

Jerome again aired these concerns in a surprisingly mild letter (after his vituperations to Eustochium on the subject) to an actual case in point; his *Letter* 117 to a mother and daughter living in Gaul. These women, widow and virgin, were living apart, both of them with 'clerical directors'; the inference is that they found each other much harder to live with and in any case preferred their independence, since they seem to have been supporting the men. Jerome was not actually acquainted with these women, but had been asked to write to them by the son of the older woman, (brother of the younger), who as a monk was worried by the scandal attendant upon the situation. In his letter, Jerome takes the stance that while he personally suspects nothing ill, it is incumbent on them to prevent suspicion in others. 'Even if your own consciences acquit you of misdoing, yet the very rumour of it will bring disgrace upon you' and he takes the same view as Chrysostom that this is an unnecessarily risky lifestyle, placing them gratuitously in the way of temptation: 'why must you live in a household where you must daily struggle for life and death?' And as much as Chrysostom he doubts the validity of the justifications used, saying to the daughter: 'If you are a true virgin, why do you fear your mother's careful guardianship? And if you have fallen, why do you not openly marry?' At least she should 'live in a separate building and take your meals apart; for if you remain under one roof with him, slanderers will say that you share with him your bed' (Jerome *Let.* 117, *passim*). All three of the family equally incur censure; the mother for letting her daughter leave her protection in this way and the daughter for displaying an unseemly lack of family feeling in so doing, both women for their live-in clerics, and finally, the son for not showing more decision in rebuking the women and taking steps to correct them.

This case demonstrates a further aspect to the *subintroductae* hardly likely to endear them to the Fathers; that this practice seems to have been a means whereby Christian women again liberated themselves from family restrictions and preoccupations, but with more than a suggestion that it was for their own ends rather than to free their minds for praising God. Chrysostom is also worried by the frivolity shown by many, and that, worse, they are leading their 'monks' into similar levity of mind: the men will spend their days running frivolous errands for their cohabitees, he worried, running to the shops for trivia (*Against those men who cohabit with virgins* 9), and by spending long hours with female converse they run the risk of acquiring the habits and 'subservient mentality' (*ibid.* 11) of that sex. In short, Chrysostom worries about something he seems to perceive as a process of what would nowadays be called 'role reversal', and says that the distinctive male and female characteristics are being over-turned in these invidious companionships; besides the men becoming frivolous and effete, the women are adopting lordly ways and rejoicing in dominion over men, forgetting that 'the head of woman is man' (I Cor. 11:3). Elizabeth Clark's analysis attributes this attitude to an inability in the ancient world to comprehend the concept of Platonic friendship between the sexes, since 'friendship in its truest sense meant a kind of parity between two people, and women by virtue of their inferior nature and status, could thus rarely qualify as suitable candidates for friendship with men' (Clark 1977:183–4).

This has a familiar ring to it; again women inferior by status, and by definition subject by sin, are then found wanting and castigated in their attempts to better their destiny. Not all women had the mettle – or the means – of a Melania or a Eustochium; for those of lesser substance or ambition, the appearance of this phenomenon of the *virgines subintroductae* demonstrates an attempt to wean themselves from their subjection equally to their families and the regard of the church; in many cases deriving from an evidently sincere motivation, though potentially unfortunate in result. Probably amongst many of those who fell, as with Palladius' example above, we might find a real vocation not equalled by spiritual strength. And once again, we encounter in the critics of this lifestyle the appeal to nature and the scriptures in their preoccupation with women's fitness to assigned roles. But then, 'roles' of any kind except inert accorded ill with the standards postulated for virgins proper, the ossified élite of the church, petrified in the perfection worked out according to the best theories of the theologians. But against these theories we have seen some small but illuminating vignettes of virgins finding indeed an active role, and admiration for fulfilling it.

This contradiction is always present in the theoretical writing of the period; the women inherently sinful of nature who may yet be capable of dazzling probity such as to put in their hands a crucial part of the burden for the spiritual well-being of the church; particularly the virgins who demonstrate their fitness for the legacy passed on by the Mother of God, which gave them such a powerful hold on the apocalyptic imagery of the early church. The need to confront this ambivalence rarely seems to disturb the writers of improving homilies addressed to women; but many of the women so addressed were unable to resolve the conflict, or, as we have seen, found means unacceptable within the hardening boundaries of orthodoxy. But some did find room to manoeuvre within the contradictions of the patristic conceptions of womanly virtue, so successfully as to achieve exaggerated admiration from these arbiters.

5

'THE CONTINENCE WHICH IS AWARE OF ITS OWN RIGHT'

The order of widows

You who are women have no excuse because of your nature.
You who are widows have no excuse because of the weakness
of your sex, nor can you pass off your fickleness because of the
loss of your husband's support.

(Ambrose *On Widows* 51)

Is widowhood grievous to you? Why should it be grievous at
all, to one who is soon to pass away? The appointed day is at
hand, the pain will not last long.

(Gregory of Nazianzus *Or.* 18.43)

WIDOWHOOD IN PATRISTIC THEORY

As compared with the virgins, widows represented a numerically
superior and historically more ancient tendency in the church. The
widows are attested from the earliest apostolic times in their own
category, 'the roll of widows' (I Tim. 5:9ff), along with instructions
as to their qualifications and supervision; they seem to have quickly
occupied an uneasy middle ground between being church functionaries and prime recipients of church charity, but were always viewed
in the light of a separate category. Ultimately, however, they would
prove to lack the qualities that were to put the virgins in the front
rank in the contest for the Crown of Crowns.

Historically, in Roman society the widow existed in equally
nebulous ground: while the *univira*, the woman who had known
only one man in her life, was traditionally held up as a model to be
admired as having attained some ideal of marriage, and the administration of the civic cults of *Fortuna Muliebris* and *Pudicitia* were

82

reserved for these women of superior standing in the community, there were also many indications that such regard – and such pious motives – were not always the case. Such a position could also be exploited as an opportunity to gain independence and self-determination, and might be seen less charitably by the families as an irresponsible attitude to the obligations of blood and property – an attitude which is echoed in the families of the devout women of the later period. And indeed, some of the widows of this study were being opportunistic to this extent, in refusing to marry again for their own reasons, as did Marcella and Melania the Elder; but were also adapting the principle of the *univira* by giving it an additional mystical resonance. For with belief in the resurrection came the consideration of genuine confusion as to one's position on the Last Day as the spouse of more than one partner, a confusion Macrina could exploit even as only a betrothed spouse. The choice of her marriage having been made for her by her parents when she was too young to have seriously objected, when the plans for her future were perforce deferred because of the death of her betrothed, she could quite sincerely express doubts as to her status as belonging to him in the eyes of God, and assume a standing as *univira* that was purely mystical in quality.

Macrina is something of a special case; but she does in this also express a trend in society at large in her day. The impulse of the Christian church of the fourth century was towards institutionalising the concept of loyalty after death to the single marriage, for men and women, with a heavy moral disincentive towards remarriage; the by-product of which was the provision, in the faithful bereaved, of a supply of mature church members with time, energy and experience of something of the world to channel into the service of the church. Ageruchia, a recently widowed noblewoman of Gaul, was enjoined by Jerome to maintain her widowhood and follow the example of her female forebears: her mother, Benigna, had remained a widow for fourteen years, and her grandmother Metronia for forty years. 'A widow who is "loosed from the law of her husband" has, for her one duty, to continue a widow' (Jerome *Let.* 38.3). This being so, the way of the women of the 60-fold, of modified – or belated – abnegation, by contrast with the straitened path of virginity would seem comparatively light. Widowhood was more of a movable feast; as a life choice, it could be embarked on by women without major upset in a kind of semi-official capacity in one's own home by simply preserving the status quo after the death of the husband – with the advantage to the widow of retaining the kind of independence that led the church writers to complain so bitterly of the wilful demeanour of some widows. Of Ageruchia and her relatives, 'a noble band of tried Christian women' (*Let*. 123.1), there is no suggestion that they altered by much their highborn lifestyle in Gaul. Similar praise is meted out to Juliana and Proba, mother and grandmother of Demetrias, women of notably independent and autocratic turns of mind who retained firm control over their own destinies.

However, 'there is no glory simply in widowhood, only if the virtues of widowhood are added' (Ambrose *On Widows* 3). The issue with vows of widowhood was accordingly more blurred than with vowed virginity. The instant a girl took vows as a virgin, she became a case for concern to her guardians and local church. With widows the case was rather the opposite, since Paul warned carefully about assuming too many widows at the care of the church, and they were actively encouraged, where the family circumstances allowed, to merely contain chastely under their own auspices, 'that the church may not be charged but may be free to relieve those that are widows indeed' (Jerome *Let*. 123.6). Those who count as 'widows indeed' in this context are deemed by Paul to be only those who are over three-score years old, the wife of only one husband and seen to be upright in the community; and in addition 'such as are desolate and have no relations to help them, who cannot labour with their hands, who are weakened by poverty and overcome by years, whose trust is in God and their only work prayer' (*ibid*. quoting I Tim. 5:3–5). Hence the dichotomy in the thinking about the widowed state; by these criteria few indeed qualify, and yet the Fathers are keen to stress that it does not become young Christian widows such as Ageruchia and Salvina, another recipient of Jerome's sales pitch, to marry again, merely because they were not old and poor; they could be still better witnesses to the beauty of chastity, of whom it would be said 'her youth makes her chastity all the more commendable' (Jerome *Let*. 79.1). They were advised:

> Do not be disturbed because the apostle allows none to be chosen as a widow under the age of three-score years old, neither suppose that he intends to reject those who are still young. Believe that you are indeed chosen by him who said to his disciple "Let no man despise your youth".
>
> (Jerome *Let*. 7)

So they were to remain widows within the community, not on the church roll, with less incumbent on them than the virgins. Ambrose, however, seems to share Paul's reservations that 'the younger' are perhaps 'not able to fulfil the requirements of so high a degree of righteousness', though they should not be excluded from trying; but he does allow provision for remarriage – indeed, he does not even discount the possibility of admitting the twice-married to the state: 'Nor, truly, is anyone excluded from the devotion of widowhood if, after entering into a second marriage . . . she is again loosed from her husband' (Ambrose *On Widows* 10–12).

This ambiguity about their status explains the wide disparity between the intensity of their observances. Although not an office properly speaking, within the Christian community the widowed state implied – to those inclined to heed the words of the Fathers – a quest for a perfected lifestyle and a mission to the younger women in the community. Certainly some, such as Melania, Marcella, Paula, Blesilla, regarded the station as a commandment to greater devotional and ascetic efforts; to those of a less extreme turn of mind such as Furia, Salvina, Ageruchia, Juliana, Proba and the unnamed widow to whom John Chrysostom wrote, he, Jerome, Ambrose and Augustine restrict their advice to the meat of the matter. These women should read Paul for guidance on how to behave (though the classical snob Jerome can also be found advocating Dido as a good example), do their duty by their remaining family, and principally preserve their modest demeanour and their chastity – and above all, their reputation for chastity; 'a woman's reputation is a tender plant . . . especially when she is an age to fall into temptation and she has no husband' (Jerome *Let.* 79.8). They must take great care that no opportunity for scandal should be given to unbelievers or the community; particularly because of 'too great intimacy' with 'troops of retainers' (*ibid.*). Ideally, 'you will display among us a heavenly manner of life' (John Chrysostom, *Letter to a Young Widow* 6).[1]

Several levels of thinking about widows existed, and in some cases evidence of rather a strained attitude. Some merited no admiration for their continence, for they were, slightingly, 'widows from necessity, not choice' (Jerome *Let.* 22.16) while others chose to maintain the state for the wrong reasons, preferring 'the licence of widowhood to rule by a husband' (*ibid.*). This last was in fact an incentive not infrequently offered by the patristic writers to persuade those whom they targeted of the advantages of the situation: 'Is it not far better to have a few possessions over which you have complete authority, than to have everything in the world but with it be subject to another's power?' (John Chrysostom *Against Remarriage* 5). It was none-theless regarded as an unbecoming conclusion for the women to arrive at by themselves, and the Fathers complained bitterly of their taking advantage of the situation. 'It has become a matter of indifference for widows to talk foolishly, and revile one another, and flatter, and be shameless, and appear everywhere and parade in public places'; and some 'treat priests pridefully because they are rich' – or, presumably, because of the more independent habits learned within the greater freedom of marriage (John Chrysostom *On the Priesthood* 315). There might seem to be an advantage then in re-attaching these unruly women to a man so that they would be at least notionally under authority; nonetheless, to the ascetic fathers the path of raising one's widowhood to the level of a vowed life-choice approved by the church was of necessity to be advocated to women for whom vowed virginity was no longer an option. 'A widow should be ignorant that second marriage is permitted; she should know nothing of the apostle's words "it is better to marry than to burn"' (Jerome *Let.* 79.10); she was invited instead to consider that 'digamy is preferable only to fornication' (*ibid.*) and betokened 'a weak and carnal soul' (John Chrysostom *Against Remarriage* 2). Given the comprehensive expectations of marriage and the early notions of the marriageable age already examined in Chapter 3, advice on second marriages would be relevant to a far greater proportion of the women to whom the fathers preached than their homilies on virginity. But those so addressed were widely believed to be in considerably more need of exhortation than the virgins; both those who had a reputation for behaving with too much licence and those less fortunate, who were 'widows who are placed in a position of stress and tribulation' (Jerome *Let.* 48.2), who, 'broken down by adversity' (Ambrose *On Widows* 53), were repre-sented as having a very harsh lot to endure.

In the first instance the widows were believed to be rather worse off in terms of susceptibility of the flesh than the virgins, the reasoning being that it is easier to forego that which you have not experienced. Jerome's advice to Eustochium compares her task with that of her sister Blesilla, who married but whose husband died after only seven months of marriage, and so 'lost thereby the crown of virginity and the pleasures of wedlock' and of whom Jerome did not at first hold high hopes: 'it will be harder for her than for you to forego delights once known and with a lesser reward for preserving her continence' (Jerome *Let.* 22.15). Augustine, when expostulating on the duty to maintain widowhood, seemingly ignored his own experience to insist 'it is easier to bridle than fulfil desire' – but added sourly that 'I have, however, often observed this fact of human behaviour that, with certain people, when sexuality is repressed, avarice seems to grow in its place' (Augustine *On the Good of Widowhood* 20, 25).

The other objections to continence the Fathers had to combat were more down-to-earth:

> My little patrimony is shrinking day by day, the property I inherited is being squandered, my servant insults me, my maid ignores my orders. Who will appear on my behalf before the authorities? Who will see to the education of my children and the training of my slaves?
>
> (Jerome *Let.* 54.15)

Excuses, says Jerome, sardonically: 'No woman marries to avoid cohabiting with a husband' (*ibid.*). Ambrose is similarly jaundiced: 'Do not say "I am desolate": this is the moan of someone who wants to marry' (*On Widows* 57) and he too cites worries over property and slaves and relatives as excuses. John Chrysostom, drawing on the experiences of his mother Anthusa who had been widowed at the age of twenty with two young children, had a particularly clear understanding of 'the horrors of widowhood' at that time, even amongst those who did have adequate means to support their state. He vividly represents this in *On the Priesthood*: 'she must encounter the slothfulness of domestics, and keep an eye on their misdeeds, ward off the plots of relatives, and bravely bear the insults of those who levy the public taxes, and their cruelty in the imposition of tribute' (*On the Priesthood* 315). Being also a widow with children as was his mother tended to added anxieties on their behalf, not to mention the expense. Nonetheless, in *On Remarriage* he refutes all these anxieties as 'pretexts and excuses; a ruse to hide your weakness' (*On Remarriage* 4) and he, Jerome and Ambrose took a still more dire view of the sufferings involved in marriage; the clashes of temperaments, the petty wrongs and jealousies between husband and wife, the pain, worry and expense of children. 'Why then, my daughter, do you seek again those sorrows which you dreaded before . . . ? If sorrow is so grievous, one should avoid its cause, not seek it again' (Ambrose *On Widows* 87). Chrysostom stated his belief that they were looking at their marriages, now safely in the past, through rose-coloured spectacles; 'They return to marriage to escape the trials of widowhood but they rediscover in it other tribulations even more awful and then they redouble the same old complaints' (John Chrysostom *On Remarriage* 1) and he laboured the advantages of remaining a widow (*ibid.* 5).

Those lower down the social scale were rather prone to the kind of petty, diminishing anxieties and grievances suffered by other widows of whom Chrysostom talks, who were alone, impoverished and embittered. Less rancorous than Jerome, Chrysostom seems to have had bad experiences with the order, to judge from reiterated occurrences of scolding; but he was also fully awake to the trials which must have driven many women to throw themselves on the charity of the church, those women whom Jerome sneers at as 'widows from necessity, not choice'. Chrysostom is particularly interesting in his advice to priests on the care necessary in the vetting of the widows' roll; some may try to get on it who 'have destroyed houses, spoiled marriages, and often been caught in thefts and frauds' and 'that such should be supported by the funds of the church, brings vengeance from God and utter condemnation from men' (*On the Priesthood* 297–8). For the situations of women of the humbler origins who joined the order, he is an illuminating witness; his criticisms are stringent but he takes their woes into account with a realistic and compassionate eye.

> Widows as a class, owing partly to poverty, partly to age and sex, use an unbridled freedom of speech ... and cry out unseasonably and find unnecessary fault and murmur over what they ought to be thankful for and complain about matters for which they should be grateful
>
> (John Chrysostom *On the Priesthood* 302)

such that great forbearance is necessary not to be 'provoked by their unseasonable annoyances, nor by their unreasonable complainings'; since 'through fear of want they are forced into begging, and through begging become insolent, and through insolence are again despised' (*ibid.* 306).

It is interesting to compare the examples of two more influential writers advising specific women in this position. Jerome in his letter to the noble Roman lady Furia on the duty of remaining a widow adjures her to think of her high forebears, the Furii Camilli, the wives of whom he represents as, almost to a woman, remaining faithful to one husband if widowed. If pagan women can achieve this, how much more ought not Christian women to be equally capable; and, true to form, he represents marriage as a great evil from which Furia has fortuitously escaped, full of such mundane cares as the supervision of property, the household and servants: 'you have lost your virginity to no profit; now stay chaste' (Jerome *Let.* 54.6). Chrysostom's advice is more sensitive to the situation; in his *Letter to a Young Widow* he shows far more awareness of the recipient's grief and bewilderment at her circumstances. His letter is full of comfort: rather than suggesting, with Jerome, that she must be relieved, if not happy, to have done with the turmoils of the married state, he fully appreciates and condones her feelings of grief, adjuring her not to fret 'because his greatness was cut short' and reminding his recipient that she at least was there when her husband died, unlike the wives of soldiers. He offers her the comfort that her beloved husband is now in heaven and she can still love him – and show it best by keeping her bed sacred to his memory. This loss, he says, is the worst blow she can endure, but the Lord will comfort her and she will enlighten all by how she bears it (John Chrysostom *Letter to a Young Widow* 6). Despite his poor opinion of the breed in general, this is a sensitive treatment of his correspondent, and his advice is the more palatable thereby. (It compares favourably, for instance, with Gregory of Nazianzus' advice in condolence of his mother on the death of his father appended at the head of this chapter.)

Certainly, whatever the personal griefs and hardships, from the point of view of the Church, the lot of the 60-fold seems to have been easier than the 100-fold. Despite opinions that 'virginity is the easier because virgins know nothing of the promptings of the flesh and widowhood is harder because widows cannot help thinking of the licence they have enjoyed in the past' (Jerome *Let.* 123.11) and despite troubles of the household, estate, children – or, indeed, because of them, the life of the dedicated widow, fuller and more occupied than that of the virgin, and with a grounding of greater worldly experience, seems to have been less prone to dramatic upset and the kind of scandal we have seen afflicting misled virgins.

WIDOWHOOD IN PRACTICE

In some communities, the widows had duties which placed them within the church hierarchy; possibly those later subsumed by the new order of the deaconesses (examined in Chapter 8), for Clement of Alexandria sets them after the three male orders as 'persons of distinction' (*eklekta prosopa* – *The Instructor* 3:12:97) and Origen speaks of them as ranking with those enjoying definite ecclesiastical status (*ekklesiastike time*) but says that there is no reason for them to be accorded this if their only function is foot-washing, which can be done by servants and domestics (Daniélou 1961:17). The Third century *Apostolic Church Order*[2] requires the appointment of three widows, 'two to devote themselves to prayer on behalf of all those who are tempted and to revelations, to whatever extent is necessary, one to succour women who are sick' (*Apostolic Church Order* 21); 'They must be ready to help, they must be temperate and make the necessary reports to priests' (*ibid*.).

However, the Egyptian *Church Order* states unequivocally that 'the widow is instituted for prayer which is the function of all Christians' and the *Didascalia Apostolorum* or *Teaching of the Apostles* that their mission is 'nothing else than to pray for bene-factors and for the whole church' (*Did. Ap.* 15.123); further that 'if questioned, [the widow] will not reply . . . she will refer the ques-tioner to those in the church' (*ibid*). 'Now what makes this work especially suitable to widows but their bereavement and desolate condition?' Augustine wrote to Proba (Augustine *Let.* 130.30). He then somewhat confuses the issue by imputing by a kind of rhetorical licence that everyone 'is in this world bereaved and desolate as long as he is a pilgrim absent from his Lord' and that therefore everyone should be 'careful to commit his widowhood, so to speak, to his God as his shield in continuous and most fervent prayer' (*ibid*.) – but he thus clearly preserves the association between widowhood and prayer.

This combination of the prayerful with the church functionary is reflected in some of the respects in which they were regarded as serving their communities. We can see evidence of the respect accorded them, for instance, as communicators of the 'revelations' anticipated by the *Apostolic Church Order* above, in the account of a vision, related with evident satisfaction by Evodius to Augustine, which was experienced by 'a respectable widow from Figentes, a handmaid of God . . . twelve years in widowhood' (Augustine *Let.* 158); she saw, reassuringly for her congregation, heaven receiving with honour the body of a young man who was the son of a presbyter of her church who had died the day before. Augustine himself might use a widow of the order as a messenger, as when he entrusted to the agency of the widow Galla his gift to bishop Quintilianus of relics of the protomartyr Stephen (Augustine *Let.* 212).

But as an order, their tendency to the contemplative would bring them too close to the purlieus of the virgins, with whose ideal they could not adequately compete. Ultimately, as Daniélou[3] has pointed out, as a separate tendency and practical force, the order went into decline, a victim of its own ambiguities; its contemplative aspect given greatest expression by the virgins and its quality of service held in dubious regard until finally subsumed into the flourishing office of the deaconess. Indeed, Daniélou considers the only characteristics the widows retained right up until the effective disappearance of the order around the end of the fourth century were that of a general body of aged women whom the community succoured, to whom their title gave charitable rights which they sometimes abused. If this was indeed the light in which they were mainly seen, it is understandable that writers such as Jerome were cautious in recommending younger, wealthier women to the life; this sets in context the rise of the office of deaconess.

Even more than the virgins, then, the devotional observances of widows were a matter of trial and experimentation; and as with the virgins at this time, the most notable exemplars of this group carved out their own rules and structure according to their own circumstances and inclinations. And to set against the negative evidence we have seen from the later fathers about unwilling and refractory widows, we also have a considerable showing of virtuous, restrained and eminently pious widows, not least from the pens of those who complained most about their truculence as a breed. Marcella, for instance; Jerome advises Furia if she is considering a life of avowed widowhood to set her standards by the pinnacle achieved by Marcella who 'while she maintains the glory of her family has given an example of the gospel life' when widowed after seven months (*Let.* 54.18).

Marcella does indeed seem to have been something out of the ordinary. A wealthy and youthful widow of senatorial rank disposed to asceticism, she was without precedent at Rome in her lifestyle, in which she was amongst the first of her kind, precursing the call to *ascesis* of Jerome, Pelagius and the rest. 'In those days, no highborn lady at Rome had made profession of the monastic life, or had ventured – so strange and ignominious and degrading did it then seem – publicly to call herself a nun' (*Let.*127.5); the many men and women attested afterwards in Rome practising similar disciplines were all too frequently her imitators. So also, given her lack of precedents for her rule, she was exceptional in her certainty and decision in its application. Marcella was the Anthony of her place and generation; the great instigator to a monastic lifestyle the more wonderful because sought and worked out in the centre of urban Rome amidst the wealth and property that Anthony had fled. She worked out the details of her lifestyle in large part for herself, from her own readings into the desert communities: particularly of 'the blessed Anthony, then still alive, and of the monasteries of the Thebaid, founded by Pachomius, and of the discipline laid down for virgins and for widows' (*ibid*.). Worlds away from her cushioned urban existence at the centre of known civilisation, it was an unlikely pattern to come to with such eagerness and entirely on her own initiative; only later to be endorsed, advised on and publicised by Jerome, who when he first met her was a callow young priest from Dalmatia finding the going in Rome hard, and who was drawn into her influential circle at her initiative and insistence.

When embarking on her lifestyle, she kept to her senatorial house, but lived humbly within it; she put off the clothing appropriate to her senatorial rank, selecting instead 'clothing meant to keep out the cold and not to show her figure' and put off all jewels, 'choosing to store her money in the stomachs of the poor, rather than to keep it at her own disposal' (Jerome *Let*. 127.3). She, like the virgins to whom she was then still near in age, kept close to her mother at all times, selected only virgins and widows for company 'and those women serious and staid', and avoided men; she 'would never see without witnesses such monks and clergy as she was required to interview' (*ibid*.). In common with her younger virgin sister Asella, she

> fasted in moderation, abstained from eating meat and knew the smell of wine more than its taste, taking it for the sake of her stomach and her frequent illnesses. She rarely used to go out in public and scrupulously shunned the houses of noble ladies so that she might not be forced to see that which she had renounced. She frequently visited the basilicas of apostles and martyrs for private prayer, and avoided the crowded throng of people.
>
> (Jerome *Let*. 127.4)

She also implemented 'long study' and 'constant meditation', dragging Jerome all unwilling into expanding the education of herself and her ladies in her search for knowledge, and, both before and after his departure for the Holy Land, keeping him so well plied with searching questions that he was driven to protest at the demand upon his time they required.[4] Such was her intellectual curiosity that she was drawn into controversies herself, to the extent of instructing and answering the queries of others; saving always that

> when she was thus questioned, she would reply as if her answer was not her own but from me or some other man, in order to confess that what she taught she herself had learned from others. For she knew that the apostle had said 'I do not permit a woman to teach' and she would not seem to inflict an injury on the male sex and on those priests who were enquiring about obscure and doubtful points.

(Jerome *Let.* 127.7)

Paula, a contemporary and friend of Marcella and part of her original circle of noble dévots, went on to become another widow hailed as an exemplar. What we know of Paula's ascetic life is in detail only for the period after she had left Rome with Jerome for the Holy Land for a conventual life proper. After this, her 'rule' was similar to Marcella's; she maintained the customary segregation and 'never sat at meat with a man' even if he were a bishop, 'never entered a bath except when dangerously ill' and 'even in the severest fever, she did not rest on an ordinary bed, but on the ground covered only with a rug of goat's hair' – in the little time she rested in between making 'day and night alike a time of almost unbroken prayer' (*Let.* 108.15). Paula attempted entirely to subjugate her physical needs: 'Her self-restraint was so great as to be almost immoderate; her fasts and labours were so severe as almost to weaken her constitution'; using even very little oil except on feast days, she completely eschewed 'wine, sauce, fish, honey, milk, eggs and other things agreeable to the palate' (108.17). She allowed the virgins of her community these 'indulgences' when they were sick, but 'when she fell ill herself she made no concessions to her weakness' (108.20) refusing to take even 'a little light wine' (108.21) at the special instance of her doctors and a bishop, Epiphanius, whom Jerome had hoped might sway her – nearly prevailing upon him instead to give up wine. Her discipline of study was equally voracious; she 'knew the holy scriptures by heart', learned Hebrew (a language Jerome self-deprecatingly claimed to have only 'partially acquired' after a lifetime's study) 'so well that she could chant the psalms in Hebrew and could speak the language without a trace of Latin pronunciation' (108.27) and, like Marcella, plied Jerome keenly with questions as to scriptural interpretations. She further burdened herself with personal debt, borrowing money at interest to feed the poor. It was a family tendency; her widowed daughter Blesilla, who seems to have been initially something of a 'merry widow', also succumbed eventually to her mother's prayers and Jerome's oratory and took to asceticism with such fervour that her premature death was arguably attributable to it.

Melania the Elder was equally uncompromising in her conception of the duty of the Christian widow. Widowed at twenty-two, she carefully set her family affairs in order and entrusted her son Publicola to the guardianship of the Praetorian Prefect, then decamped for the Holy Land, where for the next forty years she traversed the land, helped clerics in distress, intimidated officials, instituted a monastery with her satellite cleric, Rufinus and 'at her own expense, she assisted churches, monasteries, guests and prisons' (Palladius *LH* 46). She ministered to the Fathers of the desert 'from her own resources', tending to their need in the desert and assisting them in prison (*ibid*.); and along with their hospitality, she and Rufinus were held to have enlightened the recipients of their charity:

> both of them received those who had turned up in Jerusalem for the sake of a vow, bishops and monks and virgins; at their own expense, they edified all those who passed through. They united the four hundred monks involved in the schism over Paulinus, and having convinced every heretic who fought against the divinity of the Holy Spirit, they led them back to the church.
>
> (*LH* 54)

In later life she saw her mission as best realised in an attempt to browbeat the remaining worldlings of her family into a life of renunciation, ably seconded by her granddaughter and namesake. Her ministry and its implications will be considered in more detail in Chapter 8.

John Chrysostom also knew exemplary widows: not least the renowned Olympias. Born around 368 into the highest circles of the Constantinopolitan court, the daughter of 'the count' Seleucus (*LH* 56) and the bride of the city prefect Nebridius, Olympias, like Marcella in Rome, became infected with the zeal for renunciation despite hugely advantageous worldly circumstances, and, also like Marcella, attached herself and her possessions to the service of an influential man of God; in this case, the Patriarch John. She was certainly technically a widow, having been married if only for a brief span. But she enjoyed something of the ambiguous status attested for

Macrina of being both widow and virgin, although in reverse; for Macrina the title of widow was the complimentary one as she was merely betrothed and not actually married. Olympias, though she was widely accredited with maintaining her virginity – 'through the goodness of God she was preserved unspoiled in the flesh as in the spirit' (*Life of Olympias, Deaconess* 2)[5] – was nonetheless a widow, and a fairly formidable one. Her standing was achieved despite a far more unfavourable set of circumstances than any of the other exemplars faced; to achieve her ambition of a vocation as a widow avowed in the eyes of the church she had to resist, in seemingly complete isolation, a barrage of coercive forces, not excluding imperial displeasure. Left an orphan in the care of the prefect Procopius as her tutor, 'she was joined in marriage to a husband' Nebridius, of whom 'the debt of nature was very soon required'; reputedly 'she remained a spotless virgin to the last' (*ibid.* 2).

Subsequently she exercised her own choice: she is reported to have considered and rejected the dictat of Paul to Timothy that 'I wish young widows to marry'. But, as might be expected for one who had 'birth, affluence, the most costly education, a sweet nature and all her youthful beauty', 'her early widowhood became the cause of disquiet' and the Emperor Theodosius himself 'made great efforts to marry her off to a certain Elpidius from Spain, who was one of his own relatives' (*ibid.* 3). Upon her refusal, he placed her and her possessions under the guardianship of Clementinus, the urban prefect, until her thirtieth year; Clementinus continually urged Elpidius' suit and forbade her to visit the church or meet with clerics. When Theodosius returned from suppressing the revolt of Maximus, he discovered her still steadfastly refusing marriage, and, apparently impressed 'having heard that she practised the most rigorous asceticism' (*ibid.* 5), gave her control over her own fortune again. She promptly distributed large quantities of it in largesse to the church, entirely supporting several bishops, most notably Chrysostom himself, and set up her house as a convent.

Her ministry will be examined in greater detail in Chapter 8; for her personal rule, she followed the pattern we have seen derived from the inspiration of the desert dwellers, taken to a high degree:

> it would be impossible to better that which she achieved ...
> For she never ate meat and went almost entirely without bathing; only occasionally would she bathe if the need arose through illness (for her digestion gave her continual suffering),

when she would come to the waters with her shift on, out of modesty.

(*Life of Olympias, Deaconess* 13)

Nothing could have been cheaper than her clothes; she covered herself with garments that were all rags, unworthy of her manly courage. And such was the meekness she taught herself that she outdid even the little children ... she passed her whole intolerable life in penitence and in an ocean of tears.

(*Life of Olympias, Deaconess* 15)

In addition she is accounted as having all the requisite virtues of an ascetic life, 'her appearance was free from artifice and her face from makeup; she kept sleepless vigil, her body was nothing to her, her mind was free from pride, her intelligence was without conceit ... her generosity limitless, her garments squalid, her self-control boundless' (*ibid*. 15). In addition she 'catechized women who did not believe ... she called her multitude of household servants out of their slavery to freedom, and proclaimed their worth as great as her own nobility' (*ibid*.).

For the service such notable role-models amongst widows could offer their local community and church, the ecclesiastical canons mentioned previously provided little practical scope. Widows were encouraged to minister to each other, and to those inferior to them in the congregational pecking order, i.e. married women and penitents. For properly-conducted virgins to consort with these symbols of what they were forbidden was, as we have seen, not encouraged. However, one of the most frequently attested and important functions of the more dedicated widows became supervision of the 'more princely order' of virgins: 'I ought not to separate [the widows] from the commendation belonging to the virgins ... For instruction in virginity is strengthened by the example of widows' (Ambrose *On Widows* 1). Even the same writers who deplored easy access between the two orders bore witness to and praised their mutually beneficial effect. 'It was in Marcella's cell that Eustochium, that paragon of virgins was gradually trained' (Jerome *Let*. 127.5) in the days in which Marcella and her ladies were pioneering their route in Rome. Eustochium's training was completed by her mother in the Holy Land; her place in Marcella's enclosure was taken by the noble virgin Principia, to whom Jerome's eulogy of Marcella in *Letter* 127 was addressed. Marcella subsequently acted as her virgin companion's protectress in the sack of Rome, managing to persuade initially hostile barbarian soldiers who broke into her house to escort them safely to the basilica of St Paul in search of a refuge (*ibid*. 127.13).

Following Marcella's lead in Rome, 'monastic establishments for virgins became numerous' (*ibid*. 127.8); often headed by widows, like Marcella. Her friend in *ascesis*, Lea, also the motivating force in a religious society at Rome, though she 'as a widow she held a lower place', also surrounded herself with virgins to whom she 'showed herself a true mother' (*Let*. 23.2) and set them the example of the religious life. She 'wore rough sackcloth instead of soft clothing, spent nights sleeplessly in prayer . . . neglected her dress and hair and ate only the coarsest food. Still, in all that she did, she avoided display' (*ibid*). Paula too, in addition to personal austerity, dealt strictly with the 'girls who had accompanied her' (*Let*. 108.14). 'Surrounded by numbers of virgins, she was always the least noticeable in dress, speech, action and walk' (*ibid*.) and exemplar to those still steeped in the values of their previous life; she imposed dire regimens, and if they were 'troubled by fleshly desires' her remedy was to redouble their fasting, 'for she wished her virgins to be ill in body rather than suffer in soul' (*Let*. 108.20). She kept a hawk-like eye on the purity of her precious charges: 'So strictly did Paula keep them separate from men that she would not allow even eunuchs to approach them, in case of giving cause for slanderous people to gossip' (*ibid*.) – or because she believed with Basil of Ancyra that eunuchs could defile virgins in the belief that they were free of the consequences. She enforced strict equality of clothing and appearance, allowed none of the high-born girls to be served by maids of their own household and kept them busy with chores, portions of scripture to learn every day and garment-making. She took special care to oversee personally all they did, coaxing or scolding or morally uplifting them; and, as Elias' and Augustine's experiences seen in the previous chapter suggest was to be expected, one of her most crucial responsibilities was that 'when the sisters quarrelled amongst themselves, she reconciled them with soothing words' (*ibid*.).

Melania had round her in Jerusalem 'a group of fifty virgins' (*LH* 46) besides ministering to virgins who 'passed through', presumably on pilgrimage. For instance, typical of these may have been Eunomia, her cousin and the virgin daughter of Avita, a devout matron who had adopted a continent marriage with her husband Apronianus, a connection of Paulinus of Nola. According to Paulinus, who was related to both cousins, 'Eunomia is Melania's "sister", almost her daughter, for she delights in dogging Melania's footsteps, looking to her sister as her teacher . . . [Christ] hears Eunomia, instructed by the guiding voice of Melania' and Eunomia in her turn 'leads with her pure voice the blessed female choir'; for in Melania's triumphal return to family haunts 'a great procession of noble ladies follows, a multitude of dedicated virgins who all alike share the colour of the one fleece [of virtue]' (Paulinus of Nola *Natalicia* 21.60).

Olympias also had in her monastery 'her maids, fifty in number, who all lived in purity and virginity' in addition to 'her relation Elisanthia . . . who was herself a virgin also . . . with her sisters Martyria and Palladia, also virgins' (*Life of Olympias, Deaconess* 6). This gathering then further attracted

> many other women of senatorial family . . . such that by the grace of God there were gathered all together there in that holy spot two hundred and fifty in number, all crowned with virginity and all leading the most virtuous life.
>
> (*Life of Olympias, Deaconess* 6)

Widowed mothers of promising virgin daughters were particularly applied to in the all-important matter of guarding the vocation of their daughters, whether or not they personally were under such strenuous vows: for 'a daughter may be as religious as she pleases; still a mother who is a widow is a guarantee for her chastity' (Jerome *Let.* 117.5). So as a matter of course, in the discussions about Demetrias' vocation, Juliana is addressed as 'you who approve and rejoice in it' (Augustine *Let.* 188.6). Augustine's congratulations on Demetrias' decision to take vows and his anxious counsel that she should disregard suspect Pelagian teachings (cf. Chapter 4) are addressed to Juliana; Augustine is perhaps more cautious than Jerome in the proprieties of addressing virgins directly. Certainly he entrusts to Juliana the interpretation and transmission of his teaching to Demetrias. His widow-envoy to Quintilianus, Galla, also has with her 'her daughter Simplicia', a consecrated virgin, who is 'subject to her mother by reason of age, though above her by virtue of holiness' (Augustine *Let.* 212) in the usual formula. Paula, as we have seen, kept Eustochium under her vigilant eye; Emmelia, though cast in the role at the instigation of her seemingly dominant daughter Macrina, performed the same function:

> her father had by this time departed this life . . . she shared her mother's labours, dividing her cares with her, and lightening her heavy load of sorrows. At the same time, thanks to her

mother's guardianship, her own life remained blameless under
her mother's eye which directed and witnessed all she did.

(Gregory of Nyssa *Life of Macrina* 966)

Marcella, Melania and Olympias represent the breed of women for
whom the decision had been early made by their, in the main,
Christian families for marriage; a decision they later elect to overturn.
Many of those Jerome refers to somewhat slightingly as the 60-fold
and whose marriages Augustine says disqualify them from being able
to take Christ as their spouse, thus being in the front-rank of the
pious, we may believe to have been virgins manqué. Macrina would
have been amongst their number but for the turn of events. For all
that, for those such as Marcella, Melania, Paula, Juliana, and arguably
Olympias and Macrina, widowhood, if strictly regarded, was a
suitable channel for the ethos of holy renunciation and they
augmented it by their example. It is such women as these that
Chrysostom had in mind when he averred that 'the widow starts off
inferior only to the virgin; but at the last she equals her and joins her'
(John Chrysostom *Against Remarriage* 2). Not many shared this
view. Ultimately, the order suffered from a lack of definition and
poor regard; though these notable women carved out their own
definition of a holy life as we have seen, they still seem to derive most
of their standing from being seen primarily as guardians of a more
precious state carrying far more standing in the eyes of the male
authorities; the care of the virgins. And, despite the alacrity with
which Marcella, Melania and Olympias took to it, the state of
widowhood retained its aura of being a less than enviable condition,
even to the pious; Gregory of Nazianzus considered his sister
fortunate indeed because 'why should I say more of her compassion
to widows than that the reward she obtained was never to be called
a widow herself?' (*Or.* 8.12).

6

MARRIED SANCTITY I:
'THE BED UNDEFILED'
Christian wifehood

The marriage of the faithful is a better thing than impious virginity.

(Augustine *On the Good of Marriage* 8)

Marriage; a garment fit for mortals and slaves ... where there is death, there is marriage.

(John Chrysostom *On Virginity* 14.5, 6)

It remains to consider the lot of the 30-fold: married women, the lowest rung of the ladder of devoutness, many of whom still, within the household, displayed conspicuous piety. Because they were more hemmed about with others, their situation was more complex; added to which, there are direct grounds for comparison between them and their pagan counterparts (as there are not for institutionalised celibates) which raise some interesting problems. Was, for instance, the experience of a Christian *matrona* much different from that of the pagan *matrona* of a few generations earlier? In this age of the 'gentrification' of Christianity, were her relations with her husband, *gens* and offspring visibly altered, specifically in terms of her Christianity? And how much did this effect, if any, alter in different echelons of society? We must also consider how great was the influence in this period of ascetic Christianity on actual marriages and the concept of marriage. Peter Brown has offered a view of married couples in the later Empire as representing in their persons 'a miniature of civic order' (in Veyne 1987:248); would this idea of marriage survive the beliefs of the couple supposedly being remodelled along eschatological lines, totally at odds with the ideals of public life?

The Fathers viewed marriage as a potential 'problem' coming between the Christian and his duty. 'Originally, marriage had the two purposes [of procreation and the passion of nature]; but now ...

there is only one reason remaining for it; the prevention of indecency and licentiousness' (John Chrysostom *On Virginity* 19). Reading the mass of texts on this by a number of church writers using all their authority, there is a temptation to begin to see this as a common belief; but there is a great difficulty in knowing how far, in fact, their contemporary readership hoisted in this view. We must consider whether ordinary Christian men and women saw marriage as a 'problem', or if the Fathers modified their ideals for womanhood to suit married women they knew; if marriage could be an end in itself for the Christian couple, or if it must necessarily be a consolation for lost chastity. Some believers attempted a compromise; a celibate marriage where the couple remained together, but abstained from physical relations. Where did such continent marriages, a peculiarly Christian phenomenon, rank in the hierarchy of devotion? Was a continent marriage seen as an achievement in its own right, or as a second-best for those who could not make the final break? Then, too, when bringing up a bishop or a saint (or a family of them, in some cases) gave one reflected lustre, we will examine whether one could somehow palliate the loss of one's own chastity through the means of procreating saints; and whether the merit acquired this way might be relative or superior to the credit given for a continent marriage. And finally, a question that recurrently suggests itself on reading the Fathers on marriage; did the church foster a competition in piety – and particularly in chastity – between man and wife?

PRE-CHRISTIAN EXPECTATIONS OF MARRIAGE

While there is not the space here for an in-depth analysis of how social attitudes to marriage evolved prior to this period,[1] some background is needed for an examination into what changed with Christianity; I shall therefore offer some general considerations to set the scene before a more detailed examination of marriage under the patristic eye.

In Roman society, marriage was a private act not requiring the sanction of a public authority, having its basis, as with so much else in Roman life, in the family as a legal and social unit; the laws to do with marriage predominantly express concern over the protection of the property-base of the *familia*. While private ceremonies were usually gone through, they were not legally necessary or binding, and served mainly the purpose of indicating the intent of the couple in front of witnesses. The undertaking of this private act was for legal purposes indicated primarily in the consent of the two parties concerned – and that consent might in any case be given by the *patres* of the couple marrying, rather than by themselves (see p. 49); hence the perplexities of the jurists not infrequently seen trying to ascertain whether two individuals were in fact married or not. Ultimate proof often rested merely on intention, a difficult thing to prove – given eloquent expression in 'the usual oath regarding wives' administered at the census: 'Have you, to the best of your knowledge and belief, a wife?' (Cicero, *de Orat.* 2.260; Gellius *NA* 4.20).[2] Hence Macrina's statement that she considered herself married although her betrothed had died before they could seal the union seems less of a display of over-sensitive principle and more of an actual difficulty, when one considers the Roman legal difficulties in actually ascertaining whether a couple were married or not, based largely on the existence of consent alone. Under the Republic and early Empire, divorce was correspondingly easy, with the simple utterance by one party – usually the husband – of the words '*tuas res tibi habeto*': 'take your things' (e.g. in Martial 10.41 – spoken by a woman).[3]

There was a fairly well-established tendency amongst the aristocrats in the republic of undertaking marriage largely in order to increase property or secure political alliances; hence the need for a flexible legal attitude. High-born women were 'a "recyclable" resource', (Corbier in Rawson 1991:61) and as such prone to multiple marital alliances; indeed, to such an extent as to merit the term 'serial marriage' (Bradley in Rawson 1991:85). Nevertheless, popular notions as expressed in literature and epigraphical evidence indicate that the public's taste was for a hopeful belief in tales of marital devotion and happiness, even if they did not always experience these themselves; and in the later Imperial era, public pronouncements seem to adopt and expand on this, with increasingly paternalistic legislation on moral behaviour and literary rhetoric which frequently seems to prefigure many of the attitudes later bruited by the church in family relations. It has been argued, indeed, that this amounted to a deliberate process of working at a self-conscious concept of monogamous marriage as a moral code, by the promotion of the ideals of *homonoia* (like-mindedness) and *concordia* (harmony).[4]

The change in tone in the representation of marriage, if it is to be believed, projects more equality of emotional support, more importance placed on domestic harmony and some sharing of responsibilities: the wife as a friend, a companion in life who 'shares in your prosperity and your troubles' (Plutarch *Brutus* 13), rather than 'the accessory to the working of the citizen and *paterfamilias*' (Veyne 1987:37) that she had tended to be viewed under the republic. Seneca saw the marriage bond as comparable in every way to the pact of friendship, bringing with it an exchange of obligations. Plutarch and Pliny the younger commended the nobility of higher friendship as a form of conjugal love; Pliny wrote unusually fond and frequent letters to his wife when they happened to be parted even for a short period, and Plutarch wrote a treatise of conjugal advice advocating tolerance and patience on both sides – but specifically encouraging the bride into dependence on her spouse. 'A wife ought not to make friends of her own, but to enjoy her husband's friends with him' and 'a woman ought to do her talking either to her husband or through her husband' (Plutarch *Moralia* 140D and 142D).

These ideas of marriage as a mutual support, however, still go in tandem with notions of the wife as a 'grown child' in need of tutelage and at risk from the exigencies of the political and business world, the education of whom it was the husband's duty to complete – insofar as he saw fit. Though she might exercise a great deal of financial control if *sui iuris* (legally independent), still she must be protected from making rash statements on her tax returns; rescripts from several emperors concerning the *fiscus* were aimed at preventing people damaging their own rights by inadvisable admissions, and the high-risk groups, from inexperience and ignorance of their rights, were rustics and women.[5] Though encouraged to improve her mind, one's wife must be guarded from imbibing dangerously destabilising intellectual flim-flam; while the wife of a friend of Pliny's was puffed off for her epistolary talents (though her husband was given much of the credit), Seneca's mother was forbidden to study philosophy by her husband, who saw it as the road to dissolution. *Industria*, however, was perceived as healthy in combating temptations to the virtuous wife to improper pursuits: physicians recommended that women be given charge of the house, as running around supervising the slaves, overseeing the provisioning and housework and making sure everything was runnning smoothly was more healthful than sitting about languishing – let alone that it gave less time for intrigues.

The wife participating in this 'higher friendship' was subject to some of the same notions affecting the Victorian wives perceived as the 'Angel in the House': one's wife was to be respected as a partner in this noble endeavour, not to be treated as a mistress, that is, subjected to passion or affectionate cuddles. In an anticipation of the

Fathers of our period, Seneca gives the rationale for physical love as solely the making of babies, thus it should be performed sparingly, on a basis of reason, not fondness. Indeed, later Christian authors such as Clement of Alexandria used some stoic bases for certain of their arguments. Christian practices – and Christian couples – in their turn influenced neo-Platonist adaptations of these principles. As early as the late second century, the physician Galen was struck by the sexual austerity of the Christian communities:

> Their contempt of death is patent to us every day, and likewise their restraint in cohabitation. For they include not only men but also women who refrain from cohabiting all their lives; and they also number individuals who, in self-discipline and self-control, have attained a pitch not inferior to that of genuine philosophers.[6]

Peter Brown has argued that, lacking the clear ritual boundaries provided in Judaism by circumcision and dietary laws, this sexual abstinence expressed their need to make the distinction between theirs and alien communities and present a united front to outsiders: that, in fact, 'they make their exceptional sexual discipline bear the full burden of expressing the difference between themselves and the pagan world', expecting that 'a person who is an exception on this point will be an exception in other respects as well' (in Veyne 1987:264). How far this was perceptibly borne out in the experience of Christian married couples we will examine later in this chapter; but I consider that rather too much can be made of this distinction. That issues of sexual control were heightened 'in a community anxious to avoid marriage with pagans' (*ibid.*) does not chime with many of the examples we have of Christian girls married to pagans, in the humbler sections of society no less than in the aristocracy, as we will examine in detail with Nonna, Gorgonia and Monica (see pp. 115ff).

Despite what looks like a change in public rhetoric regarding the married state, however, Roman expectations of the realities of marriage from the husband's point of view seem to have remained on the whole low. While approvingly highlighting legends of conspicuous marital devotion, with spouses sharing exile, opprobrium and death, nonetheless Roman society had a very matter-of-fact attitude to the likelihood of actual marital harmony; as there was less option about the matter of whether or not to marry, so it seems, less choosiness about the object of marriage. Epigraphically, 'she never gave me cause to complain' is as frequent a comment as 'very dear wife'[7] . Pre-Christian Roman marriage ideas still owed more to notions of civic duty than the kind of theories that would emerge from Christianity of the 'help-meet'; Pliny and Seneca's 'higher friendship' had strong undercurrents of the desirability of public observation of this praiseworthy ideal. Antipater of Tarsus regarded marriage as a duty in order to provide one's country with new citizens, and because the divine plan of the universe required the propagation of the human race; according to Musonius, the foundation of marriage was procreation and mutual support. Observing this, Peter Brown considers that the married couple came to assume in public something of a miniature of civic order: 'The *eunoia*, the *sumpatheia*, the *praotes* of the relations of husband and wife echoed the expectations of grave affability and unquestioning class loyalty with which the powerful man both lovingly embraced and firmly controlled his city' (Brown in Veyne 1987:248). For besides being a civic duty in itself, marriage, particularly if up the social scale, as a venture into 'respectability' and an obvious move away from the irresponsibilities of youth, often carried with it enrolment into the ranks of worthy burgherdom. For a provincial it could entail expectations of undertaking liabilities in keeping with one's increased dignity as a householder: of serving on the town council, collecting taxes, or undertaking civic improvements. Small wonder that some – even from the more solidly worthy ranks of provincial respectability, like Augustine – balked at the prospect of being part of a socio-civic unit as 'Husband' and opted instead for a 'second-class marriage' – a monogamous liaison, often of lasting duration, with a concubine.

Concubinage must be considered in the context of notions on marriage, having something of the every-day quality and acceptedness of the 'common-law marriage' unions of today. Notwithstanding Plutarch making Brutus' wife Porcia insist on the difference between the concubine who merely uses the material benefits of the household and provides sex, and the wife who 'shares your prosperity and your troubles', it seems to have been a viable and well-regarded alternative to all the implications of marriage. Porcia's view may express the anxieties of the legitimate wife, but from the male point of view such an arrangement had much to recommend it, for instance for those yet with their way to make who were not interested in local ties, like Augustine, or for widowers, maybe with a family anxious not to be supplanted. Jane Gardner has pointed out a tendency for the men in such unions to be of higher status than the women (Gardner 1986:58); concubinage also provided an outlet for relationships which, if sanctioned by the form of marriage would have been regarded as shocking mésalliances, or simply illegal, such as those of citizens with *probrosae* (morally reprehensible women such as actresses or prostitutes) or women with no *conubium* (the legal capacity for marriage). But the boot could be on the other foot: Callixtus, a former slave who became pope from 214–218 'authorised' senatorial women who did not wish to lose their privileges for marrying below their class (since women legally were assumed into the class, with all its advantages or disadvantages, of the man they married) to live in concubinage with plebeians and freedmen (Hippolytus *Refutation of all Heresies* 24). This, seemingly because of a shortage of eligible men, may have its origins in Callixtus' own standpoint as a former slave; or may indicate a view that living with a believer without *conubium* was better than undertaking marriage in proper form with a more socially equal pagan.

This kind of liaison was not without its risks: Ulpian warned that sexual relations with one's concubine might legally be regarded as *stuprum* (debauchery, unlawful intercourse) unless the woman was *probrosa*, and warns men off living with free or freedwomen – both of whom occur in noticeable numbers as concubines (*D.* 25.7.1.1). The status was, however, regarded as honourable to a fair degree, assuming an altogether stable and monogamous relationship; enough to confer on the women concerned the dignity and almost the status of *matronae*. If this were not so, there would have been no call for the procedure which existed for prosecuting the unfaithful concubine for adultery, very much as a wife; as long as she was of good standing, and only as a third party (*D.* 48.5.14). These women appear legitimately on tombstones after the wife, or in their own right. Libanius' figures in his autobiographical oration, Augustine's in his *Confessions*. 'Even the Catholic Church was prepared to recognize it, provided the couple remained faithful to one another' (Brown 1967:62). Hippolytus of Rome in the *Apostolic Tradition* ruled that 'a concubine who is a slave and has reared her children and has been faithful to her master alone may become a hearer [in the church]' although 'the man who is with a concubine must desist and marry legally' (*Apostolic Tradition* 16). The probability exists that Augustine's concubine may have been a catholic catechumen throughout the years of her liaison with him (Brown 1967:62–3); she was described as 'devout' and when finally parted from him she went home to Africa vowing to observe the abstinence of a widow. She was with him for some thirteen years; her influence on his waverings should evidently be considered in the same context as that of a Christian wife on a pagan husband.

More negative suppositions of the husband from his union were bolstered by an extensive corpus of law on adultery. This preoccupation initially reflects more insecurity about property ownership than moral opprobrium. Epictetus reflects prevailing views in describing adultery as theft: taking away the wife of a neighbour is as inconsiderate as pilfering his portion of pork from his plate. 'Similarly, for women, the portions have been distributed among men' (cited in Veyne 1987:46). The attitudes husbands expected from their spouses in the opposite case are exemplified in the advice that Plutarch addresses to young wives (evidently as one of the duties that go with the privileges of the higher friendship): they should be sweetly indulgent and shut their eyes to a little philandering rather than wreck a marriage; though he does also exhort the husband not to enrage his wife unduly – both should consider the holiness of procreation (Plutarch *Moralia* 140B–144F). In saying this Plutarch is simply giving a utilitarian rationalisation of the well-documented legal double standard with regard to adultery: that a man might prosecute his wife for adultery – but not she him.[8] Further, if the wife was adulterous – or under common suspicion of being so – and her husband did not divorce and prosecute her, he might himself be liable to prosecution under the *lex Iulia de adulteriis coercendis* for *lenocinium* (pimping). In marriage or attempting to escape it, the odds were stacked against Roman women; it is small wonder that so many in our era, having been married at first when barely at puberty, subsequently made a choice against the social norm.

In this respect Christian writers from Hermas onwards did take a completely new line to advise behaviour actually counter to the law: canvassing the unprecedented view that an adulterous wife could repent, in which case, her husband should forgive her and take her back. This view was not shared by the legal authorities; as against the emerging leniency of the Christian theorists, the laws against adultery of wives became even more oppressive with the establishment of Christianity.[9] But this was part of a school of thought pioneered by Christian ideology, dedicated to combating the Roman belief in marriage as 'disposable' at one's convenience; something that, as we have seen, could be assumed or dispensed with according to one's whim. Christian theorists began to purvey the idea (rare, but not unknown in the pagan eras) that marriage was for life; hence the wholesale condemnation meted out to Fabiola (see p. 32) who, of good family but also a good daughter of the church, released herself from a difficult marriage (coincidentally, to 'an adulterer' believed also to be 'a sodomite' – Jerome *Let.* 55.3) to remarry. Remarriage after death was, if not approved by the more austere Fathers, tolerated; but the church writers were propagating the unheard of concept that while both spouses yet lived, they were bound one to another. Even in the case of adultery, the Christian should cleave to his or her spouse while at all possible, separate if absolutely neces-sary, but at all costs not divorce and re-marry. This being said, they applied the logic to both parties equally; the seriousness of male adultery was an issue on which the patristic writers took the humane advantage over the view of enlightened paganism (as they did not invariably in consideration of family life). In pre-Christian Roman belief it might be held as better not to indulge in extramarital sex, as a courtesy more than a due to one's partner, or because character was believed to derive from having the strength to resist vice (with the additional disincentive of the possible consequences of being caught – acts of revenge on those so found out included mutilation, castration and homosexual rape;[10] but, such rationalisations aside, male inchastity did not *matter* as such. Female inchastity could threaten bloodlines and property transfer, and so from the earliest times very much did matter: the moral odium coming secondarily and in support of the 'portion of pork' thinking seen in Epictetus.

Christian theorists in the later period took, and published abroad, the ground-breaking attitude that faithfulness was the responsibility of both partners. 'Yes, I say, I command you . . .' thundered Augustine, 'We have baptised all these many men for years now, to no effect if none of them here preserve the vows of chastity they took'; and, far from advising the women to be compliant to preserve the marriage, 'I do not want Christian wives to give in over this' (Augustine *Sermons* 392.4). Chrysostom, too, pressed for a single sexual standard:

> . . . just as we punish women when, although they are married to us, they give themselves to others, so too are we punished, if not by Roman laws, then by God . . . The sexual act is adulterous not only when the woman is bound to another man; it is also adultery for the man who is himself bound to a wife.
>
> (*Hom.* 5 on I Thess. 2; trans. Elizabeth Clark)

Further, he stresses that this is so even when the other woman is free and unmarried; in fact, Chrysostom refutes in detail the legal position that only women's inchastity signified in marriage, in a passage so full of reproach and repetition (– 'pay close attention to what I say. Even if my speech becomes tedious to many, it is still necessary for me to utter it to set you straight in future' – *ibid.*) that we may infer that he too is meeting a dead weight of inertia, if not active opposition, from his hearers.

This brings us to the first major distinction in the study of Christian era wifedom: thus far we have dealt with the expectations to be encountered in the husband, as does most of Roman tradition – even Plutarch's advice to the Bride has a subtext of how she should comport herself to least inconvenience her spouse. What begins to distinguish our period is writers addressing themselves to and about wives, in more and greater detail, with advice to them about their actual experiences, admonishing, trying to fit and tailor their behaviour and expectations (occasionally confusingly and at cross purposes): Tertullian's *Exhortation to his Wife* and *On the Female Dress*, Augustine's *On the Good of Marriage, On Marriage and Concupiscence*, John Chrysostom's *What sort of women ought to be taken as wives*, besides all the homilies, letters and treatises dealing with them incidentally. Nor is this body of advice necessarily preferential to the male view. The earlier attitude – that it behoved the husband to behave well as the rational half of the partnership, but that even if he did not, the wife must observe her proper station – has lost its purchase; wives are to be seen admonishing their husbands and instructing them, and even drawing praise for doing so. The wife, in the new Christian rhetoric, has a far more important place than formerly, just as the couple has a more significant place in the community as a representation of 'proper relations', of Christian to Christian and man to God: in Peter Brown's resonant prose, 'married couples were expected to bear in their own persons nothing less than an analogue in microcosm of the group's single-hearted solidarity' (in Veyne 1987:263). In this analogue, the position of the wife was altering: we must look at what altered directly in a wife's experience.

THE CHRISTIAN *MATRONA* AND HER *GENS*

A Roman wife married without *manus*[11] derived all her own standing, as her property, from her *gens*, her own birth-family; regarded throughout marriage (or multiple marriages) as remaining 'her' family to which she would return in the case of divorce or the death of her husband. It was almost as if a woman's family merely loaned her to her husband; her father (or oldest male relative from her *gens*) retained his *patria potestas* over her, with legal control over her actions, to the extent of dissolving her marriage if he saw fit, as one of the 'consenting' parties (*see* p. 49). While she lived in and on her husband's property, she only had the use of it, inasmuch as he allowed her, and it remained absolutely his – as did any children she had, which were deemed to have been born into 'his' family. Though she might marry up the social scale and acquire glory from her husband's status, this was as much a loan as any material property with which he might favour her; and gifts between husband and wife were not valid in law, since each derived their property from the *familia*, which must not be diminished. Her husband's family would always regard her to a certain extent as an outsider; and even if she died after a lifetime married to the same man, to the day she died, she and they would consider her 'real' family to be her *gens*.[12]

Her standing in the family she married into was thus precarious on all sides; and she need not expect that this position would be made any easier by sympathy from those who might seem to be her natural allies, the women of her new family. Her mother-in-law, if still *in situ*, would have established her own standing in the family from a similarly precarious start, and a great deal of any influence she had would have stemmed from her relations with her male children; only to become vulnerable again through the injection of an outsider with greater claims on her son. Small wonder then if some brides experienced further alienation at the hands of the one person who might be expected to have the deepest understanding of their plight; hence Terence's dictum that 'all mothers-in-law hate their daughters-in-law' (*Hecyra* 2.1.4). Plutarch tells that in Lepcis, in Africa, the situation was formalised into ritual: the new bride on the day after her marriage would send to her mother-in-law to ask for the loan of a pot, which the mother-in-law would refuse her, and, further, declare that she had none; the pot in this case being symbolic of assistance and support. For, says Plutarch,

> her purpose being that the bride may from the outset realise the stepmother's attitude in her mother-in-law, and in the event of some harsher incident later on, may not feel indignant or resentful ... The one way to cure this trouble is to create an affection for herself personally on the part of her husband, and at the same time not to divert or lessen his attention for his mother.
>
> (Plutarch *Moralia* 2.143; trans. F. C. Babbitt)

This exactly encapsulates the experience of an African bride from our period at Thagaste; that of Augustine's mother Monica on marrying Patricius. Not only did she have to win over her 'hot-tempered' husband, but also a jealous mother-in-law egged on by 'tale-bearing servants'. As if she had read Plutarch, Monica did exactly as he prescribed, and 'won over the older woman by dutiful attentions and patience and gentleness' until her won-over mother-in-law complained to Patricius instead about the servants and had him punish them; after which the two women 'lived in wonderful harmony' (Augustine *Confessions* 9.9). The situation was not, therefore, irremediable; but it must have been tense for many new brides, and contributory in turn to reinforcing their dependence on their own *gens* after their marriage.

This tradition of the importance of birth and the family of origin was taken over by the Christian writers; it is a recurring theme in the sources. This is particularly true in the cases of the women from out of the top drawer of nobility; it was a minor obsession with the Fathers of the church just how well-born some of their most devout female adherents were. They trumpet their lineages with all the satisfaction of those who have three centuries of taunts that their flocks were 'slaves, criminals and greeklings' to avenge. Thus Jerome on Paula's inherited distinction: 'Of the stock of the Gracchi and descended from the Scipios, the heir and representative of that Paulus whose name she bore, the true and legitimate daughter of that Martia Papyria who was mother to Africanus' (Jerome *Let.*. 108.1). Of Marcella, he says 'I will not set forth' in true Ciceronian style 'her illustrious family and lofty lineage ... her pedigree through a line of consuls and praetorian prefects' (*Let.* 127.1). Paulinus of Nola on Melania the Elder, as a family connection had an interest in publishing abroad her resounding lineage – with appropriately pious disclaimers: 'I proclaim the worldly nobility of this servant of God as much as her spiritual glory, for it is evident that her preeminence came from the Lord ... Here was a woman of the highest rank who had lowered herself ... a rich woman who embraced poverty, a noblewoman who embraced humility ... Her grandfather was the consul Marcellinus' (Paulinus of Nola *Let.* 29.7); and he makes the most of the extraordinary scene of her arrival in Rome, with a multitude of glittering senators anxious not to be behindhand with appropriate courtesies to this sackcloth-clad scion of a noble house (*ibid.* 29.12). Palladius, who travelled in her retinue, also attaches much importance to her background, though his information is more sketchy: 'She was a daughter of Marcellinus, one of the consuls' he thinks, and evidently considers this more noteworthy than being also 'wife of a high-ranking man (I do not quite remember which one)' (*LH* 46).

Augustine, from less elevated social origins himself, seemed to be similarly aware of birth and indeed slightly overwhelmed by the advent into his limited circle of the likes of Proba, Juliana and Albina, the cream of the aristocracy; it is not difficult to catch echoes of the young rhetor scrambling for place in Milan in the tone of his letters to these ladies. To Proba, addressed as 'noble lady, deservedly illustrious' he enthuses 'it might indeed appear wonderful that solicitude about prayer should occupy your heart and claim the first place in it when you are noble and wealthy and the mother of such an illustrious family, as this world reckons such things' (Augustine *Let*. 130.1); and to Proba and Juliana 'my daughters, most worthy of that honour due to your rank' (*Let*. 150). Gregory of Nyssa laid down that 'as for family distinction, he will not boast of that which devolves mundanely even to numbers of the worthless' – nonetheless, an aristocrat himself, he was in no doubt about the distinction of his own family and of its right to rule the roost, nor reticent about the distinguished derivations of his subjects Macrina and Basil; and thus, incidentally, his own. Though all stress that birth should be outweighed by nobility of life, still they cannot leave it alone; but the view of Gregory of Nazianzus, well-born himself, was that true nobility should be judged 'according to a better than the ordinary rule of noble or ignoble blood, whose distinctions depend not on blood, but on character; not does it classify their families but as individuals' (*Or*. 8.6).

For, boasting apart, we are witnessing a new development of the old concept of birth. It has become a double-barrelled weapon for the Fathers with a newly visible concept of an 'aristocracy of piety'. It has become something to boast about to have forebears, whether or not of distinguished lineage, of distinguished piety – even of mere length of days in the church, in this era where many were now turning to Christianity only in the wake of its establishment by the state. Thus Gregory of Nazianzus' mother Nonna's crucial inheritance from her *gens* (in the context of which the above statement came) was not land, nor jewels, nor even blood, but 'the faith that is pleasing to God' (*Or*. 7.4). In just the same tone as descendants of well-born families would boast of a consular tradition in their *gens* and antique habits of virtue, Gregory parades his mother's patrimony: she 'was consecrated to God by virtue of her descent from a saintly family, and was possessed of piety as a necessary inheritance' (*ibid.*). This it was, most precious in the writer's eyes, and presumably in those of his audience, which she 'had inherited from her ancestors'; and in accordance with traditional notions of husbanding the property of the *familia*, 'this she increased and amplified' – by the conversion of her husband (*ibid.*). And, 'having received virtue as her patrimony', in due form according to what was owed to the *familia* she increased her patrimony and passed it on: 'this golden chain she cast around her children' (*Concerning Himself* 116). Moreover, his mother's inheritance bore favourable comparison with that of his father, Gregory the Elder: though 'every inch a gentleman' (*Or.* 7.4) in his own person, his blood, it seems was not so good, for 'he sprang from a stock unrenowned and not well-suited for piety' (*Or.* 18.5) – but in attaching himself to Nonna he married above himself into her 'pious lineage', and was 'well grafted out of the wild olive tree to the good one' (*Or.* 7.4). Nonna, as will be shown, had a great deal of say in the working-out of her marriage; her son Gregory the Younger's attitude was almost that, just as an aristocratic woman who had married beneath her rank might lord it over her socially inferior spouse, so Nonna's 'pious lineage' accorded her seniority of status in their home.

Ageruchia also, who received Jerome's exhortation on remaining a widow, though we do not know for certain her *gens*, is vaunted as a third-generation devout Christian woman, as well as a 'high-born lady'; 'around her stand her grandmother, her mother and her aunt, a noble band of tried Christian women' (Jerome *Let.* 123.1) – and wives – and *univirae*. They are a true aristocracy of piety, accorded a potent and benign influence by their standing; 'do not your grandmother, your mother and your aunt enjoy even more than their old influence and respect, looked up to as they are by the whole province and the leaders of the churches?' (*ibid.* 123.14). Ambrose exhorted his sister, Marcellina, to be 'an heir of virtue' worthy of 'your martyred ancester' (and his), Sotheris. Emmelia, mother of Gregory of Nyssa, Basil of Caesarea and Macrina, was also guided by such considerations. A century earlier, a woman in her station might have chosen to name her daughter for the wife of a consular forebear whose courage in times of trial was still retold in the family, maintaining continuity and reinforcing at once remembrance of the admired woman's name and the proud family history; just so in the later period, 'directed at all times by divine will' she named Macrina for her paternal grandmother, a renowned woman who had 'confessed

Christ like a good athlete in the time of the Persecutions' (Gregory of Nyssa *Life of Macrina* 962). Just so Melania the Younger's notions of piety – and her subsequent dictating of terms to her husband and family – were a species of legacy, as her name, from her grandmother; tales of whom told to her in her youth inspired her to emulation of her admirable forebear and namesake though her equally Christian parents tried to curb the wilder excesses of her zeal. Her ultimate victory owed much to that formidable lady's return from the wilderness (*LH* 61).

Just as aristocratic women of preceding centuries took their family pride and their dowry with them to a marriage (and, often, away from it again) and maintained the one and controlled the other in the face of their husbands, so Christian women brought their special legacy to their new families and maintained their own ways. Sometimes their in-laws welcomed these, particularly if they had a similar history, as Gregory of Nyssa's mother Emmelia found when she married Basil the elder. Laeta also, herself a product of a Christian mother and a pagan father, when she married Toxotius, the son of Paula, found much in common with her in-laws; more in fact than she had with her husband, as Toxotius, withstanding the combined example of Paula, Paulina, Blesilla and Eustochium, was a pagan when she first married him. But sometimes, as Monica with Patricius, and Nonna with Gregory, these women were grafted on from alien stock – and were working against the grain.

THE CHRISTIAN *MATRONA* AND HER HUSBAND

What, then, in a world only newly Christian, were husbands to expect from their wives? Might they no longer necessarily count on subservience as of right, if their wives were motivated by new priorities of value? Being male in a man's world might no longer guarantee sway in one's own household – the men might even be regarded as disadvantaged, having less status with the Faithful in a new world of Faith. Evidence that men were in fact early alert to the possibilities of upsets in their own household because of new loyalties comes as early as Plutarch, who stressed in his *Conjugalia Praecepta*:

A wife ought to ... enjoy her husband's friends in common with him. The first and most important friends are the gods; so it is most suitable for a wife to know and worship only the gods that her husband believes in and to steer well clear of weird rituals and outlandish superstitions. For secret rites performed stealthily by women find no favour with any god.

(Plutarch *Moralia* 140D)

Though this might have obliquely referred to a number of cults with sinister reputations – Isis worship, for instance, or Bacchic rites – Momigliano considers this to indicate that Plutarch was aware of a danger specifically from Christianity, which he 'must have known' was 'one of those cults which both attracted and accepted unaccompanied women' (in Eadie & Ober 1985:443). In our era, we can see this disparity in religion between married couples becoming open to discussion, and even used by patristic writers, in a way not at all envisaged by Plutarch, as a reproach to the wife's faith.

This is not to say that Gregory the Elder and Toxotius' experience was uniformly that of pagan husbands married to Christian wives: of the couples we actually know about, the responses varied, and many husbands will have experienced little change in what they regarded as the natural order. The experience of the well-born women can tend to mislead one about the nature of the struggle to devotion; many Christian women must have fought a quiet, unsung campaign – if they fought at all – against the inertia of an unnoticing husband. Augustine tells of the many women in his mother's circle who endured harsh treatment at the hands of their husbands and relates that it behoved Monica to exercise great tact in views not chiming with her pagan husband, since Patricius was fiercer than the husbands of many of those who so suffered. But Monica in fact found nothing to cavil at in such a situation: her attitude, says her son, was rather that her friends were in the wrong to 'take the upper hand against their masters'; that 'from the time they heard read aloud to them the matrimonial tablets, they should consider them instruments by which they had been made servants' (Augustine *Confessions* 9.9). Monica's victory – for, sure enough 'at last she won for You even her own husband, at the end of his earthly life' (*ibid.*) – was the victory of diplomacy, of the silent witness. From Augustine's account of his parents' married life, there is no evidence that Monica employed towards Patricius the same proselytising zeal with which she pursued her wayward son; possibly in Augustine she scented a more certain hope of success than in her 'fierce' and 'wrathful' husband. In her conduct with Patricius, nothing more is implied than merely silently enduring his unbelief as his bad temper, and maintaining her own faith; though it may be that years of silent disapproval had a cumulative effect on Patricius and wore his resistance down more than Augustine indicates.

Comparable with Nonna is Gorgonia, the sister of Gregory of Nazianzus, and unremarkable daughter of the peerless Nonna. Her situation as a married woman indicates some similarities with that of Monica: in the unexceptional quality of her married life, and the undocumented struggle she waged with the similarly unpromising material of her 'unreasonable master', her husband Alypius – of whom Gregory merely says dismissively 'and if you wish me briefly to describe the man, I don't know what more to say of him than that he was her husband' (*Or.* 8.20). To Gorgonia also is attributed the attitude that truly 'her husband was her head' (*ibid.* 8.8) and of 'confining herself within the due limits of a woman' (*ibid.* 8.11). She, too, achieved some kind of spiritual improvement in her husband, that of 'her one remaining desire', given as 'her husband's perfection' (*ibid.* 8.20). But with this as with Alypius' details, Gregory is uncharacteristically tight-lipped: 'nor did she fail of this' (*ibid.*) is all the notice this potentially meaty subject receives. There is something more in all this than we are learning; it would be interesting to know whether the so-pious Nonna had married her worthy daughter off to a pagan, or a man of heterodox tendencies; or whether Gregory's disapproval is for a believer guilty of backsliding.

The reticence with which Gorgonia's relations with her husband are treated is highlighted by comparison with Gregory's florid exposition of those of his mother and father – 'the Abraham and Sarah of these, our latter days' (*ibid.* 8.4). He relates her to have been the active agent in the matter of her husband: she directly converted him, by her 'prayers, influences and example' (*ibid.* 8.5). Gregory the Elder's beliefs were as dubious as those of Alypius, or possibly more so; he was a a Hypsistarian – an obscure sect whose existence in fact we only know about from Gregory's funeral oration on him. Gregory enters into few details about their beliefs, saying only that his father, before he met Nonna, 'lived his life among idols' and that the sect was a combination of 'Greek error and legal imposture' (*Or.* 18.5), worshipping fire and lights, observing cleanliness, but despising circumcision. Nonna was married to him while he was still a Hypsistarian; another example of the daughter of a settled Christian family being married off to a man suitable socially but not religiously. But Nonna was made of stern stuff:

though exceeding all others in endurance and bravery, she could not bear being only half united to God, because he who was a part of her was estranged; so that their bodily union was not completed by being joined in the spirit. To this end, she prostrated herself before God day and night, pleading for the salvation of her head with many fasts and much weeping; and she assiduously devoted herself to her husband, using many means to influence him, by reproaches, warnings, attentions, estrangements, and above all, by her own character, with its ardour for piety, which especially works upon the soul and softens it so that it willingly submits to virtuous pressure.

(*Or.* 18.11)

– a process that Gregory likens to water wearing away stone. Not surprisingly, Gregory the Elder soon started to respond to this conditioning, and had a vision of his own, of himself singing psalms, 'which was foreign to him'. Nonna 'seized the opportunity' (*ibid.* 18.12) and the convenient proximity just then of a convocation of bishops, and Gregory was received into the church in short order by Leontius, the metropolitan.

It was only then, Gregory says 'when he gave himself to the Lord, she both called him her husband and regarded him as such' (*Or.* 8.4) – a frank re-statement of the church's sanction of disregard for societal priorities and an implication that Nonna perhaps had not been at one with her distinguished family in her assessment of the criteria that made up a fitting husband. Small wonder, at all events, that 'some have both believed and said . . . that even her husband's perfection has been the work of none other than herself' (*Or.* 7.4) and 'from her he learned his ideal of a good shepherd's life' (*Or.* 8.5). Her strong influence continued through to his later work as a bishop:

not only . . . his helper, but even his leader, by her influence in words and deeds she led him on to the highest excellence; . . . she was not ashamed where piety was concerned to offer herself even as his teacher. As wonderful as her conduct was, it was still more wonderful that he should readily agree to it.

(*Or.* 18.8)

In this respect, in fact, Gregory of Nazianzus declares that she was superior to Eve, who was only sent to be a helpmeet to Adam. Gregory the Elder seems to have been more promising material for 'making over' in the first place than Gorgonia's Alypius, but Nonna must have been a force to be reckoned with. Gregory of Nazianzus is a good, because a firsthand, witness; his account may be smoothed out of any ruffles and full of the formulae proper to such *encomia*, but more telling than any of his rhetoric is his unquestioning acceptance of feminine influence as the driving power in the family.

A direct contrast to Monica's gentle traction, and Nonna's irresistible force of will, is the outright assumption of independence of Melania the Younger in Rome – as portrayed by her biographer Gerontius and her follower Palladius of Helenopolis, who knew her only after the break with the world had been made. This was another case of a daughter in opposition to family marriage plans; in this case the husband in question was Christian, but not of extreme enough a persuasion to suit her taste. After reluctantly complying with family dynastic planning, and the failure of two pregnancies to produce an heir (see p. 146), Melania offered her husband a direct choice. If he wished to marry her, he must 'practise asceticism with me according to the fashion of chastity', only under which condition would he be 'my lord and master'; leaving him otherwise an option couched in terms perilously close to the formula of divorce: 'take my belongings and set my body free' (Palladius *LH* 61). Pinianus was conspicuously unwilling to do either – Augustine attributes him with 'a strong natural capacity for enjoying this world' (Augustine *Let.* 126.7) – 'but at last God had mercy on the young man and laid on him also an ardour for renunciation' (*LH* 61). Even after his conversion, however, Melania is to be found criticising him in his manner of implementing it, correcting his dress code and admonishing him in the correct disposal of their property (Gerontius *Life of Melania the Younger* 8, 15).

Highhanded aristocratic young lady though she may have been, Melania's apparently dominant influence in her marriage thus approvingly portrayed is quite striking in the context of the attributes accorded to other Christian married women – even the formidable Nonna – of still revering their husband as 'her head', of valuing the meekness proper to women, and so on. The rest of the passage in Palladius relates entirely to Melania's ascetic doings without reference to Pinianus – how she gave away upwards of 25,000 pieces of silver and gold to various churches, she freed 8,000 slaves, she sold off property in Spain, Aquitania, Taraconia and Gaul; though we know her husband was with her at this time, for Palladius she is the protagonist and motivating force. The women are more often seen as the victims of marital politics, from which position Melania started out; but it is worth considering how much choice Pinianus had in the matter. As the nearly sole heirs of two of the wealthiest families of the Christian aristocracy, the match was a fitting one; but there is not much to indicate that Melania and Pinianus' parents gave its Christian fitness as much thought as its dynastic suitability. Pinianus' actual opinion of the match goes unrecorded, but he did show signs of considerable devotion to Melania. Though patently reluctant to have the consequences of his Christian beliefs pushed to their logical conclusions, he did not give her up. But, bearing in mind the condemnation meted out to Fabiola, who gave up on a more obviously infamous spouse, he would have been unwise to do so once attached to Melania by the bonds of a union that, even amongst the aristocracy, has in our period moved a long way from the casualness of the classical era.

These are examples of women of faith gaining the upper hand over husbands represented as being (at least initially) in some sort a drag on their piety. There is, however, equal evidence for Christian *matronae* finding wifely roles in being the support and back-up of a husband of conspicuous piety, and implementing this in more active areas than merely complementary worship; but at a potential risk to their own devotions. Nonna, once she had made a bishop of Gregory, took on all the duties of running their household and estate, the better to liberate him for the burdens of being a bishop. This she seems to have done remarkably ably: though Gregory the Elder and she 'rivalled each other' in deeds of charity with their property, when it came to its actual management 'he entrusted the greater part of this bounty to her hand, as being a most excellent and trusty steward of such matters' (*Or.* 18.21), in which capacity 'by her skill, she secured the prosperity of the household' (*ibid.* 18.8), their liberality notwithstanding.

There is a tension here of which Gregory the younger, writing about it, shows himself to be aware; for a great deal of rhetoric was being generated by some of the more stringent ascetic Christians of his time concerned to prove that care devoted to the management of property, even the business of one's own household, was by extension care for things of the world, and that properly pious men and women in the new mould would despise such preoccupations as a distraction from the path of prayer, rather than manifest such as ostentatious aptitude for them. Gregory, however, carries out a neat job of tailoring his account of mundane household management into received ascetic ideals. He does indeed indicate their inherently contradictory nature – Nonna displayed 'as great a degree of skill' in household management 'as if she had no knowledge of piety; and she applied herself to God and Divine things as closely as if she were absolutely released from household cares' (*ibid.* 18.8). Nonetheless, he neatly manages to fit square peg into round hole, essentially by sidestepping the argument completely: 'allowing neither branch of her duty to interfere with the other, but, rather making each of them support the other', she is exceptional – merely because she *is* exceptional, he says, with breathtaking circularity of argument.

> Some women have excelled in thrifty management, others in piety, while she, difficult as it is to unite the two virtues, has surpassed all in both of them, both by her eminence in each, and by the fact that she alone has combined them together.
>
> (*Or.* 18.8)

The necessity to care for the flesh while not neglecting to tend the spirit was seen as a dilemma, affecting both sexes. Paulinus of Nola gives a more realistic assessment of a similar case when writing to his friends Aper and Amanda; married, but having recently decided to continue their marriage in continence, Aper exercised some kind of ministry, and Amanda had undertaken the duties of their household and estate, again to release him for the proper observance of his devotions and duties. Paulinus' attitude is signally different from Gregory's and less doggedly idealistic. It *is* a burden for Amanda, and one that will inevitably draw her more into the world; she is shouldering it as a sacrifice of herself, 'by interposing her holy slavery so that you [Aper] may be shielded . . . She takes charge of secular business so that you may forget it' (Paulinus of Nola *Let.* 44.4) so that Aper may be better able to fulfil his vocation – at the expense of her piety. But her sacrifice will better her in the eyes of God; though lacking as much time for the piety of contemplation, still, 'in the transactions of the world she serves not the world but Christ, for whose sake she endures the world that you may avoid enduring it' and so 'she will not lose her share in your reward because of the exemplary scale of values by which she sought not her inclination but your salvation' (*ibid.*). This, says Paulinus, is not at all the same thing as putting the world before Christ; and he praises Amanda for leading Aper away from effeminacy and towards self-discipline (*ibid.* 44.3). This last compliment is a direct paraphrase, in fact, of Augustine's praise of Paulinus' own wife, Therasia; another case (of which we know tantalisingly little) of a pious wife acting as a prop and mainstay for a pious husband's devotions. In writing to Paulinus, Augustine congratulates him on possessing 'a wife who does not bring her husband to effeminacy' (*Let.* 27.2) and who is one with him in spiritual ties, the stronger because of their purity – a reference to Paulinus and Therasia's continent marriage.

THE DEBATE OVER MARRIED CELIBACY

> We keep at home all the time the woman who often seduces us and makes us against our will commit uncounted sins; or we are convicted of adultery if we think of divorcing her.
>
> (John Chrysostom *On Virginity* 44.1)

This brings us naturally to the whole issue of celibate marriages: a necessary part of any consideration of the relations between husband and wife at this time, particularly if both were Christians, is their attitude towards sexuality and producing children. As we have seen Galen commenting, the Christian communities were conspicuously more 'body conscious' than their pagan forebears had been, whether to demonstrate a 'concern for order and cohesion in the more domestic sphere of sexual self-discipline', or because the conquering of the sexual drive, more significantly than any other human transformation was held to symbolise 'a state of unhesitating availability to God and one's fellows, associated with the ideal of the single-hearted person' (Brown in Veyne 1987:265ff). It was for this reason that after fifteen-odd years of concubinage, Augustine made the decision that 'there is nothing I must flee more than the conjugal bed' (*Soliloquia* 38.347); and Chrysostom scolded that even if intercourse with a woman did not lead to impurity, it was still 'a waste of time' (*On Virginity* 30.2). The public adoption of such a transformation was pre-eminently one of the leadership ideals of the early church, to denote proper distance and dedication in a celibate clergy; but with the spread of the appeal of asceticism, it may be seen that the struggle was being broadened in the increasingly eschatological mentality of the late Empire. Writers such as Chrysostom averred that marriage was no longer appropriate in this later age, 'as the present time hastens to its end and the resurrection is at the door, it is not the time for marrying and piling up possessions' (*ibid.* 73.1), and played on men's fears about what marriage represented: arguments, poverty, the ties of household and the impossibility of leading a quiet, private life – and also a vivid, exact and extensive analysis of sexual jealousy which, as he says 'only those who have been through this experience understand it well' (*ibid.* 44, 52–54).

To some in this climate, then, the simple act of taking a wife represented the lure of the world and the devil. The venerated desert monastics regarded illicit fornication as a temporary, and therefore venial, fall from grace, admitting of penitence and a return to the fold; for them, the really serious threat was from the lawful and apostolically provided-for institution of marriage – representing the retreat into the world. Hence an anonymous 'great man' of the desert whose disciple was tempted and went off to get married is portrayed in the *Sayings* as having prayed that the disciple might not be polluted, with such success that 'the moment he was bound to the woman' the young man died – 'and so was not polluted' (*Anon. Apoph.* 82). The same viewpoint heroised the stance of Abba Theonas, who deserted his wife as a seductress when she resisted his suggestion of a celibate marriage; a scheme Abba Amoun thought also to impose on his new bride, with more success (see p. 50).

At such a time then, the view of Augustine was relatively moderate: he stressed the view that, ideally, intercourse should take place only to conceive children, which was no more than austere pagans had demanded; that man was, after all, a social animal, that children were the glory of marriage, and that obedience was better than continence. Nevertheless, to view sexual congress as inevitable was not in any way to promote it; since he regarded sexual feeling as a punishment for the disobedience engendered by Original Sin and in itself emblematic of the Fall of Adam and Eve, he also advised his congregation that they should love the sexuality of their wives and the physical bonds of their families only as a Christian must love his enemies.[13] Peter Brown's analysis is that Augustine in fact feared all the symptoms of sexuality as tokens 'of the wrath of God against the pride of Adam and Eve in cutting themselves off from the will of God' (in Veyne 1987:308). With such rhetoric present in varying degrees in all the great orthodox writers, however it was portrayed an active choice – for full married life keeping (solely for the purposes of progeny) 'the bed undefiled' (Jerome *Let.* 66.2), or for continence and 'the great emulation of God's marriage with the Church' (Paulinus of Nola *Let.* 44.3) – was incumbent on all Christian married couples.

And so, scattered all over the sources are references – some for edification, but often just a passing mention – to couples like Paulinus and Therasia, and Aper and Amanda, making the effort to renounce their sexuality within their marriage. But there seem to have been different notions current amongst Christian couples, just as there were in the writings of the Fathers, of the level of Christian obligation in this respect. Amongst our top-drawer *matronae* vaunted for piety, for instance, Paula had children, five of them in fact; reportedly because her husband wanted an heir and she did not succeed in producing a boy until the fifth child. Three of her daughters Blesilla, Rufina and Paulina went on to marry in proper form, with no evident pressure to do otherwise from Paula; the fourth, Eustochium, was sufficiently young at the time of her decision for vowed virginity that it could be attributable to any variety of emotional causes, not least a desire not to leave her mother. (It is also worth bearing in mind that Eustochium was amongst the first few generations which, following the Christian Emperors' prohibition on the exposure of unwanted children, may have been witnessing the start of a new demographic phenomenon; that of 'surplus' daughters. In the following centuries, such a resort to the nunnery for daughters surplus to marriageable requirements would become quite the norm.) Of Paula's married daughters, Jerome does attribute to Paulina the desire that 'as soon as her union was blessed with children, she would live henceforth in the second degree of chastity' (Jerome *Let.* 66.3), i.e. continence in marriage; but his is not a witness to take on trust in such matters, and despite these attributed scruples, he makes no claim that she entered the union reluctantly, or even tried for children reluctantly.

Melania the Elder also dutifully married and produced, and like Marcella, showed no signs of eschewing her obligations to the family until 'released' by the death of her husband and two small boys. Melania the Younger was 'forced into marriage' (Gerontius *Life of Melania the Younger* 1) and persuaded to try for heirs, though only with reluctance; family obligation initially taking precedence over Christian even for as motivated and strong-willed a young woman as Melania. Therasia also had a child with Paulinus, a son Celsus, who had died before she and Paulinus opted for continence – the death of a child was frequently the precursor to a decision for a marriage of continence. Olympias and Macrina, though they are represented by their biographers/hagiographers as heaving a sigh of relief when their projected nuptials did not come off as planned, had been lined up for marriage in the usual fashion for girls of their status, with no reported opposition beforehand such as Demetrias ultimately displayed. To Demetrias' final decision against marriage, the sources do not relate Juliana's and Proba's actual reaction, they only infer it: such devout widows must of course be delighted – though both had previously demonstrated all the proper dynastic feeling in family matters, and their ascetic fervour was restricted to remaining *univirae* after the deaths of their husbands, and writing elegant letters to the fashionable Christian philosophers of their day. Likewise, there never seems to have been any question of whether the immensely pious and strong-willed Nonna would keep 'the bed undefiled', or her daughter Gorgonia, who had two sons and three daughters.

Indeed, Gregory of Nazianzus' position on Gorgonia's married state is illuminating. In his funeral oration on her, while tackling the issue of celibacy and acknowledging the grounds for divergence he then sidesteps the main issue again, as he did with the question over Nonna's household management. Rather than adopting one or other of the positions, as to whether marriage was as good as celibacy or necessarily inferior, he accepts both sides of the argument and simply unites the virtues of each of them in his subject – in this case the rather unlikely person of Gorgonia.

> . . . as regards the two divisions in life, that is, the married and the unmarried state – of which the latter is more exalted and closer to the divine but more difficult and dangerous, while the former is more humble but safer – she was able to avoid the disadvantages of each, and to choose and combine the best of both conditions; to wit, the superiority of the one and the security of the other . . . For though she was in a carnal union, she was not cut off from the spirit because of it, nor because she had a husband as her head, did she forget the foremost Head: but while she fulfilled those duties due to the world and nature, according to the will of the law of the flesh . . . she still dedicated herself entirely to God.
>
> (Gregory of Nazianzus *Or.* 8.8)

Gregory is thus very much aware of the distinction; but in his thinking, as in that of Gregory of Nyssa in his *On Virginity*, concepts of chastity and virginity have become more spiritualised qualities and less simply represented by sexual abstinence. Many thinkers of the time like Gregory were aware of the dangers in the ascetic disparagement of the flesh, of tending too far towards suspect gnostic ideas of dualism – of dividing the world completely into fleshly and spiritual elements and rejecting the former by equating it absolutely and in its entirety with evil. For Gregory of Nazianzus, drawing back from this black and white equation, it is not the body and its functions that are essentially evil but rather the 'fleshly will': likewise a life of bodily virginity is merely the 'substructure' for the virtuous, truly 'virginal' life (Gregory of Nyssa *On Virginity* 17). He could then posit the possibility of a 'virginal' lifestyle for those who remained in and of the world, keeping, however, a 'love of virginity' before them; and he projected this reconciliation of the married and the 'virginal' life on to his sister Gorgonia: '[She] proved that neither [the married nor the unmarried state] binds us or separates us from God or the world . . . but that it is mind which nobly presides over both marriage and virginity, and orders and works upon them as the raw material of virtue under the master-hand of reason' (Gregory of Nazianzus *Or.* 8.8).

Virginity for Gregory had thus become a much more theoretical quality, an inner property rather than a mere external, physical state: 'let no-one suppose . . . one little observance of the flesh could settle so vital a matter' (Gregory of Nyssa *On Virginity* 18), echoing Jerome and Chrysostom's 'virginity of mind, not body' argument (see p. 58). Gregory, however, not only takes the idea to its logical conclusions but, uniquely, relates it to a specific example, his sister Gorgonia. His belief, deriving more from the philosophy he had so extensively studied than a homiletic background such as that of Jerome and Chrysostom, is that virginity is best served by the philosophic ideal of *apatheia*; 'balance in all feeling', 'the ordered control, by wisdom and prudence, over every emotion of the soul' (*ibid.* 18) and freedom from slavery to the passions. This should be the prime objective, of married and unmarried alike. Having forsworn marriage was a more helpful precondition, but did not necessarily betoken this ideal; by the same argument it was possible to achieve *apatheia* within the married state, though more difficult because of the carnal aspect and the distractions and concerns of spouse and children. But Gregory believed it was possible to live in the world 'as if not', performing the duties of nature but not allowing one's will and desire to settle there so that they did not become ends in themselves (Ruether 1969:141). This happy estate he represents Gorgonia as having achieved, as we have seen; though he is markedly unforthcoming with the proofs of this, indeed far more reticent about the actual details of her domestic life than he is about his mother's.

Nonna's stance in this all-important aspect Gregory also spends time in justifying. Nonna was not merely tolerant of carnality, she specifically wanted children herself – 'she was anxious to see a man-child in the house; that is indeed a wish common to many people' – and it is represented as being acceptable for her to pray for them, 'imitating the cry of the holy Anna' (Gregory of Nazianzus *Concerning Himself* 425). Even the staunchest, most misanthropic ascetics are seen to connive at this: the austere hermit Hilarion in his wilderness matter-of-factly cured women of sterility – as told us by Jerome, whose opinion of childbirth we have already seen (*Life of St Hilarion* 13). But Nonna allegedly wished to have children in order to dedicate them to Christ. Gregory thus manages to knit two conflicting stances yet again by claiming that her procreation was actually consecrated, by her own pious descent, and by having children for God, specifically and avowedly: both these notions are tied together when Gregory talks of the 'noble inheritance of fulfilling her vow' (Gregory of Nazianzus *On His Own Life* 65). Gregory's future was accordingly decided from birth: 'as soon as I made my appearance, straightway in the noblest of contracts I became another's' (*ibid*. 80).

Nonetheless, full marriage followed by procreation in the view of orthodoxy was at best a consolation prize for the absence of the capacity to live celibately – which was, all agreed, a gift of God. Paula's married daughter, Paulina, is evidently seen as disadvantaged in piety: Paulinus of Nola, writing fondly of her after her death in consolation to her husband Pammachius, who had decided to become a monk, says that her soul is precious chiefly because she was 'the wife of faith, the sister of virginity, and the daughter of perfection – Paula, her mother, Eustochium, her sister, and you her husband' (Paulinus of Nola *Let*. 13.28) – which said little for the qualities of Paulina herself. A woman praised for her own piety and charitableness by Paulinus and Jerome, still as a married woman her place in the scheme of things is markedly diminished by comparison with her more austere family-members. So, despite Gregory of Nazianzus' fast footwork with the impossibly pious Nonna, still 'there is a difference', he affirms solemnly; and for all his claims that she was capable of the highest ascetic exigencies, in actuality Nonna was still on the wrong side of the divide. As proof of her rightmindedness it must be asserted that she 'had a greater love for virginity' than marriage and was perforce merely 'patient of the marriage bond herself' (*Or*. 18.9), just as it must be indicated that Gorgonia was cognizant of the preeminent virtues of virginity, however implausibly it is claimed that she combined them with marriage.

Indeed, it is rather impertinent of Gregory to make that claim for Gorgonia in the face of the many who accepted fully the consequences of the Apostle Paul's often repeated statement that those who were married could not be concerned for the things of the Lord: the basis for the decisions of Therasia, Melania the Younger, Amanda, and Avita to opt out of the carnal aspect of their marriages. And in opting out, they achieved new equality of status with their husbands in the eyes of the writers of the age: in terms that specifically recall the dogma that 'God is the Head of man and man of woman' (Eph. 5:23). Therasia and Amanda we have seen being commended for combatting 'effeminacy' in their husbands. Another such woman, Theodora, who had vowed continence with her husband Lucinius was written to by Jerome in 399 that she was 'once a woman but now a man: once an inferior, but now an equal' (Jerome *Let.* 71.3), Jerome is emphatic, 'for the difference of sex, while essential to marriage is not so to a continent tie'. Further this sanctified androgyny has eschatological resonance: continence in marriage is the prefiguration of that time when 'there will be no longer bond or free, Greek or barbarian, male or female, all will be one in Him' (*Let.* 75.2).

Among the *humiliores*, with considerably less drum-beating and banner-waving, we find an even greater level of observance of this ideal – a far more routine assimilation of it into otherwise inconspicuous lifestyles. The *Apophthegmata* or Sayings of the Desert Fathers give many examples of lowly couples living quiet and unsung lives of continence and charity: indeed, showing themselves markedly reluctant to break into its serenity by speaking of it even at the urgent request of the monks. One Eucharisticos, cognomened 'the Secular' because he was living still 'in the world', nonetheless merits a place in the *Alphabetical Collection* of the Sayings specifically for this achievement; it and the humility in its observance he displays, by implication place him above the two abbas who were sent to him at heavenly prompting, evidently because they could learn from his instruction. The lifestyle of Eucharisticos, a shepherd, and his wife consisted mainly of practising charity and chastity. Besides dividing anything in the way of profit from their small flock of sheep into three equal portions, for the poor, for hospitality and for personal needs, 'since I married my wife, we have not had intercourse with each other, for she is a virgin; we each live alone. At night we wear hair-shirts and our ordinary clothes by day. No-one has known of this till now' (*Alph.* Eucharisticos). (Note that he makes the claim for virginity only for her; presumably, like Augustine, chastity was granted to him only after the expected ardour of the youthful male had been indulged, and its attractions diminished.) Before his ultimate retreat into the desert, Abba Amoun and his wife were also of this number for eighteen years after he had persuaded her in their bridal chamber to observe sexual abstinence. Amoun and his wife, however, made the final leap and separated completely; a conclusion that after some years of celibacy Amoun had wished for and suggested, but (unlike Theonas) shelved in deference to his wife's resistance. Ultimately, however, it came at her own instigation:

> The prayers of Amoun at last succeeded and she said to him ". . . It is right that we should live apart – you practising righteousness as a man, and I too eagerly following the same path. For it is absurd that you should live with me in chastity and yet conceal such virtue as yours." So he, thanking God, said to her: "Then you keep this house; and I will make myself another house." And he went away and settled in the inner region of the mountain of Nitria . . . He used to see that blessed lady his wife twice each year.
>
> (*LH* 8)

Some seculars opted for this practice later on in life, either needing longer to arrive at sufficient motivation, or taking time to fulfil familial or public obligations first. Abba Paphnutius was directed, again by divine instruction, to visit the headman of a neighbouring village who had given up conjugal relations after begetting three sons to help him: 'It is now thirty years since I separated from my wife. I slept with her for only three years and had three sons by her' (*HM* 14.10–13). He also practised hospitality and charity and was renowned locally for his upright judgements.

But again, more interesting (and again less subject to pious dogma) are the tales of those who failed in this ideal: those who absorbed the prevalent ascetic attitudes to the extent of attempting to practise this 'second degree of chastity' but whose faith – or instruction – was evidently lacking in some vital respect. Augustine wrote to a *matrona* called Ecdicia who took it upon herself to attempt to impose the condition of continence upon her marriage; her unwilling (and Christian) husband had subsequently resorted to adulterous liaisons, thereby transgressing in a far more serious way than merely maintaining marital carnality. Jerome also intervened in 408 in what was evidently a very similar case, in this instance writing to the husband concerned, Rusticus. The attitudes displayed by the writers differed as one might expect from these two. Jerome, though writing as 'a stranger to a stranger', wrung his hands over the back-sliding Rusticus and begged him to reconsider and repent: he had been applied to by Rusticus' wife, Artemia, 'now no longer your wife but your sister and fellow-servant', egged on a friend who was yet another of Jerome's keen female correspondents from Gaul, 'that servant of Christ, Hedibia' (Jerome *Let.* 122.1). These ladies begged him to intercede and turn Rusticus back to the virtue he seemed in danger of departing from – a task after Jerome's own heart. Rusticus and Artemia, by her account, had taken a vow 'by consent' to live apart, 'that you might give yourselves to prayer' (*ibid.* 122.4); but apparently his will in the matter had not been equal to hers, and he 'gave way altogether' while she stood firm. Subsequently, when they were about to be separated by a threat of barbarian invasion, Rusticus had vowed an oath that if Artemia made her way to the Holy Land, he would follow her there when he could and do penance; but he had not carried out this promise, which was the occasion for Jerome's involvement. Jerome accepted Artemia's view of the affair completely. For him the issues are quite simple: Artemia holds the moral high ground, and her object is so worthy that Rusticus must be in the wrong to cavil at it. He admonishes Rusticus that it should be enough for him that 'you can still be joined in spirit to her to whom you were once joined in body.' The only option open to Rusticus in his view is to make haste to fulfil his vow and take Artemia as his instructress and example and

> imitate her whose teacher you ought to have been. For shame! The weaker vessel overcomes the world and yet the stronger is overcome by it! "A woman leads in the high endeavour" (*Aeneid* I.364) and yet you will not follow her when her salvation leads you to the threshold of the faith!
>
> (*Ibid.*)

Certainly, this is an area in which women seem to have had little difficulty in becoming the stronger vessel. Though perhaps less in evidence in the anecdotes told of the desert experience, in Western examples from the middle to upper classes, it seems to have been more the rule for the wife to take the initiative. Thus, besides Artemia and Ecdicia, Melania the Younger with Pinianus; and Aline Rousselle speculates that Therasia may have been the motivator towards continence with Paulinus. Certainly Ausonius referred to her as Tanaquil – the name of Tarquin's wife who was responsible for persuading him to leave his native town and take Rome (Rousselle 1988:191).

The case of Ecdicia and her (unnamed) husband directly echoes that of Artemia and Rusticus: Augustine's response, however, is signally different, and considerably more developed. In this case, the impulse towards maintaining a continent marriage was definitely Ecdicia's (where we can only suspect it to have been Artemia's responsibility); her husband was apparently persuaded only reluctantly, and after some kind of initial attempt resorted to purchasing physical consolation elsewhere. At the time of her applying to Augustine, they seem to have been living apart and Ecdicia was denying her husband access to their son. Augustine took a firm line: far from admonishing her husband for backsliding, he takes the stance that both the sin of her husband and the resulting rupture are wholly Ecdicia's fault, and something for which she must express a wholehearted repentance.

> I am greatly grieved that you chose to behave in such a way towards your husband that the edifice of chastity, which had begun to be constructed in him, has fallen into the wretched ruin of adultery because of his failure in perseverance ... This great evil has happened because you failed to treat his state of mind with the moderation you should have ... I know that you took upon yourself the continent state when he had not yet consented, which is not in accordance with sound teaching; for he should not have been cheated of the debt you owed him of your body before his will joined yours in that good that is above marital chastity ... even if he had wished to practise continence and you had not, he would have been bound to render you the observance of the debt; and God would have given him the credit for continence if he, giving way to your infirmity, not his, did not deny you the marriage bed, so that you should not fall into the damnable sin of adultery. How much more then you, from whom more subjection is fitting, should have fallen in with his desire of paying this debt ... so that your husband did not perish.
>
> (Augustine *Let*. 262.1–2)

This is a theme which Augustine felt needed reinforcing: the view of women such as Ecdicia may have been provoked by, and certainly found justification in, contentious ideas put around at this time by Pollentius, with whom Augustine took issue in *On Adulterous*

Unions, that 'the separation of spouses is admissible not only when there has been adultery on the part of one of the partners, but also where there is incompatibility or if the rejection of the conjugal act makes it too difficult to live together' (Rousselle 1988:192).

In addition to her defiance over the marriage bed, however, Ecdicia had still further provoked her husband by unilaterally making the decision to observe other stringent ascetic practices, to wit giving away their property and wearing mean and shabby clothing. The outlandish scenario suddenly foisted on him must have still further alienated her husband and influenced his fall from grace, and Augustine rebukes her roundly for the whole: since her husband had conceded, however unwillingly, in the most important matter of chastity, she should not have further tried him. 'You should have given way to him in your domestic concerns with greater obedience and humility, since he had so conscientiously conceded to you such a great thing . . .' (Augustine *Let*. 262.4) '. . . is the good you have done in tending to the bodies of the poor with your excessive almsgiving as great as the evil you have done in turning your husband's mind away from his worthy resolution? (262.6) . . . it was your duty to consult with your husband, who was a believer' (262.9).

The contrast with Jerome could not be more striking. For Augustine it is not nearly such a clear-cut issue; not for him the stance to which Jerome leans, of the end ultimately justifying the means, the objective of chastity so hallowed that it takes precedence over the problems of one of those involved. Nor is there any of the predictable breast-beating over the more obvious sinner, he who has committed fornication and adultery: the sin is laid at the feet of the person who occasioned it, however overtly blameless in her own life. Compare this with the case of Abba Theonas, whose wife used just the same reasoning on him; and the admiring way in which John Cassian tells us of his complete disregard of it. When he proposed a life of continence to his wife, she refused it, arguing that 'in all the bloom of youth she could not do without her husband. If she fell into bad ways because he had abandoned her, it would be his fault for breaking his marriage vows'. Hearing this, he considered her 'a seductress' and himself quite justified in deserting her (Cassian *Coll*. 21.8–9). Abba Paphnutius also encouraged a former disciple, who had left the coenobium to marry, to desert his wife in order to return to righteousness (*Alph*. Paphnutius 4). The Fathers of the desert evidently took a more stringent attitude to personal salvation at the risk of occasioning sin in others; though it is difficult also to avoid the conclusion that the difference in the way the writers treat of these cases is due to the difference in sex in the person attempting to unilaterally impose continence.

For Augustine, however, theoretically it did not matter which spouse was the initiator if the other spouse objected. Ecdicia, as a wife and as a believer – even though in this she was firmly convinced he was in the wrong – should have demonstrated proper subjection to her husband: but even if the boot had been on the other foot and it had been his idea, he must have sought her agreement and bowed to her wishes. Augustine was careful to emphasise that, in this practice, the decision must be equally arrived at by both partners, or not take place at all. This is a theme in which all the writers on continence were careful to follow the apostle's dictum that neither husband nor wife must deprive the other of sexual relations if unwilling. 'If one wishes to refrain, he cannot withdraw his head from the yoke, for he is subject to the incontinence of the other' (Ambrose *On Widows* 69). John Chrysostom also takes this line, reiterating the apostolic 'do not deprive one another except perhaps by consent' (*On Virginity* 40.2) and, like Augustine, felt himself obliged to preach conjugal duty to wives whom he considered 'responsible for their husbands' misdemeanours' and reproved spouses who had adopted continence without the agreement of their partners. He also concluded that 'great evils arise from this sort of continence; adultery, fornication and the ruin of family life' – and yet 'this is a thing which many women do' (*Hom.* 19 on I Cor. 7, 3). Yet it is possible to mistake John's message in this matter (as perhaps some of the women in such cases did): for this is the same writer who also said quite unequivocally, 'she will not be able to save her husband by living with him as a wife' and, further that 'if she continues to make the demands of a wife, she will not help her husband and may even harm him' – before stressing that she must, of course do as he wishes in the matter (*On Virginity* 47.2, 48). For Augustine and Ambrose (with Chrysostom at least paying lip-service), the equality incumbent in this crucial decision arose logically out of patristic theology: neither partner must backslide, hence both must be fit for it, and consent. Better that both remain in the lower degree of virtue than that one achieve the heights while the other slide to destruction; but the emphasis, and the hectoring tone with which this idea is reiterated may well result from having to apply it to the many cases of petticoat rebellion which the ascetic movement unwittingly sparked off. In practice, as Theonas' wife,

Ecdicia's husband and Rusticus found, the actual decision resided with the more dominant partner – and even if imposed willy-nilly on a reluctant spouse, in the cases of Theonas and Artemia, there are writers very ready to praise such an arbitrary, unilateral stance.

Augustine returned to this theme when writing to Boniface, the Count of Africa, in the 420s. After the death of Boniface's first wife, a devout Catholic and a line of communication between the Bishop of Hippo and the Count, Boniface had vowed to remain chaste, even contemplating becoming a monk; but, falling out of Augustine's orbit, his determination had dropped away and he had remarried – and to add insult to injury, the new wife was an Arian heretic. Augustine, seeing his influential contact drifting inexorably away from him, sent him one last, rather forlorn letter of admonishment, expressing disillusionment and grief at the gap between Boniface's expressions of intent and his actions. Since he has sinned, in vowing chastity and remarrying, he should, if possible persuade his wife to agree to a vow of continence, that what had been vowed to God might rightfully be returned to him. However, this is advocated with the important reservation that it must be with his wife's consent, and not a unilateral decision, and Augustine restates the thinking he had applied to Ecdicia: 'I am prevented from exhorting you to [continence] by your having a wife, since without her consent it is not lawful for you to live under a vow of continence' (Augustine *Let.* 220.12) – and this despite the wife being a despised heretic. The aspect of the importance of individual choice for women in the working-out of their Christianity, even for married women, and girls *in tutela* who were not accustomed to exercise it, in the eyes of influential Western church writers, was a very important, and self-consciously novel concept.

7

MARRIED SANCTITY II:
CHRISTIAN
MOTHERHOOD

Parents should bring up their children with mildness and
forbearance, "in the discipline and rectitude of the Lord", and,
as far as possible, give them no cause for anguish or grief.
(Basil the Great *Moralia* 76, quoting Eph. 6:4)

[Of my mother] Libanius would say, "Heavens! What women
there are among the Christians!"
(John Chrysostom *Letter to a Young Widow* 2)

The exercise of greater influence in their marital relations must have
been of no small importance to those Christian wives who did have
children. Because of their position in Roman law, as essentially
outside their husband's family, constituting in some sort their own
individual family unit; and because of the comprehensive nature of
patria potestas, Roman women were at a considerable legal disadvantage in their relations with their children. Jane Gardner has
rightly pointed out that where *patria potestas* included custody of
and disciplinary powers over the child concerned, ownership of the
child's property and ultimate right of decision on education, marriage and domicile of the child, and where in the case of dis-
agreements between the parents concerning the child's welfare the
mother's wishes carried no legal weight, the extent of the mother's
influence on the child was decided by her relationship with her
husband.[1] In this respect, then, Christian wives were beginning to
have some advantage over their pagan counterparts. It is now
necessary to examine to what extent they used their increasing
centrality in the specifically Christian perception of the family to
influence their children according to the lights of their beliefs; and
in what respects their relations with their children differed from
those of their pagan counterparts of a century or two earlier – and

what trends in maternal thinking we can see that are specifically Christian in origin.

THE NEXT GENERATION: TRAINING, EDUCATION AND CONDITIONING

The first indications seem to show that Christianity had less effect on the children of pious matrons than one would think. Surprisingly, with some of the women from whom one would most expect it, there is little obvious change: however pressing they regarded the need for personal observances and sacrifice, some of our high-profile pious *matronae* show signs of regarding their Christian obligations as being apart from their family obligations. Mothers such as Paula and Albina, conspicuous for personal devotion – ultimately to the extent of extreme ascetic observance – yet produced sons, Toxotius and Volusianus, who were brought up in impeccable paganism in the best tradition of their *gens*. This might indicate that the 'belief' tradition was better transmitted through daughters, but even this was not invariably so. Three of four of Paula's daughters maintained an unexceptionable lifestyle far removed from her extreme form of worship; in particular the hedonistic behaviour of Blesilla after marriage and widowhood suggests a fair degree of licence from the influence and opinions of her austere mother, before severe illness led to what looks like a 'dark night of the soul' and a revision of her lifestyle. These instances may be indicative more of the particular level of pressure on women in the capital and out of the top-drawer of society to prop up at least a semblance of the *status quo*; but they are also a barometer indicating the wind of change. Toxotius and Volusianus were later subject to indirect pressure arriving because of their mothers: both were targeted by their mothers' respective mentors, Jerome and Augustine, using the personal connection to try for an illustrious conversion, whether with or without the connivance of their mothers is not clear. All that is certain is that these women left behind sons in the traditional mould, implying either that the pious woman's influence failed – perhaps in the case of her husband, perhaps of her son – or that she, as well as they, still saw other concerns as preeminent in the case of those who were to carry on the *gens*; but that despite her scruples, if any, in any case these traditional men later come under pressure to change, because of their devout mothers.

Other devout married women show signs that a certainty in moral orientation towards Christianity was not necessarily backed up by a similar certainty in its application in the practical sphere. For it is clear that while for some the duties of the Roman family no longer started and ended with the *gens*, that one of the maternal duties was now perceived to be the instilling of the sense of obligations due to the next world, still there were great difficulties in rejecting the paraphernalia of this one. Further, this ambiguity was being transmitted to the next generation, particularly through uncertainty over the precepts to be followed in their training.

The signals that Augustine received as a child were evidently confusing to the growing boy: while his mother clearly wished him to be in good standing in the eyes of the church, she was still ambitious for his future. She as much as Patricius was preoccupied with the need for a good, classical education for her son, although in her case Augustine does attribute her with the idea that it would also help him towards God; but with hindsight he saw it as a retarding factor in his journey towards God, for which he blamed them equally. Because 'both my parents were unduly eager for me to learn' (Augustine *Conf.* 2.3), the young Augustine imbibed with his learning what he later regarded as the wrong priorities – 'their only concern was that I should learn how to make a good speech and persuade others by my words' (*ibid.* 2.2).[2] It was not the usefulness of this training that Augustine was querying; it would stand him in good stead as a bishop as much as it helped a struggling young rhetor. But this happy conclusion was in no sense thanks to 'those who compelled me to study', Augustine considered,

> For they had not the insight to see that I might put the lessons which they forced me to learn to any other purpose than the satisfaction of man's insatiable desire for the poverty he calls wealth and the infamy he knows as fame.
>
> (Augustine *Conf.* 1.12)

And he condemns the emphasis placed on it as an end in itself; even by the mother who 'did all she could to see that you, my God, should be a father to me' (*ibid.* 1.11) and by whom in this respect he feels the more let down. For with all her pious scruples how could she, he asked with the bitterness of hindsight, attach value to 'a training which taught me to have a horror of faulty grammar' such that 'a man . . . gives greater scandal if he drops the aitch from 'human being' than if he breaks Your rules and hates another human being' (*ibid.* 1.18)?

As a catechumen, 'I had been told of the eternal life promised to us by Our Lord, who humbled himself and came down amongst us proud sinners' (*ibid.* 1.11): as a schoolboy 'the traditional education taught me that Jupiter punishes the wicked with his thunderbolts and yet commits adultery himself' (*ibid.* 1.16). Augustine agreed the necessity of learning one's letters but deplored the use made of them: 'the words ... are like choice and costly glasses, but they contained the wine of error' which 'if we refused to drink, we were beaten for it' whereas if 'I learned all these things gladly and took a sinful pleasure in them ... I was called a promising boy' (*ibid.*) – this he regards as definitely culpable in 'those who insisted on making me study', particularly Monica. He implies, in fact, that while she was weeping, praying and seeking out the advice of bishops on his behalf, her respect for old-style notions of education was acting against her own ends: the young Augustine's ready intellect had quickly absorbed the lesson that to tell a lie more eloquently than the next boy was to gain more merit than to tell the truth – a hard lesson to unlearn. The upright servant of God she may have been, but more than once in the *Confessions* we get a strong sense from her son that Monica's years of tears for Augustine that he calls her 'legacy of Eve' were of her own making.

This was an ambivalence perceived by others of his contemporaries, evidently. Jerome confessed that after giving up family, friends, home 'and – hardest of all – fine food' to follow the path of asceticism, the one sacrifice he had been utterly unable to bring himself to make had been 'to give up the library which I had put together for myself at Rome with such work and care' (Jerome *Let.* 22.30). This was the real hardship for the educated Christian; for after reading Plautus and Cicero he found 'when I started to read the prophets again, their style seemed barbaric and repellent' (*ibid*). The guilt Jerome experienced at this dilemma, combined with his lifestyle of deprivation, brought on a highly-charged vision in which he was brought to the seat of Judgement and condemned because he was found out as 'Non Christianus, sed Ciceronianus' – a follower not of Christ, but of Cicero. This bitter *cri de coeur* encapsulates the divergence he and Augustine experienced, for to succumb to the temptation of reading the mellifluous pagan authors rather than more crudely expressed devotional works was to the good Christian 'what I may call adultery of the tongue' (*ibid.* 22.19). Jerome's cry is a protest not just against the untruthful content of their works but also against the unconscious assumptions that were received with a traditional classical education: of ultimately putting the training in which they figure to use in the secular, self-concerned world they had evolved to serve. Though Jerome fought against this motivation, the young Augustine assimilated it readily, too readily for at least one of the parents who had pushed him into the way of it; small wonder he complained of mixed messages.

Gregory of Nazianzus also was much concerned with the tension between Christian belief and classical culture; it is an issue that he considers much in his writings, though from a more apologetic standpoint than Augustine. It is something he treats of in his works on the family; but as so often in the intimate sphere, he is anxious to gloss over something identified in advance as an issue of concern. For herself Nonna, just as she never touched the person of any heathen women, would have no truck with 'Grecian tales or theatrical songs, on the ground that what is unholy is unbecoming to holy things' (*Or.* 18.10); but with regard to her male children there was a difference, and Gregory is less stridently honest than Augustine about his own training and conflict of interests. If Nonna held this view so absolutely, and if she had the influence in the household and children that Gregory represents her as having, it might have been thought that she would make a push to de-contaminate her children from the contagion of pagan cultural notions; but there is little in the outline of Gregory's education and aspirations to suggest that she held this view in fact. Certainly his tutor, Carterius, subsequently became a monk, which suggests an early pedagogic influence more in harmony with the maternal bias than was the case with Augustine's small-town schoolmasters, but the educational matter Carterius used was traditional enough. And in Gregory's subsequent career at Athens and in his rhetorical aspirations, he was simply following the common run of classical further education; although his autobiographical writings highlight the tension between the life of the rhetorician and the life of the Christian contemplative. Ultimately, though he taught rhetoric briefly (as did his friend and fellow-student at Athens, Basil of Caesarea), he came to consider the rhetorician's art incompatible with a serious Christian vocation; but still his writings, in the structure of his language, his stylistic devices and his development of ideas, indicate that he was thoroughly imbued with contemporary sophistic culture. 'Rhetoric formed his education, moulded his literary style, and gave him oratorical tools to fight his enemies, praise his friends and enhance his daily correspondence' (Ruether 1969:156). Later on, however, he too perceived the need to justify his style of education and his preference for the classical philosophy and poetry against the attacks of more stringent Christian critics; and though his attitude is less condemnatory of the materials of the classical education than that of Augustine, it is at best ambivalent about the effect of pagan culture on Christian youth. He and his friend and colleague in the bishopric, Basil of Caesarea, preferred to think that pagan classical literature need not be wholly set aside, but could even be used in a proper Christian education. 'Both advocated plucking literature from its native value system and transferring it to the value system of philosophy. Both would envisage a *paideia* [training] in which literature, "purged" of its indecency, could be used to buttress morality and introduce the student to the higher life' (Ruether 1969:174).[3]

In this area, *matronae* of the Christian families observed a limit to what they could practicably achieve by their increased influence in the family circle. In the higher social strata, their sons seem to be wholly or partly exempt from any proselytising notions of their mothers, as the daughters were not: Paula and Albina brought up pagan sons. Where they did succeed in drawing their sons away from the preferred religion of the paternal *gens*, this influencing confined itself entirely to the personal sphere, the immediate concern of the soul's well-being: they seem not to have recognised – or at least, not tried to redress – the divergence between the domestic and didactic conditioning. Monica strove desperately to imbue Christianity and the Christian value-system in her son, and yet also wished him permeated with a 'good grounding in the classics', as was proper for a middle-class provincial lad with his way in the world to make. Nonna's ostentatious eschewing of pagan culture was entirely personal, as was proper for women of the newly conscious Christian households; even the most spiritual of them seem to have had few notions – as few means – of directing the training of their sons into paths more in keeping with Christian cultural notions. Hence the dilemma inherited by their more educated sons, perceived so acutely by Augustine and Jerome, Gregory and Basil, of the actual pain and shame afforded them in finding their holy writings, of such immense spiritual value, couched in such basic and primitive language; of seeing them derided by educated pagans, and experiencing a sneaking and guilt-ridden sense of communion with this derision, as their own education had trained them to do. Hence their guilty preference for reading Cicero and Virgil – and furtively reproducing their 'hall-marked marmoreal phrases'[4] in writings devoted to Christian ends. For these were the tags and allusions which denoted an educated man the length and breadth of the civilised world; and to give up the appurtenances of education was a sacrifice that in the final analysis these great Christian thinkers could not make, even for their souls' sake. And over this dilemma, maternal religious conditioning could offer little help and did not offer any visible struggle.

MATERNAL RELATIONSHIPS

If found wanting by their offspring for not attaching enough significance to their cultural conditioning, these mothers do express in other spheres notions which would seem dangerously anti-familial to opinions formed by the traditional view of the *mos maiorum*: in the personal, if not the didactic arena, and particularly in the area of property, the idea of 'putting God before the children' became a well-aired patristic notion. Melania the Elder and Paula are excellent cases in point. Though Jerome, who relates these parts of their stories, is capable of exaggerating the impulsive haste of their flights from the world such as to imply they gave no thought at all to those they left, they did leave behind fairly careful provision for their deserted children – but did not in the least consider themselves obliged to be held back by them. In this respect, Jerome's narrative on Paula touches on, and boasts of, exactly those aspects – of the duty of the Christian negating that of the mother – that would be seized upon for their shock value by opponents. Her own personal devoutness notwithstanding, Paula was neglecting her maternal obligations in not staying to see Toxotius into maturity and Rufina into marriage as reportedly with tears they begged her to do; nor was taking the youthful Julia Eustochium with her considered a palliating factor by those who thought with her aunt Praetextata that the little girl ought to have been offered at least the chance of seeing the kind of life girls of her station were normally leading (Jerome *Let.* 108.6).

Gregory of Nazianzus also attributed the notion of 'God before the children', with the customary lavish praise to his own mother, that model for Christian mothers. For once, however, the wife is presented as being at one with the spouse on this point: 'Lovers of their children and of Christ as they both were, what is most extraordinary, they were far greater lovers of Christ than of their children', says Gregory fondly, 'their one measure of blessedness in their children was their virtue and close association with the chief Good' (*Or.* 7.4) – but Nonna never seems to have had to challenge this singlemindedness with a practical test. Monica, on the other hand, though never related as espousing this view, when pushed exhibited it in practice in forbidding Augustine her house while he was a practising Manichee (Augustine *Conf.* 3.11).

Not that all Christian matrons saw such extremes as the proper end of Christian motherhood; many perfectly devout matrons were neither committed to absolutism themselves nor consenting to such extremes on the part of their children; some attempted to act as a brake on the piety of the next generation. Albina, mother of Melania the Younger, though herself 'saintly' by Melania's biographer Gerontius' standards, presents the case for moderate and bewildered, if devout, Christian parenthood. Though accompanying Melania in her chosen lifestyle, Albina frequently disagreed with her daughter on the practicalities of its observance, particularly as to fasting and hours of prayer and labour, and was genuinely tormented by the spectacle of the extremes of self-immolation Melania put herself through. She was 'greatly grieved' at the extent of Melania's fasting and attempted to persuade her to modify it: at Easter 'she barely succeeded in convincing her blessed daughter to take some oil at least for the three days of the feast' (Gerontius *Life of Melania the Younger* 25): for the rest, she failed entirely.

> Embracing her, her mother would say, weeping, "I have faith that I also share your sufferings, my daughter; for if the mother of the seven Maccabees, for having watched for a single hour the torments of her sons possessed with them eternal joy, shouldn't I have this reward so much more, because every day I suffer more torments than she, watching you consume yourself without ever any relief from such cruel labours?"
>
> (Gerontius *Life of Melania the Younger* 33)

Though devout herself, Albina evidently did not find such excesses either fitting or necessary.

Among the desert coenobites there are also tales of mothers of a similarly uncomprehending frame of mind deploring or resisting the exigencies their flesh and blood wished to impose on themselves. These women were usually represented as extra crosses for the monks to bear. The renowned ascetic Mark had a mother out of sympathy with his ideals who went to his cell and pestered his abba, Sylvanus, that she might be able to see him, against Mark's will. In this case, Sylvanus is represented as entertaining her wish patiently, directing Mark to let his mother see him, and comforting her subsequently when she had obtained her wish at small consolation to herself. Her mission had been abortive, for when Mark arrived, thin, dirty and much altered, and greeted her in an unresponsive monotone while closing his eyes so as not to see her, she did not even recognise him, thinking him just an attendant. At a second request from her, Mark refused pointblank to see his mother and Sylvanus sent her away (*Alph*. Mark 3–4). The mother of Abba Poemen, who had lost all seven of her sons to asceticism, was similarly reluctant to just let her boys go, but met with even harsher treatment. When she went to see them, they shut the door of the *coenobium* in her face, and would not open it for all her crying, bidding her to content herself with the prospect of seeing them in the next world (*Alph*. Poemen 76). John Chrysostom's mother, Anthusa, also fell a victim to the notion of the family tie as millstone: a sufficiently devoted mother – and *univira* – to attract the admiring attention of his pagan teacher Libanius, (see p. 134)) she still rated him, and family life, above God in her order of priorities when she begged him not to leave her and enter the monastic life. Imputing her chief motive as an unbecoming fear of being a lone widow, he warned sternly about the legacy of Eve, and properly ignored her feminine weakness (John Chrysostom *On the Priesthood* 11–23).

The polarisation of standpoints, of traditional as opposed to Christian-ascetic affecting the wife and mother's obligations towards her children was still more positively demarcated when it came to the highly emotive issue of property: an issue fundamental equally to the traditions of the *familia* and to the new teaching. As a legal unit and as a social entity the *familia* was defined by its property, and all the individuals in it were hedged about by obligations thereto. Now devout men and women of standing were being asked to consider – and act upon – the idea that their property was not theirs or the family's, but held in trust for Christ and his needy people; resulting in far heavier obligations of civic relief and *largitio*, or largesse, than when it was merely believed to be being held for the family and future generations. Christian parents were, if they took the teaching literally, called upon to beggar the seed of their loins in this world on the promise of a requital in the next; to give up their children's material security as a species of down payment on their heavenly mortgage – a new and interesting twist to concepts of parental duty and safeguarding the interests of the *familia*.

Of course, opinion could vary as to the best methods of doing this, amongst which making the bulk over to the Church to dispose of did not necessarily rank very highly. Many who were considered to be following this teaching elected to interpret it in the manner of keeping their wealth under their own hand – the better to dispense their charity in a fitting way, as did Juliana, Albina, mother of Melania, Pammachius and many another. In this spirit, then, some notable cases of mothers advertised as setting out to 'impoverish' their descendants should be taken with a pinch of salt: Jerome frequently makes this claim on behalf of his female followers, with dubious reliability. Paula, for instance, is depicted as expressing the ascetic orthodoxy on this issue when he says of her 'so lavish was her charity that she robbed her children; and when her relatives remonstrated with her for so doing, she declared she was leaving them to a better inheritance in the mercy of Christ' (Jerome *Let*. 108.5). Similarly, of Albina, mother of Marcella, Jerome claims:

> so obedient was [Marcella] to her mother that she acted against her own personal wishes. For Albina was all set to neglect her own offspring and was preparing to alienate all her property from her own children and grandchildren to confer it on her brother's family

> (Jerome *Let*. 127.4)

– though Marcella's chief objection was that it should go to complete strangers, and not to 'persons already rich' – otherwise she was 'content to throw away her money'. For, as Jill Harries has pointed out, both Paula and Albina, though dispossessing themselves – and that of only part of their wealth, evidently retaining enough to set up monasteries in their new lives – were still observing conventional methods of property transfer (Harries in Craik 1984:61–2).

For Paula evidently had not entirely plundered her family vaults; directly after the allegation that she had 'robbed' her children, Jerome says almost in the next breath that 'before setting out she gave them all that she had' (Jerome *Let*. 108.6), 'disinheriting', in fact, only 'herself upon earth that she might find an inheritance in heaven' (*ibid*.). Jerome also may be misleading in implying that she had deprived even herself of the vast mass of the family estate, for likely it was not hers to shed; a widow was dependent on her husband's generosity in his will for any share in the marital property and if he died intestate, she ranked after the children according to the laws of inheritance. Albina similarly was merely abiding by the principles of intestate succession, since with no certain descendants apart from Asella, vowed to virginity, and Marcella who was refusing to remarry, her brother's children would be the heirs, as agnates.

Melania the Elder, another great example of extreme devotion to Christian mothers, scrupulously upheld family priorities when she 'surrendered all she possessed' (though again, she evidently still had enough for the building and provisioning of monasteries in the Holy Land) to 'her only son' Valerius Publicola (*Let.* 39.5). Emmelia, mother of Basil the Great, Gregory of Nyssa and Macrina (and four others) is another case in point of the mother who observes ascetic self-abnegation while preserving the family's precedence of consideration: in this case, influenced and prompted by her offspring rather than drawing them willy-nilly after her. Egged on most notably by Macrina, says Gregory of Nyssa, who 'weaned her off luxury into equality' to give up 'all showy styles of living and the services of domestics . . . and to share the life of the maids' (*Life of Macrina* 966), she divested herself of what does seem to have been her hold on the family wealth: 'the property – a frequent cause of worldliness – she divided between the children' (*ibid.* 970) though Macrina, the instigator, 'kept nothing of the things from the equal division . . . but all her share was put into the priest's hands by divine command' (*ibid.* 982). Like Marcella, Macrina would have no direct descendants so her perception of her obligations was different.

What is perhaps more surprising is how many women really did seem to want to fulfil this teaching, or who wished to be accorded the repute of doing so, given that it was so subversive to received ideas of what was due to the *familia*. Palladius met a nobleman called Verus in Ancyra who, together with his wife Bosporia, were reckoned to have 'defrauded even their children' in their Christian zeal:

> For they spent the income from their estates on the poor, although they have two daughters and four sons, to whom they give no portion except to the married daughter; saying "After we are gone, everything is yours." But when they receive the revenue of their estates, they spend it on the churches of the towns and villages.

All they seem to have been depriving their children of, in fact, is the income from their estates; there is no suggestion of them selling off the family holdings and donating the proceeds, and thus genuinely impoverishing their progeny – but it is instructive that they wish to be thought of as doing so. Most interesting of all are those such as Nonna who are accorded every intention of pauperising their progeny by the very children in question, and with approbation, not reproach:

unable to satisfy her zeal for benevolence, [Nonna] not only considered all the property which [she and Gregory] possessed and which came to them later as insufficient to satisfy her own longing, but she would, as I have often heard her say, have gladly sold herself into slavery, had there been any way of doing so, to use the proceeds for the poor. Thus entirely did she give rein to her generosity.

(Gregory of Nazanzus *Or.* 18.21)

Gorgonia, too, is accredited with following her mother's example: she 'opened her house to the Godly' and 'helped the needy' to the extent that 'she left nothing behind on earth except her body. She bartered everything for the hopes above: the sole wealth she left to her children was the imitation of her example and emulation of her merits' (*Or.* 8.12). This has a fine ring to it, and sounds like a genuine case of 'Christ before the children' – up to a point. Gorgonia predeceased her husband; and since Gregory nowhere says of her, unlike Nonna, that she was entrusted by her husband with complete control of her household finances, the farthest extent of her liberality in this case would have been to have expended her dowry and personal money upon worthy causes. The children would still have received their father's estate. Nor is there any concrete evidence that Nonna seriously imperilled the material well-being of her children in actuality, for all Gregory says she wanted to: though she and Gregory 'rivalled each other' 'in considering their wealth to be communal to all and in liberality in bestowing it', when he 'entrusted the greater part of this bounty to her hand', it was 'as being a most excellent and trusty steward of such matters' (*Or.* 18.21), which, taken with her excellence in managing household resources already noted (see p. 119), implies that her forte was in carefulness and forethought, not to say husbanding of resources in the bestowing of their charity, rather than a headlong spree of abandoning wealth. Gregory does not seem to have been left destitute; nor does he say of either of his parents even as much as he says of Gorgonia of their depriving their children. Yet he considers it commendable to stress their charitableness in terms which imply a dereliction of family dues which would have been deeply disturbing to the more traditional-minded of his readers.

A more genuine example of the will to deprive the family is found in the actions of Melania and Pinianus. This young couple are seemingly unique in our sources for the extreme nature of their charity and their absolute observance of the commandment to 'sell all that you have and give to the poor' – 'all' in this case being one of the largest aristocratic fortunes of the time. And far from praising their actions, their family did their utmost to prevent them. But on looking closer, once again hazarding the security of their lineage is not really an issue: Melania and Pinianus had no heirs, Melania having had one daughter who died in infancy, and one miscarriage; she was probably her father, Valerius Publicola's only child[5] and he had no brothers to whom would go testamentary precedence. When they first married, Pinianus had expressed perfectly proper notions concerning the transfer of their wealth: when Melania, ever the more energetic Christian of the two, tried to talk him into a continent marriage, he replied sturdily, 'as soon as, by the will of God, we have two children to inherit our possessions, then together we will both renounce the world' (Gerontius *Life of Melania the Younger* 1). But given their unhappy experiences in trying to encompass this, it is not altogether surprising that Pinianus was finally convinced that this was not what God intended for them; following Melania's miscarriage, she was so ill that her life was despaired of, and Pinianus promised continence against her recovery. In this instance, his perceptions of the needs of the family, as promoted by the traditional outlook of Publicola, were outweighed by hers, as promoted by the formidable exponent of the new sanctity, Melania the Elder: Melania the Younger and Pinianus, two scions of noble Christian houses, were caught in a straight clash of ideologies between authoritative elders over the correct conception of Christian aristocratic family duty. For Melania as for Pinianus, family pride and glory were not negligible – she maintained a high profile in her later charitable and ascetic works, brushing shoulders with aristocrats, imperial officials and empresses – but she was still playing with different goal-posts. For her, family glory could, and should, be obtained through alternative means than procreation and property rights.

The consequences of this distinguished victory for extremism were far more wide-ranging than they had been when Melania the Elder opted out of the aristocratic life, or her relatives Paulinus and Therasia in similar circumstances. Melania the Younger and Pinianus made their gesture at a far more desperate time in Rome's history; and in them had been vested far more concentrated family hopes for precisely the continuity that they rejected. Publicola threatened them with disinheritance – a fairly redundant threat, given the lack of any other direct relatives to whom to leave the property, and a measure against which Melania might successfully have appealed in any case because of her entitlement, as *suus heres* to Publicola, to a quarter of the estate. Severus, Pinianus' brother, seems to have been equally aghast at their plans, with even more justice since in view of Pinianus' renunciation of his conjugal rights, he had the best claim on the estate in the case of intestate succession, and should, by convention, have been offered first refusal by the young couple in their disposal of their estate. Instigated by him, says Gerontius (and he himself instigated by the devil), the slaves on one of Pinianus' properties rebelled against being sold: 'Severus . . . goaded the slaves to say, "No, we should not be sold; but if we are forced to let ourselves be sold, it is your brother Severus our master who should buy us"' (*ibid*. 10). The embattled couple appealed for support to Serena, the wife of the chief minister, Stilicho; she had previously shown interest in them though they had then declined to meet her. They succeeded in obtaining her help, resulting in the speeding-up of the sale of their extensive estates in the provinces; only to find themselves, just as they were trying to leave the City, at odds with the Prefect of the City, Gabinius Barbarus Pompeianus, 'a man of strong pagan beliefs, who had decided with the agreement of the whole Senate that their goods should revert to the public treasury' (*ibid*. 19).

It is revealing that the biographer concedes that Pompeianus had the support of the whole (predominantly Christian) Senate in this spoiling action: it has been surmised that Melania and Pinianus' schemes can have had little to recommend them to 'moderate Christians in the Senate, as Publicola had been, who combined Christian belief with a tenacious adherence to the rights of property' (Harries 1984:68). To add point to this, there was a financial crisis in the city, brought on by the need to find money to attempt to buy off the encroaching Gothic invasion; and the couple's supporter, Serena, had just been executed at the order of the Senate for suspected treason. However, Pompeianus did not live to put the issue to the test: while performing the duties of his office he was caught up in rioting following a bread shortage and 'by the providence of God' says Gerontius, 'he was attacked on all sides and lynched in the heart of the city' (*ibid*. 19). Without him, the Senate did not pursue his measure, and Melania and Pinianus achieved the tactical coup of ridding themselves of the majority of their property just before the bottom dropped out of the market with Alaric's invasion of Italy in 408.

Melania and Pinianus chose to retain their own disposition of their wealth, feeding the poor on a grand, senatorial scale, ransoming prisoners and endowing African churches – with the result of finding themselves forcibly detained at Hippo, to Augustine's mortification, by parishioners who hoped to stave off their own incipient economic crisis by means of the anticipated largesse of their aristocratic visitors. Despite Augustine's version, that his flock were moved to attempt to coerce Pinianus into ordination in their church rather by his evident piety than by his equally evident material resources, it is not hard to read their hopes that if he became a priest in their diocese, their church would have first claim on the disposition of his property (Augustine *Let*. 125, 126). Melania and Pinianus' devotion to Augustine and his ends, however, went only so far: although placing piety above family in liquidating their assets for pious purposes, they did not interpret it as being of necessity filtered through the approval of the prelates of Mother Church. Though lavish with their resources, they retained their own personal interest in their disposal.

Paula too does qualify for the category of ultimately placing piety above family, despite leaving those dependants in Rome catered for. One of her offspring she genuinely did not only deprive but in fact impoverish: her daughter Eustochium, closest to her and, in fact, most dependant on her. This is given as her avowed motive in fact: 'my plea is that I may die a beggar, not leaving a penny to my daughter' and was the result of charitable self-deprivation, in which motive Eustochium was expected to participate, when 'she left those dependant on her poor, but not so poor as she was herself' (Jerome *Let*. 108.15.). In this, her charitable impulses have gone beyond even her teacher Jerome's ideas of what is proper: 'so anxious was she to turn away no needy person that she borrowed money at interest, and often contracted new loans to pay off old ones' for which 'I reproved her . . . I wished her to be more careful in managing her concerns' (*ibid*.). But 'she overruled me' and so 'she obtained her wish at last and died leaving her daughter overwhelmed with a mass of debt. This Eustochium still owes, and indeed cannot hope to pay off by her own efforts; only the mercy of Christ can free her from it' (*ibid*.). Jerome presents this sobering statement in the context of a panegyric, and, understandably reluctant to backtrack on his previous sentiments on the right disposition of property, finds matter in it to commend: 'her faith was greater' than his (*ibid*.). But he had evidently had a shock at how far his precepts had been taken in practice; it is debatable whether vexation or approbation is the stronger motive in this passage.

One other case is pertinent of a woman obeying the behest to impoverish oneself absolutely for God, and a stark story it is: Paësia, an heiress from near Scetis in Egypt who, according to the Sayings of the Fathers 'exhausted her resources till she began to be in want' because she 'made her house a hospice for the use of the fathers of Scetis' (*Alph.* John the Dwarf 40). Far from being morally supported by them in this crisis, as Paula was by Jerome and others, having used up her fortune they left her alone with her destitution; it was not until she had taken up prostitution to support herself that they again interested themselves in her, and then to reproach her for her descent from her former 'blessed', exploited status. Abba John 'the Dwarf' visited her, reproached her and drew her out of her evil life only in time for her to die penitent.

Paësia was suffered to behave so because she was a woman on her own. Paula was suffered to behave as she did because she was effectively a woman on her own, her family largely provided for, ruining the prospects only of another woman on her own. Melania was suffered to behave so because she won Pinianus' backing and had no progeny with prospects to ruin. Contrast their treatment in the hands of our writers with that of Ecdicia, who won sharp criticism from Augustine for attempting unilaterally to initiate this state of abnegation, with a present and unwilling husband and infant son.

> You should have given way to him in domestic concerns with greater obedience and submission, since he had so conscientiously conceded to you over such a great thing . . . You should not, therefore, have given away any of your clothes, any of your gold and silver, any money whatever, or any of your earthly belongings, without his agreement . . . When the apostle speaks of almsgiving, he says 'I do not mean that other men should be eased and you burdened' (2 Cor. 8:13); you should decide on all these concerns together, you should administer your treasures in heaven together . . . in carrying out almsgiving and expending your property on the poor . . . you should have consulted with your husband, who was a believer.
>
> . . . there is a certain kind of proper matronly dress – distinct from widows' dress – which is becoming to the status of married women who are believers, while preserving religious decorum. If your husband did not want you to discard this and make a spectacle of yourself by dressing as a widow while he was still living, I think he should not have been driven to a scandalous quarrel with you about this matter.
>
> (Augustine *Let.* 262.4–9)

Perhaps Ecdicia had been influenced by the tales the Fathers told of such examples to her sex as Melania the Elder and Marcella in their 'wretched' clothing, and Paula, who thought 'a clean dress signifies an unclean soul': but despite such edifying tales, discarding the trappings – and disregarding the consent – of the world, as represented by one's family, was not in fact such a personal decision as the Fathers often represented it. Ecdicia might well have been following a diet of Jerome's advice from what we can glean of her actions; it brought her short shrift from Augustine. The commandment to 'sell all you have', though far more central to Christian doctrine than the vexed question of celibacy, should still not be undertaken by the *matrona* without the actively participating consent of her spouse – by this checkpoint, Nonna was praised and Ecdicia rebuked – and even given this, would find it very hard without the consent of the rest of the family. Not lightly was it said that those with husbands and families could not take thought for piety: and yet Gregory of Nazianzus maintained that such women could and did. The matter was less straight-forward: women with unwilling husband and family found they could not.

WORKING WITH AND AGAINST THE GRAIN – SOME CONCLUSIONS

It is evident, then that some of the more notable Christian women of this period became highly regarded in their milieu by setting their influence to work with the status quo, for and on behalf of the family nucleus. There is evidence for a number of formidable Christian matrons who were stiff with family loyalty and put their piety to work in its behalf. Albina, Proba and Juliana are examples of *matronae* whose outlook is not perceptibly much different from what might have been expected of them a century earlier. They embraced the traditionally admired stance of the *univira*; they admired and wrote elegant letters to the fashionable thinkers of their day, and dabbled in approved intellectual pursuits; in escape from an unfortunate political situation, they travelled to visit friends, relatives and places admired by their peers. So doing, they were lauded as venerable widows, as devout seekers after Christian guidance, as pilgrims. Proportionate to their wealth, they were not even outstandingly charitable – these women well understood family tenacity over property. Proba, after all, was 'the heiress of a vast agricultural empire, acquired by rapine and maintained with a selfishness that had

aggravated the miseries and resentments of the Gothic disaster'
(Brown 1967:351). Augustine's exaggerated respect for them nowhere reflects this. He can only say rather feebly to Proba, 'though
you are very wealthy, pray as a poor person' and instruct her to
'account yourself desolate in this world, however great the prosperity of your lot may be' (Augustine *Let*. 130.30). Jerome likewise
exalted Proba as a 'staid and holy woman (Jerome *Let*. 130.5) 'whose
holy life and universal charity have won for her esteem even among
the barbarians' (*ibid*. 7) and advised Demetrias to follow the
'sweetness' of Juliana and Proba as 'models of virtue'.

Their devotion was tepid compared with the example of either
Melania, both of whom Augustine knew, or even with that of his own
mother; he still addresses them in glowing terms. 'Venerable handmaid of God' he wrote to Albina, 'devoted handmaid of God' to
Proba; and this despite the readiness with which they took issue with
him. Albina had obviously taken him firmly – if indirectly – to task
for allowing her family to be coerced by his disorderly flock to the
discomfiture of Pinianus: 'We must not be indignant against you as
you are against the people of Hippo', wrote Augustine with injured
dignity and a sting of reproach that 'you, saints of God, have believed
such things about us';[6] and he thanked her sardonically because 'from
humility and modesty you did not presume to correct a bishop, but
left it to be discovered by indirect inferences' (Augustine *Let*. 126.9).
Obviously her strictures had found their mark – he was humiliated
and defensive to Alypius on the subject, and bitter that she had been
vilifying his name around the neighbourhood; since, to add insult to
injury, they had removed only as far as 'the exceedingly small and
poor town' of Thagaste, preferring to remain under the aegis of
Augustine's good friend, Bishop Alypius, whom they found to be
'most skilled in interpreting the Holy Scriptures' – as opposed,
presumably, to Augustine (*Life of Melania the Younger* 21). Juliana,
too, showed an aptitude for putting down prelates: when Augustine
wrote to her to warn her of the pernicious nature of the Pelagian
treatise to her daughter Demetrias, she gave him a top-lofty and
dismissive answer, that though she thanked him for his care in
warning them against heretical thinkers, 'your Reverence knows that
I and my household are entirely separated from persons of this
description; and all our family follow so strictly the catholic faith as
never at any time to have wandered from it or fallen into any heresy',
even 'the most trivial' (Augustine *Let*. 188.3). Augustine's reply that
he had felt it incumbent upon him to write, given the danger, is in a

distinctly nettled tone. Matrons like these, well-ensconced within the world and identifying strongly with family interests seem to have conceded little to current models for female sanctity as advanced by the Fathers: it is informative, then to note the regard in which the Fathers held them.

A brief but illuminating cameo of another such matron can be found in Jerome's *Life of St Hilarion* : this is one Aristaenete, 'a woman well known among her people' as the wife of the upwardly mobile Elpidius 'who later became Praetorian Prefect' (*Life of St Hilarion* 14). Aristaenete and Elpidius with their three sons were returning from fashionable pilgrimage to visit the famous Anthony in his seclusion, when her three children were struck down at Gaza with a 'semi-tertian ague'. When their lives were despaired of, she went to the hermit Hilarion, who was then living in the near-by desert, to beg him to come to Gaza and cure them; and despite his refusals, she would not take no for an answer.

> At first he refused and said that he never left his cell and was not accustomed to enter a house, much less the city; but she threw herself upon the ground and cried repeatedly, "Hilarion, servant of Christ, give me back my children". All present were weeping, and the saint himself wept as he denied her. What need to say more? The woman did not leave him until he promised that he would enter Gaza after sunset.
>
> (Jerome *Life of St Hilarion* 14)

Aristaenete is an example of a *matrona* not infrequent in the sources of this time, achieving devotion to the work of piety in conjunction with devotion to her ties in the world. Like Albina, Proba, and Juliana, she had no idea of following the model adopted by Paula and abandoning the city and her family in her piety. Rather she made them accomplices in it: the World visiting the Desert – and on more than one occasion, as Jerome relates that she was on her way to visit Anthony again when Hilarion informed her by miraculous intuition of his fellow-hermit's death. Hence when in need, she had no hesitation in calling upon the resources of the Desert to assist her World-based family: this pious matron would move heaven and earth – and a recalcitrant hermit out of the Desert, against his strong opposition – in their interests.

Some such women of family, indeed, exercised their manipulative powers on behalf of clerics from inside a normal social circumstance; Augustine wrote to one Italica in 409, for instance, with exaggerated respect, canvassing her views in a theological debate: she obviously was a woman of some repute and many contacts (Augustine *Let.* 92, 99). John Chrysostom also wrote to an Italica in 406; though it is not now thought that she was the same person, this was another matron of no small respect, since Chrysostom expects her to be able to influence the Pope and possibly the Emperor in his behalf (John Chrysostom *Let.* 170). Not all pious Christian matrons felt impelled to either abandon or alter their family circumstances; some could manipulate their pious lifestyle – and others' – from inside a safely orthodox family environment.

Others, in the name of the *familia*, prove to be in practice a remarkably adept fifth column in the interests of their beliefs. Monica, as we have seen, drew Patricius intractably away from his civic-based paganism. Laeta seems to have done the same for Toxotius' class-based paganism – and in so doing, was more successful than his mother and sisters had been. Unfortunately, we know very little about the process in his case; only that Jerome wrote to Laeta commending her devotion in the face of resistance from her father, Publilius Caecina Albinus, and Toxotius 'before he came to believe' (Jerome *Let.* 107.1). Nonna exercised similar traction on Gregory the Elder: though his beliefs may seem to have been a little closer to hers to start with, they were not seen as having anything in common with catholic Christianity, and Gregory the Younger stressed that for her 'he went out from his kindred and his home' and 'she was the occasion of his exile' (*Or.* 8.4). Melania the Younger turned Pinianus around completely from his cheerful worldliness to her own dark intensity, until he 'obeyed her blithely' in everything; 'as she was a truly good instructor' (Gerontius *Life of Melania the Younger* 37). Avita is credited by Paulinus of Nola with being the motivating force behind the conversion of her husband Apronianus and her daughter Eunomia to asceticism (Paulinus of Nola *Let.* 29): a family Palladius noted as being

> all so desirous to please God that they were publicly converted to the life of continence and virtue and were held worthy on this account to fall asleep in Christ freed from all sin, having become possessed of knowledge and leaving their life in good remembrance

> (*LH* 61)

– evidently the family that prayed together stayed together.

It is a pattern one finds over and over again; sometimes in unlikely quarters. Fritigil, 'a certain queen of the Marcomanni' came under Ambrose's influence, according to Paulinus' *Life* of Ambrose, having heard of his fame from a Christian traveller; when she wrote to him 'asking that she be informed in his own writing as to what she ought to believe', he wrote back 'a most noteworthy letter in the form of a catechism' in which besides advice on personal observances, he urged her to use her influence 'to persuade her husband to entrust himself along with his people to the Romans' (Paulinus of Milan *Life of Ambrose* 36) – as represented by their most catholic bishop Ambrose. It is small wonder, then, that Epiphanius laid the responsibility for the heretical beliefs of many men at the doors of their women: 'the persuasion and perverted advice of a woman bring death on her own husband – and not only him, but her children also' (Epiphanius *Medicine Box* 79.8). So Count Boniface we have observed being got at in the interests of piety by Augustine through the agency of his first, catholic wife; and subsequently drawn from the fold again by his second, arian wife. Volusianus was rendered susceptible to approaches by Augustine because of his connections with his pious mother, Albina, and niece, Melania. Gorgonia exercised some kind of influence on her husband; in this case it is impossible to tell how much or of what kind since Gregory is unaccustomedly reticent on the state of this man's spiritual welfare, only saying elliptically that when it came to her husband, Gorgonia was anxious not to 'leave behind her imperfect anything that was hers' (Gregory of Nazianzus *Or.* 8.20). Evidently something was lacking since 'her husband's perfection was her one remaining desire'; happily for her, however, 'she did not fail even in this petition' (*ibid.*), as befitted her mother's daughter.

A case of influence of this kind even more interesting in its implications is that of Augustine and his concubine of fifteen-odd years. Peter Brown has assessed that 'throughout her partner's Manichaean enthusiasms, Augustine's concubine may have remained a devout Catholic catechumen' (Brown 1967:62). Certainly she was described as devout, and named their son Adeodatus, or 'given by God', seemingly a popular name amongst Carthaginian Christians; and when sent away from him at the instance of Monica, she went back to Africa 'vowing never to give herself to a man again' (Augustine *Conf.* 6.15) – a species of widow, just as she had been a species of *matrona*. Her influence, if this is so, must have complimented Monica's in these turbulent years, particularly when Monica forbade Augustine her house because of his Manichaeism; if so, a common-law marriage imitating the real thing in more respects than Augustine allowed for.

As far as the Christian community was concerned, these devout matrons were the practical vanguard of devotion, far more than Jerome's beloved virgins, whose work was so nebulous and whose care Chrysostom advised was so draining. The motivated *matronae* did their best mostly from within society; and a pretty formidable best it could be. Sometimes, indeed, their drive for piety proved simply overwhelming rather than reforming, as Artemia and Ecdicia discovered, the latter receiving only direful rebukes from Augustine for her over-activity where he had found much to praise in Proba and Juliana's inertia. However, being noted for piety while in a supportive peer-group could certainly silence a husband: from being in historical terms a 'women's' religion, Christianity had become the dominant cult; but, as throughout its history till then, it was something that the men, Patricius, Toxotius, Gregory the Elder, Volusianus, Albinus, and so on, must needs learn from their women-folk. So women also put their talents to work in the interests of the next generation, producing an impressive array of saintly bishops who admitted that they owed their convictions to their mothers, aunts, sisters.

Not that their Christian progeny were necessarily conspicuously grateful for this privileged upbringing; some of their judgements on these determined matrons indicate wariness of their influence and a distrust of petticoat government perhaps passed on from their fathers. Augustine wrote wearily to another young man oppressed by a mother: 'What is the difference? Whether it is in a wife or a mother, it is still Eve (the temptress) that we must beware of in any woman' (Augustine *Let.* 243.10) and even wrote of Monica's love for him (described as *cupiditate*, with its overtones of tenacity and avarice) as being 'a scourge of sorrow for her just punishment' for 'she inherited the legacy of Eve' (Augustine *Conf.* 5.8). John Chrysostom also regarded his mother Anthusa, despite her devout-ness, as a potential source of worldly sorrows and considered it necessary to 'flee from [her] as an enemy' – appending revealingly that since her early, abortive attempt to dissuade him from the priesthood, 'we live apart and have never quarrelled' (*On the Priesthood* 542). This is the attitude reflected by Mark and Poemen and his brothers in their harsh dealings with their mothers' importun-ings: and in the scrupulosity of an anonymous desert monk who, we are told, though conceding to family ties so far as to be accompanying his mother on a journey, carried her solicitously across the river but would not suffer his hands to touch her, wrapping them in his cloak before picking her up; because; even if his mother, 'the body of a woman is fire, and even from my touching you came the memory of other women into my soul' (*PJ* 4.68).

But perhaps the ultimate example of the cleric dogged into salvation by (and despite) an importuning mother is from the anonymous series of Sayings, which relates the tale of a young man who wanted to be a monk, but whose mother for a long time held him close to her, resisting his arguments; he stuck to his guns, however, saying 'I want to save my soul' until ultimately 'she could not prevent him going' (*Anon. Apoph.* 135). Having gone into the wilderness and commenced the arduous lifestyle, he subsequently became negligent about his observances; until, when ill, he had a vision that he beheld the place of judgement and his mother there awaiting judgement, and she said to him 'Have you been condemned to this place too? What about that phrase you used to use – "I want to save my soul"?' Upon recovering, he made haste to make up his deficiencies, saying 'If I cannot endure my mother's reproach, how shall I endure on the day of judgement?' (*ibid.*).

In sum, not all married women were buying themselves a master with their dowries: many of the Christian women of the later period were using their position to direct morals and redirect career choices and life-choices, of their menfolk as well as themselves. They did this from different viewpoints of the nature of marriage itself: whether operating within the environs of a full marriage, or from a half-and-half position of married cohabitation while in denial of the physical and worldly side; even, in the case of concubines like Augustine's, from a curious state of pseudo-marriage. Their influence was tangible and abiding: in the latent witness of the alterations of their husbands and children; in the overt witness of the writings and epigraphic evidence that attest to the strength of their piety; and in the implications of their menfolk needing to flee them, physically and mentally, for peace of mind.

8

'NOT BY OFFICE BUT BY GIFTS OF THE SPIRIT'

The ministries of women

The point of all these segregations and divides on the life of the Christian female was to denote status and worth, innate or acquired. To what end? How best to express their pious intent? What could women of this period who had acquired a name for piety actually *do*? Deprived of entitlement to participate in the (orthodox) canon of Christian offices, what was left for them must be considered: the extent of their Christian service, what positions of responsibility they could find or create, above all, their relationship with authority in the church. What kind of ministry was possible for women of this age?

This highlights particularly those women with a definite vocation towards a more devotional lifestyle. Their social role as 'holy', set-apart individuals had some resonance within their communities: in some contexts this in itself was perceived as ministering to the community, but to what extent? And did it preclude or complement service of a more practical, 'hands-on' nature? For some women the two marched alongside, as they occupied definable positions as leaders of organised religious communities with a ministry implicit therein. Others lived pious lives in private and outside a structure sanctioned by church recognition; but were nonethless reckoned by interested neighbours to be exercising a definite role which was considered of great use to their locale, although devoid of a title or a legitimising scriptural canon.

Whether women turned to the church, as has sometimes been alleged, for 'something pagan society did not afford: a set of standards by which to judge themselves that did not depend on their success as sexual and reproductive beings' (Kraemer 1992:12) or to fulfil perceived needs for purpose and roles, must be examined. Other historians have argued that the fourth century saw a quelling of a process of perceptible 'emancipation' of women that was being

157

ushered in during the preceding centuries[1] while there are some suggestions that contemporaries viewed the church as potentially parasitical in its relations with independent women and saw a need to legislate to protect women against ecclesiastical exploitation (Clark 1993:54–5). Whether the church fostered or discouraged a liberating effect for women is then a contentious issue; and the expression of this 'emancipation' (or its absence) in practical terms a still more vexed question.

Certainly in earlier centuries, Christian women had not been backward in seeking a sanctioned 'role' in the eyes of their fellow-believers in the distinction of martyrdom, as an area in which, as well as men, they could aspire to the very pinnacle of Christian regard. The phenomenon of female martyrdom is written of in confrontational terms that certainly evoke a real sense of 'liberation' for the women concerned (albeit through fairly extreme means); and in carrying this grim enterprise through they both earned the adulation of others of their opinions and provided important focal-points for their Christian communities. For women of the fourth century, however, there is evidently more tension implicit in serving the church. With legitimation came an increasing preoccupation amongst the great and good with hierarchy and structure, in emulation of lay society; and this movement followed a well-noted tendency of such processes to squeeze out extremist or dubious fringe elements – such as those advocating an equal female ministry. This chapter sets out to examine whether women would be able to perform services of any moment within this increasingly rigid structure and within a theology which, while encouraging women in their individual gifts of the spirit and special metaphysical talents, oppressed their conception and disposition of their bodies and strictly limited both their public involvement and physical movement.

The practical activities of Christian women of the fourth and fifth centuries are usually assessed in their own terms. Yet they were also the product of a more long-term context of traditional expectations of what women did and what kinds of women could be expected to be active in certain occupations. Attempting to exercise any kind of executive role against tight and detailed control would have been something of an art alike for pre-Christian women as for those in the later period. It is thus valuable to examine the areas in which they manifested any directorial control or professional skill, and whether the lessons and manipulative skills earlier generations learned could be usefully transmitted to descendants whose abilities were liable to be judged by a more doctrinally based oppression. Certainly the areas of ministry in which women of the later period are attested were crucially affected by expectations of the areas in which women had traditionally found occupations and routes to responsibility. Certain ways of thinking and a *corpus* of law had grown up around females with 'employment'; and these trends had a direct bearing on the age that was to come after. The 'jobs' maintained by women in the earlier era, the limitations and the enablements they indicate were echoed by Christian female experience of positions of responsibility.

THE BACKGROUND OF PRE-CHRISTIAN FEMALE RESPONSIBILITIES

In business and commerce, thinking was reasonably liberal on the capacity of some women with regard to their acumen and practical abilities. The law acknowledged women's right to transact business, and was indifferent to the sex of an *institutor*; thus many women are to be found in papyri and tablets buying, selling, leasing and loaning and seemingly overseeing their own business interests. That they owned ships, leased clay-yards, lent money, dealt in precious metals and participated in a variety of large-scale business ventures is well documented.[2]

Given an initially favourable circumstance for undertaking a commercial enterprise, some difficulties were likely to arise from female legal disabilities. Unless possessed of a very supportive or liberal family, a woman would need to be *sui iuris* to contemplate entering the sphere of business; and then was still subject to tutorial consent for certain transactions. However, the number of women attested as being active in business indicates that the restrictions were not that prohibitive. The lessons learned from the forays into various commercial enterprises seem to have shown to the contrary that, given a pliant family or spouse – or, maybe by preference, no family or spouse needing consideration – and given also at least one biddable male agent, their money was as good as anyone else's for mutual profit; a lesson that the aristocratic pious women of the later age would be seen putting into practice, although dictated to by a signally different understanding of profit.

The bulk of 'women at work' however were to be found in spheres that may be classed as 'service industries' of one sort and another; or procuring or maintaining commodities, or providing personal care. More has been written on the occupations of lower class women and freedwomen, and we find epigraphic attestations to the *ornatrices* (hairdressers), *pedisequae* (attendants), *quasillariae* (spinners), *sarcinatrices* (clothes-menders), *nutrices* (wet-nurses) and those employed in attendant industries, clothes-folders, bath-attendants, weavers, nannies, and so on. Women are also attested, though more rarely in 'white collar' professional areas. Though at less responsible levels than male professionals, they appear as *librariae*, *a manu* and *amanuenses* (scribes, clerks and secretaries) and *lectrices* (readers). And in the area of Roman medicine, women were in certain respects indispensable; *opstetrices*, midwives, were always female, and they were, ideally, highly trained, highly responsible and highly thought of by the male doctors who perforce placed a great deal of reliance in their judgement. For 'women's troubles', Roman women went to their midwives, who would supervise pregnancy and parturition and treat gynaecological disorders; not to the male doctors whom Galen and Soranus show hiding behind a curtain during childbirth, questioning the midwife as to the stage reached, and apparently ready to intervene in the case of an emergency. Women also appear in general medicine, however, freelance and employed privately in households, freed and freeborn, not just as *opstetrices* but also as *medicae*, physicians, implying yet another level of learning, training, and application in an area traditionally the domain of the menfolk. Aemilia Hilaria, aunt of the poet Ausonius, became, it seems, a 'dedicated virgin' in order that she might more freely follow such a career, and 'occupied herself in the art of healing, like a man' (Ausonius *Parentalia* 6). Aemilia Hilaria is also interesting in indicating what may have helped in undertaking a man's profession: seemingly she 'hated the female sex'. Another dedicated virgin, Nicarete, one of Olympias and Chrysostom's circle in Constantinople, also enjoyed a high reputation for skill in this field; she compounded her own drugs for free dispensation amongst the poor, and it was claimed by her admirers that she had cured many patients abandoned as hopeless by members of the medical faculty (Sozomen *EH* 8.23).

An area in which women by cultural expectation were required to be active to uphold the *status quo* as well as the men was that of religion. Roman traditional religions made place for women celebrants, though fewer, and on a strictly segregated basis; and in fact prefigured Christian ideas by sorting women and their right to worship by marital and social status. There were separate cults for virgins (Vesta and Fortuna Virginalis), for matrons (the Bona Dea and Fortuna Primigenia) and for *univirae* – both those widowed and those still married (Fortuna Muliebris and Pudicitia, for patrician *univirae*; Plebeian women celebrated rites of Plebeian Chastity). Slave women celebrated the rites of the Nonae Caprotinae, prostitutes those of Fortuna Virilis. There are also inscriptions commemorating female priestesses of the Imperial cult, and of civic deities, in which capacity there is much evidence that they 'bank-rolled' the cultic exigencies; evidently being possessed of adequate financial means was more than enough compensation for being women (Kraemer 1992:84–5).

It has been suggested, however, that later, more suspect additions to the pantheon offered women more scope in their worship, most seriously in the cult of Isis. In her worship, women could not merely mingle with men but exercise ministry. All had an immortal soul, despite social status or sex; her priests could be either women or men. Further, this freedom was open to all women; besides being a wife and mother, Isis had, according to her legend, been a prostitute for ten years and her doors were not closed even to *probrosae*. In some vital respects, evidently, this cult bore more than a passing resemblance to Christianity: another egalitarian doctrine of universal love and common (un)worthiness. But in this vital respect they were very different: for Christians, not all could exercise ministry, specifically not women, and maintain orthodoxy (Humbert 1972:42 ff.).

Feminist historians tend to find this aspect of Isis worship of great importance as evidence of an attempted sea-change in the climate of opinion in Rome towards greater freedom and authority for women. The new religions, we are told, 'helped women escape the restricting conditions that the ancient cults told them were inevitable' (Cantarella 1987:155); adducing *prima facie* that women of the time saw them as restrictive and experienced a need to escape. The concept of 'liberation' being applied in such a way to women of this era has a somewhat anachronistic ring to it: I think it is more probable that respectable *matronae* would have seen such a venture as an infringement of their élite status. This kind of 'emancipation' cut across all the barriers they had been brought up to believe in and believe, further, that they were special for upholding; distinctions with which much of their *amour propre* was bound up. The notion that such women felt a sense of community with other women simply by virtue of being female is a peculiarly late twentieth century construct. It is also a cliché that those who have escaped themselves from oppression all too often make the best oppressors of others in compensation. Prostitutes and other *probrosae* might be only too happy to believe themselves 'equal to freeborn persons and men respectively' (*ibid.*) but the 'freeborn persons' stood only to lose.

If not quite proving their grasp of a universally applicable concept of 'emancipation' by developing a mass taste for weird Eastern cult religions, however, it is evident that as individuals women of the pre-Christian Empire were demonstrating increasing interest and discernment in religious orientation; as manifested by the interest in and patronage of various philosophical schools shown by a number of well-born women. Galen wrote of Arria, the wife of N. Nonnius Macrinus, said to be the friend of emperors, who was interested in Platonic philosophy. Philostratus claimed the interest of Julia Domna, the wife of Septimius Severus, in his life of Apollonius of Tyana: Julia Mamaea, the mother of Alexander Severus, invited Origen to Antioch so that she could hear him, and gave him a military escort. C. Diogenes Laertius dedicated his lives of the Greek philosophers to a woman who was a follower of Plato but whom he wanted to interest in other philosophy, especially that of the Epicureans. This is not emancipation made manifest: this is the kind of intelligent interest habitually encouraged by the Romans in the women in whom they found it – given that they were well-born enough to be able to afford the education to support it. And these distinguished women supporting intellectual causes paved the way for their descendants of the fourth century, who played leading roles in defending paganism in retreat, as witness Hypatia of Alexandria, as well as promoting ascetic Christianity.

In conclusion, Roman women showed a high level of activity traditionally in fields involving nurturing, providing and purveying. This could be taken to fairly elevated levels of responsibility, in white collar spheres and even in the emotive matter of property administration; given a free rein from familial or tutorial restraint, the commercial world was reasonably open to them. But even so there would always have been the necessity to employ a male agent for the many tasks they would have been unable to deal with directly in 'their' businesses; in some cases they were evidently in the situation of providing the capital and interest in businesses with which in practice they had very little to do, as 'sleeping' partners.

The other strong pattern demonstrated is, as might be expected, the preferential class bias. Given that only limited options were open to women generally, some women had advantages of birth and situation that enabled them to circumvent the traditional obstacles to a certain extent. Their home circumstances were influential to a high degree. The legal and social disallowances were common to all: but some women owned their own property, had a more reasonable spouse or family, or no spouse or family but a good inheritance, while tutelage was a formality for some but not for others. Though in some ways restricted by the segregation required by their high birth, women of higher status possessed more ways of extending the boundaries or evading the consequences of infringing them. There was little possibility for the generality of women of rising from humble origins by talent through service the way their brothers might.

However, influence even as wielded by women of distinction only went so far; their wealth and powers of purveyance were preferred to their skills, a preference frequently perceptible also in our later era. By definition, as creatures without *civilia officia*, women were precluded from exercising any determinative say in policy or the fates of others. They could not participate in the *cursus honorem*, or as their own executives in the courts; even to defend themselves in the courts was seen as a matter for tutorial approval. For an Emperor or public official to take female counsel over a decision was seen as something best covered over: Augustus' dependence on Livia was marvelled at in a good Emperor, Nero's on Agrippina derided as shameful in a bad one.

'CAREER' CHOICES FOR DEVOUT CHRISTIAN WOMEN OF THE LATER EMPIRE

These are patterns that are echoed in the active roles played by the pious women of the fourth and fifth centuries. There were still no-go areas for women and different kinds and levels of personal restraint which they had to negotiate. The church conformed to conventions of Roman society in prohibiting the ministry of women; once again they became most instrumental in the capacity of support and service, either personal or organisational. The businesswomen and *patronae* of the second and third centuries become the church patronesses of the fourth and fifth, mobilising satellite clerics as their predecessors used business agents. Those previously in what we would term 'service industries' became those playing Martha: tending the community and its derelicts, but borrowing from Mary so far as to provide prayer as a function of their service, as we shall further examine. Also very much in evidence is the class divergence. The phenomenon of well-born and well-to-do matrons using their resources to circumvent gender restrictions is eminently applicable to a study of aristocratic Christian women, with their proclivity for creating their own pressure points on the boundaries of legitimate authority; though there was in addition great scope in the new religion for the recognition of merit and example in pious members of the *humiliores*. Given a situation, further, where many of the roles and systems that would become central to the church hierarchy were still being hammered out, birth, money and contacts were even more useful than in previous centuries for influencing the creation of functions for women in the absence of given models.

At first glance, Christianity would seem disadvantageous to women of the upper ranks in this respect. Deprived of the roles and status that had been theirs in the pagan cults earmarked for women, Christian worship was markedly devoid of activities appropriate to women of status, who might be expected to find it less seemly to involve themselves in some of the more menial functions of piety – for instance the cleaning and tending of the church fabric and bodily needs of the clerics – the way devotees of lesser caste could. Women of the *humiliores*, too, were in the forefront of the ascetic movement: earlier than the aristocratic women, and earlier than the generality of the men. From the middle of the third century, thriving congregations of women existed; Anthony, accredited with being the father of monasticism, already knew of the women's community in which he could place his sister before his own withdrawal from the world (Athanasius *Life of Anthony* 3). But as with the development of the religion itself, this was a trend which would start from the bottom of society and only gradually percolate upward, until it reached the classes elevated enough to merit literary attention and so figure more prominently in our sources. The women who receive much of the attention in the ascetic impulse of the fourth century were not necessarily the trail-blazers in their chosen means of expression of piety: but they were innovators because they were aristocrats and because it was they who took the initiative, and in being women creating communities for women and overtly exercising *dynameis* – the power, capacity, and resources for their own creative leadership. What seems to have been the experience at first of Melania, Paula and her family and Marcella and Asella, hemmed in by the expectations of the *haute monde*, was the round of Christianity of the polite salons, where inspiring works were read and fashionable clerics like Epiphanius, Athanasius, Jerome and Pelagius, lionised; in which pursuits they were the intellectual heiresses of Julia Maesa, Julia Domna and Arria, as representatives of the polite world airing the new philosophical and ethical concerns.

For many of them, this was enough. Proba, Juliana and Albina only branched out from this urbane and *mondaine* variety of Christianity when the 'security blanket' represented by Roma aeterna was abruptly whipped away from them. For those for whom it was not enough, those who wanted to actually apply the messages they learned at these discussions, there were few readily available routes of expression of the new ideals. So they set about making up their own – and hence the need for their creating their own models for pious employment. When Marcella embraced avowed widowhood and Ambrose's sister Marcellina took the veil as a virgin, 'not being of the sex which lives in common' (Ambrose *On Virginity* 1.60), there were no convents in Rome; inspired by accounts of more remote coenobitic life in the provinces and wishing to implement it in conjunction with what they knew best, they retired to live as in a cell within their family houses, living a life of study, devotional exercises and abstinence (Jerome *Let.* 127.1; Paulinus of Milan *Life of Ambrose* 4). Marcellina was still living conventually in the family house in Rome some thirty years later when Ambrose received her hospitality while attending the Council of Rome in 382 (*ibid.* 9). Having little example for a pattern of an alternative, devotional life but the alien lifestyle of the desert ascetics, they used these as inspiration while turning to what they found around them; and in doing so attracted others and imitators. By the end of the century, Rome was well-stocked with convents;[3] and a generation after their initiative, Olympias would follow the same course at Constantinople, and like them inspire others by her example. Macrina and Emmelia also followed this path and turned their family property at Annesi into their convent.

Some women, however, wished to go even further. Many took as their apostolic model the legendary St Thecla, apocryphal disciple of St Paul, who was heavily drawn on in this period in writings directed at women; Ambrose directed virgins to take her along with Christ's mother as their role-model (*On Virginity* 2.19). Her name was regularly called on as a talisman: at Macrina's birth, her mother was vouchsafed a vision in which Macrina was hailed as the new Thecla (Gregory of Nyssa *Life of Macrina* 962); Melania the Elder was written of as 'the new Thecla' (*Chronici Canones* 329) by Jerome, before he fell out with her; and Egeria counted her visit to Thecla's *martyrium* as one of the highpoints of her pilgrimage (*Egeria's*

Pilgrimage 23.3). This canvassing of the legend of Thecla is significant for the evolution of asceticism as practised by women: Thecla, in the apocryphal *Acts of Paul and Thecla*, sacrificed home, family and fiancé to follow Paul. She cut her hair in order to be able to travel as a man and was impervious to pressure from family or state to give up her vocation. She escaped miraculously from various encounters with wild beasts in the arena and even claimed the right to baptise herself; ultimately the *Acts* has Paul authorising her to be an apostle of the Gospel (that same Paul who so firmly turned his face and his church away from any kind of female ministry – there is a pleasing irony in the legend of such a revolutionary and dynamically emancipated female model being attached to the coat-tails of the apostle who did so much to permeate Christianity with his own misogynistic mindset) and depicts her ending up as a contemplative in a mountain cave, teaching and healing those who came to her.[4] It has been speculated that the first and second letters to Timothy, so trenchantly condemnatory of female teaching, were, if not written by Paul, a later attempt to redirect Pauline authority against such a trend (MacDonald 1983:59ff.); nonetheless, she remained an inspirational exemplar to Christian women, and went on being regularly referred to by male preachers (as seen above) for their edification. Inspired by such an audacious, but fêted, example in addition to the lives of such as Anthony and Pachomius, some women chose a more absolute renunciation of the world; combining this with following to its logical conclusion the contemporary vogue for acquiring virtue by association, in hunting up the saints in their desert habitats. Melania the Elder and Paula gave the lead in enthusiastically selling all that they had, to relocate close to their role-models – and create entirely, under their own hands, the kind of systems they thought meet.

In these new, largescale monastic ventures, the class bias is yet further accentuated: aristocratic advantages were something of a *sine qua non*. The prerequisites necessary to make these enterprises successful were only to be found in the gift of a Melania or Paula: a capacity for mobility of oneself and one's resources from one part of the empire to another; support from and alliance with notable ecclesiastics; the ability to bring pressure to bear on local government and governors of provinces to ensure survival and assistance for the embryonic communities. In displaying this 'creative leadership', these well-born women provided for themselves the opportunity to establish the real and public personal authority that previously they had been denied the right to exercise overtly. The reverse side of this coin was that the new foundations were then firmly established in a style most likely to guard their founders' aristocratic leadership: exercising what Rosemary Ruether sees as 'the highest self-development as autonomous persons' (Ruether and McLaughlin 1979:73), Melania, Paula, Macrina and Olympias were firmly in control of their own institutions; taking the example of, but also taking the spotlight from, the older and humbler female communities which had long existed in the Holy Land under the aegis of less high-profile leadership. For further consideration of women of authority in ministry it is thus necessary to commence with a divide of class and background.

ARISTOCRATIC *DYNAMEIS*: THE MONASTIC FOUNDRESS AND HER INFLUENCE

One of the major tasks discovered by devout women of status, then, was heading a community. We have taken as the obvious starting-point those who were at the forefront of the drive to create the community life and their own position in it; naturally, examples of those not so circumstanced were more numerous. Nonetheless it makes a logical starting-point for the examination of the task of heading a community, for the information given (rather more abundant for those who started their own) about what women who were in a position to dictate considered their priorities; and at what stage they stopped being able to decide policy and simply turned into subordinates of the local bishop. These aristocratic women were singular in their influence, wealth and coverage in our sources: but it is interesting to observe how after their initial period of creative leadership necessary to give a monastic foundation its impetus they very often became in some sort servants of their own scheme; merely the housekeeper of an entity deemed greater than the sum of their contributions to it.

For the female monastic process from its roots, much can be learned from the monasteries instigated by Paula and Melania the Elder: these women stand out as the primary establishers of sizeable monastic communities built from scratch, as opposed to foundations grown gradually from domestic roots as in the case of such as Marcella's and Macrina's. (Albina and Melania the Younger's contribution will also be considered; but their degree of creative leadership lay in building additions to the foundations initiated by their illustrious forebear, rather than creating from grassroots.) Both

Melania the Elder and Paula settled and built following a period, quite prolonged in Melania's case, of peregrinations: part pilgrimage, part sight-seeing, part, it would seem, a search for the just and proper end for their embarrassment of riches. Melania tried several outlets for her awesome almsgiving, with mixed receptions, (see p. 178) before finally settling to creating a concrete investment in prayer and its propagation with her mentor and factotum, Rufinus. Both women found suitably inspirational sites for prayerful deposits. Melania settled her convent with Rufinus at Jerusalem, on the Mount of Olives; Paula, despite being drawn towards starting her establishment at Nitria, near the esteemed Abba Serapion and other inspirational monks, finally succumbed to Jerome's persuasion and settled at Bethlehem, which had also moved her deeply. This hint of a tug-of-war between Fathers of different provinces and outlook is perhaps to account for the sourness of the attitude of Palladius towards Jerome in connection with Paula; a devotee of the Egyptian coenobites, this is maybe what Palladius had in mind when he wrote of Paula that 'a certain Jerome hindered her by his jealousy, having induced her to serve his own plan' (*LH* 41.1). Melania and Rufinus' establishment of twin houses for men and women, constructed probably around 379–80 may well have been guided by the rules of St Basil, which Rufinus was later to translate and spread to the West;[5] and they in their turn lent their influence to Jerome and Paula, who stayed there in 385 before constructing their own establishment – and before falling into a bitter, and permanent, rift over Origenism with their erstwhile hosts, only a few short years after their visit.

The rule observed in both houses was certainly rigorous enough. The day was spent in a mixture of prayer, manual work, charitable work for the poor and pilgrims, and the study of scripture. They observed six hours of prayer: at dawn, at the third, sixth and ninth hours, at evening and midnight. The intervening hours were filled with Bible reading, the menial tasks of the convent and other manual tasks such as sewing. Writing in 398, Jerome described how Paula and Eustochium, 'shabbily and sombrely clad, positive heroines in comparison with their former selves, trim lamps, light fires, sweep floors, clean vegetables, put cabbages into the boiling pot, lay tables, hand round cups, serve food, and run to and fro to wait on others' (Jerome *Let.* 66.13.).

And besides the ongoing round of practical disciplines and monastic housekeeping, they allotted much time to a gruelling schedule of study of scripture and theology; in these their own houses, the women had no intention of being restricted to the 'women's work' of nurturing and manual service. The emphasis for Melania and Paula both was on the 'better part' of Mary, and their ability to bring this aspect to fruition was another result and advantage of their upbringing. While their male colleagues studied and squabbled[6] the women followed equally demanding academic schedules. Melania

> turned night into day perusing every writing of the ancient commentators, including 3,000,000 lines of Origen and 2,500,000 lines of Gregory, Stephen, Pierius, Basil and other standard writers. Nor did she read them once only and casually, but she laboriously went through each book seven or eight times.
>
> (*LH* 60)

Paula and Eustochium studied Hebrew until they could chant psalms in it without a trace of a Latin accent and their knowledge of it bettered Jerome's, as he freely admitted; and, like Marcella, they kept Jerome at full pitch, supplying exegeses, analyses and answers to textual and spiritual queries. For all her evident linguistic ability, Paula's interest was not the textually literalist approach of Marcella, with her scholarly disquisitions into obscure words and phrases. She placed more value, according to Jerome, on the morally or spiritually edifying messages which, by deft use of allegory, could be extracted from texts. And in pursuit of these, she and Eustochium kept Jerome working at breakneck speed. It was in response to their urgent petitions, he averred, that he embarked on his translation and commentary of Origen's *Homilies on Luke*, interrupting other work on which he was engaged; at their instigation, after some resistance, he tried his hand as a biblical commentator, when they clamoured for expositions of St Paul, culminating in his commentaries *On Philemon*, *On Galatians*, *On Ephesians* and *On Titus*, as he indicates in the prefaces to these works; they also pestered him for commentaries on the Old Testament prophets and most of those he produced are to their dedication. Paula also talked him reluctantly into supervising her and Eustochium's studies of the Old and New Testaments and pushed him to the limits of his learning in her own quest. 'Whenever I stuck fast and honestly confessed myself at fault, she would by no means rest content, but would force me by fresh questions to point out to her which of many different solutions seemed to me most probable' (Jerome *Let.* 108.27).

The rigours of their schedule of activities were compounded by a dietary and personal regimen of much hardship and deprivation.

Melania wore 'rags', eschewed bathing, slept on the ground and avoided anything that smacked of personal indulgence; she asserted her ascendancy in this respect over an unwary cleric, Jovinus, whom she had caught cooling his limbs with cold water during a heatwave, declaring:

> How dare you at your age, when your blood is still vigorous, coddle your flesh like this, taking no account of the danger it allows for? Be quite sure of this: I am in the sixtieth year of my life, and no part of my body except for the tips of my fingers, not my feet nor my face nor any one of my limbs have touched water, although I am a victim to various ailments and the doctors try to force me. I have not consented to make the customary concessions to the flesh and never in my travels have I rested on a bed or used a litter.
>
> (*LH* 55)

Nonetheless, Jerome seems to have thought the ascetic standards observed on the Mount of Olives much laxer and less demanding than he considered suitable (*Apology Against Rufinus* 3.4; *Let.* 125.18). Certainly Melania's vigour was not noticeably diminished by this behaviour. Paula, on the other hand, mortified her flesh to the point of endangering her health and alarming those around her. Jerome, despite being an enthusiastic admirer of extreme practices of dietary abstinence and personal slovenliness and squalor, says of Paula's extremes in this respect 'I admit that in this she was too determined, refusing to spare herself or listen to advice' (Jerome *Let.* 108.21). Bishop Epiphanius even intervened on an occasion when she was ill to induce her to take some wine; instead of being persuaded herself, she nearly prevailed upon him to give up the practice.

In this, she and her acolytes were proving the capacity of women to follow exemplary ascetic practices established by the desert Fathers they so much admired: on the basis of established medical theories of the time of the chastening effect of a diet calculated to 'dry' the 'wet humours' of the body, they, like Anthony and Pachomius, ate little and coarse food, and went without the sleep that Oribasius wrote moistened the body; in the belief that 'the drier the body, the more it flourishes' (*Medical Collections* 6.3, 6.4). It rendered the body more fit to pray by starving it of the physical fuel for emotional and sexual impulses. On an every-day level, the ascetics, women as much as men, controlled their passions and sexuality through a lifestyle based on physiology and a carefully chosen diet. Jerome's theory that previously married women were more at risk from temptation to fornication because of their knowledge of exactly what they were missing out on might thus have influenced Paula's insistence on an extreme of *ascesis*; if her body was more at risk, she may have felt it all the more important to forestall any risk of temptation through physical comfort. It does not, however, seem to have been effective in drying up her tendency to emotional excesses that Jerome had deplored in the aftermath of Blesilla's death – even under the effects of this regime of deprivation, she evidently retained enough 'wet humours' to remain 'easily moved to sorrow and crushed by the deaths of her kinsfolk' so that 'when one after another her husband and daughters fell asleep, on each occasion the shock of their loss nearly endangered her life' (Jerome *Let*. 108.21).

Outside the personal and devotional sphere, however, things did not necessarily run so smoothly. Julia Eustochium quietly took over from her formidable mother after her death in 404, under conditions rendered considerably less favourable by her mother's actions: as we have seen, Paula had run her foundation into considerable debt which 'Eustochium . . . cannot hope to pay off by her own exertions' (*ibid*. 15) in her contempt for worldly securities; latterly, when her resources failed, Jerome had had to resort himself to attempting to sell off a few 'ruinous' family properties through the agency of his brother to make ends meet (Jerome *Let*. 66.14). Eustochium was admonished by Jerome nonetheless not to abandon the 'crowd of needy brothers and sisters whom it is hard for her to support but whom it would be undutiful to cast off' (*Let*. 108.31). Seemingly she shouldered this burden with Christian submission. Jerome's biographer Kelly has surmised, however, that the situation may have been improved by some providential advice; which Jerome discovered when in the year of Paula's death, at the solicitations of a priest named Silvanus he translated some fundamental writings of Pachomius, including his Rule and the extremely important *Instruction on Monastic Institutions* of his second successor, Horsiesi. These contained a wealth of practical, down-to-earth regulations concerning not only the daily worship and conduct of the monks and the organisation of the various houses, but also the agricultural tasks or numerous trades in which the various monks were engaged, with everyone allocated work in proportion to his strength – providing a solid economic foundation which it seems Jerome's and Paula's houses lacked, with their amateurish arrangements originally based on their foundress' seemingly boundless wealth. Jerome noted in his preface that in breaking his long silence, one of his objects was to provide Eustochium with something she might pass on to her sisters to put into practice, and to enable his own brothers in religion to imitate the life of the Egyptian monks: we may conjecture that this practical advice, come at the most opportune moment, may have done much to help Eustochium put the convent on a more practical financial footing. About her time in charge of the convent we really know very little; she merits little more attention from Jerome in his letters. Having helped to initiate the house she would be well-placed to maintain it; and she left the foundation in good heart to Paula the Younger, her niece, who had been partly brought up there, on her own death in 419 (Jerome *Let.* 143).

In contrast to Eustochium's retiring ways, Melania the Younger – heir to the spiritual legacy and duties of her grandmother, Melania the Elder – remained conspicuous even after terminating her visits to the desert coenobites and settling to ruling her convent of ninety women, twin to Pinianus' house of men. Though lecturing her cousin Paula the Younger on the true humility necessary in an ascetic (Gerontius *Life of Melania the Younger* 40), Melania remained a high-profile figure, noted for her church-building, her visits to and influence upon temporal authorities and her healing powers, brought to bear on, amongst others, the Empress Eudocia who visited Melania's convent on her pilgrimage to Jerusalem (*ibid.* 59); and on a young woman afflicted with a dead foetus which she could not deliver – made the occasion for an object lesson to her virgins on the curses of childbearing, from which chastity had delivered them (*ibid.* 61). Though her mother Albina had instituted and completed the new monastery on the Mount of Olives, we know Melania developed the rule for the governance of the convent, detailing the daily round of prayer and the rules of spiritual growth. Yet there is a brief but intriguing passage in the *Life of Melania the Younger* where it is alleged that she would not take over the running of the monastery on her mother's death, out of her 'excessive humility' but chose another woman 'who was very spiritual and consumed with love for God'; so that she, Melania, could devote herself to prayer. If true, this experiment was short-lived, and Melania seems to have found it more difficult to give up her preeminence in fact than in her pious longings. Subsequently this woman was judged by the sisters to be 'too rigid' and Melania further undermined her authority by covertly tending to the needs and comforts of her nuns 'without the mother superior's knowledge'; with the predictable result that they 'bound themselves still closer to [Melania] and devoted themselves to obeying her in all things' (*ibid.* 41). There is no further mention of this unfortunate proxy and in the rest of the account of the monastery, Melania is very much in the driving seat; the deaths of Albina and Pinianus in 431–2 left her in exclusive charge of these church and monastic compounds, responsible for the welfare, instruction and discipline of her nuns. She also oversaw the construction of another monastery for men, dedicated to the chanting of continuous psalmody (*ibid.* 49). She herself followed a study schedule at least as demanding as her grandmother's, reading both Testaments three or four times a year, plus lives of saints and the Fathers, homilies and canonical books: 'such was her erudition that when she read in Latin, she seemed to have no knowledge of Greek, but then she read Greek so that it seemed she could not be even acquainted with Latin' (*ibid.* 26). Further, she copied out texts of which she had need, and distributed copies to others; she was known for the elegance and correctness of her manuscripts. She slept only about two hours a night, according to Gerontius, to fit in her exacting timetable. Her ascetic regimen was similarly demanding, following those she had read of in the *Lives* of the Fathers, with special deprivations for Easter and the feast of the Resurrection.

One salient feature of such dynamic leadership by women of the aristocracy is how the communities it served became subservient to dynastic ends. They became an expression of what in later medieval times would come to be termed *eigenkirchen*; the church or community as a family concern, in very much the same way as a business interest. Paula handed on the reins to Eustochium, and she to Paula the Younger; Melania the Elder to Albina and she to Melania the Younger. Olympias handed over her community before her exile and subsequent death to 'her relative and spiritual daughter' Marina, who then passed it on in her turn to Elisanthia, who was related to both of them. Elisanthia is related to have 'preserved the rule which she had received entirely unchanged' – conceivably one of the advantages of leaving it to a less high-powered relative, that she might be relied on not to outshine the original foundress (*Life of Olympias, the Deaconess* 8,12). Marcella and Macrina regarded their mothers as notionally their superiors in religion and had they had obvious female kinsfolk surviving, it is a reasonable inference that these would have succeeded them. Even the church came to serve this end of dynastic empire-building in piety. These women had proved their more absolute devoutness than the pious sight-seers whom the desert Fathers had regarded as such an annoyance; those for whom making the pilgrimage to the holy places before returning to comfortable domesticity, and some almsgiving, were the ultimate expression of piety. The reward for their superior performance was the validation by the church and church writers of their superior status – which had its origins in the superior birth all affected to despise as part of the new Christian commonalty.

Significantly, this thinking is overtly manifested in the attitude of Paula the Younger, whom Melania the Younger rebuked for being prideful and comporting herself with too much of the hauteur of her family and class, and undertook her guidance, to turn her from 'Roman pomp' to true humility (*Life of Melania the Younger* 40). The real piquancy in this is in the remembrance that it was Melania who had been brought up in grandeur in the centre of the civilised world and Paula who from an early age had been raised by her saintly aunt Eustochium in the midst of humble community life (and in straitened circumstances) at Bethlehem. Being as it were a second generation monastic does not seem to have removed any of the familial inclination to hauteur in this girl; rather, by virtue of her assured place in the new 'aristocracy of piety' she might have thought she had still more reason to indulge it. It is revealing also how automatic was the assumption that she was to take over from her aunt; Eustochium's death was sudden, when she can hardly have been more than fifty, and Paula the Younger was only eighteen. And yet there was no question for Jerome, the community or her, who was to succeed Eustochium; and 'forlorn and wretched' (Jerome *Let.* 143.2), the untried girl was called upon to assume responsibilities beyond her years.

This is a tendency reflected in other religious foundations of the time, and not just those that were called into existence to answer the pious empire-building of the high aristocracy. The same strain of associated holiness by kinship is visible in many female community leaders who had not personally created their domains; most of whom we only know in fact from their association with more eminent relatives. There was a great sorority of women leading convents who were relatives of noted patristic thinkers – it is surely no coincidence that they tended to end up as the superiors of their establishments, if not placed there as such originally. This is evident as early as the time of Anthony, who, when he retired from the world, placed his sister in a 'house of virgins' of which she afterwards became the superior (*Life of St Anthony* 3, 54). Ambrose's strong-minded sister took to the female version of the cloth before he did and headed her own house community (see p. 165), not hindered subsequently, one imagines, by Ambrose's eminence in the same field. Augustine's sister also headed her community, which, following the best aristo-cratic models, was then passed on to the leadership of his niece; it was after the family leadership ended that the community fell into disorder, as we know from Augustine's harassed letters to it (Possidius *Life of Augustine* 26.1; Augustine *Let.* 211). Palladius related that Isidore of Alexandria's sisters had a community of seventy virgins; also that when Isidore died, 'he left no money or goods to his sisters who were·virgins, but he commended them to Christ' (*LH* 1). Paulinus of Nola's friend and fellow-monastic Sulpicius Severus, author of the widely-read *Life of St Martin of Tours*, perhaps lacking closer female connections, relied on his mother-in-law, Bassula, to run the female end of things at his foundation at Primuliacum (Paulinus of Nola *Let.* 5, 31). Not much later, this tradition would culminate, most famously, in the great monastic exemplar, St Benedict, heading his monastery with his sister St Scholastica, in charge of the complementary female convent. Having often been 'placed' in these positions by interested parties, these women did not merit so much wooing by their distinguished relatives as did the independent-minded aristocratic monastics, and consequently figure less in our source material; though we may fairly assume that they were just as authoritative, and probably more efficient given the situation of Jerome and Eustochium feeling the need for lessons from the systems employed by Pachomius and his sister on viable monastic life.

The exercise of female authority

The proper end for the officially publicised activities of these women was seen as largely ministry to their own sex; exercising the functions of teaching, lecturing, catechising and administering assistance prior to baptism were quite proper when the objects of these ministrations were other women. Both Melanias, Marcella and Olympias were duly attested instructing and converting notable women and their maidservants, and catechising women and preparing them for bap-tism.[7] But these were amongst the least of the respects in which these women were exceptional. These more high-profile proponents of monastic leadership are distinctive for immense practical influence quite outside their briefs and their definable areas of control. They displayed, in fact, a considerable licence for interference with both church and secular affairs, evidently quite sublimely unconscious of any thought that their position as women might undermine their position as church functionaries; therefore it is necessary to try and determine how much was due to their personal singularities and aristocratic individualism, and how much came within the official scope of their *auctoritas* as a species of church office-bearer.

These august monastic foundresses demonstrated, for instance, a great tendency to dominate church functionaries; and, conversely, a definite ability to resist being directed by those representing the church. Melania the Elder was instrumental in healing a festering Antiochan schism, according to Palladius, assisting in the 'edification' of 'some 400 monks in all and, winning over every heretic that denied the Holy Spirit, [Melania and Rufinus] brought him to the church'; what is more, 'without offending anyone' (*LH* 46). This is another sideswipe at Jerome, who conducted his disputes with maximum offence on all sides, and who accredited Melania with a malign influence in the Origenist dispute he had with Rufinus – a sign of the extent he accorded her influence. Palladius is a further witness that she did not scruple in lecturing officials of the church about procedure in a manner which owed little respect for their inherently superior status as being men and ordained; we have already noted her hectoring Jovinus, then a deacon, subsequently bishop of Ascalon, 'a devout and learned man' when she caught him indulging himself (as she regarded it) with a wash in hot weather. She also had a short way with backsliders. When Evagrius Ponticus, an upwardly-mobile arch-deacon of Constantinople, fell out of health and political favour seemingly as a result of an illicit affair of the heart and fled to Jerusalem, Palladius credits Melania with healing his mental and physical anguish:

> When the physicians were at a loss and could not find any cure, the blessed Melania said to him, "Son, your long illness displeases me. So tell me what is in your mind; for this sickness of yours perhaps comes from God." So he confessed the whole affair to her. Then she said to him: "Promise me before the Lord that you will keep to the standard of the monastic life, and sinner though I am, I will pray that you may be granted a longer life." So he agreed. And within a few days he became well, and got up and received from the hands of the lady herself a change of clothes [i.e. clerical, which he had abandoned] and he went away and exiled himself in the mountains of Nitria, in Egypt.
>
> (*LH* 38)

Olympias is another example: it was related of her, in Palladius' glowing account, that she 'addressed priests reverently, and honoured bishops' (*LH* 56). For all that, she set Theophilus, bishop of Alexandria, at defiance in defence of her adored Chrysostom whom Theophilus had been instrumental in deposing; she received monks he had expelled and held herself and her community in secession from communion with Arsacius, John's replacement as bishop of Constantinople (Sozomen *EH* 8.24). Nectarius, bishop of Constantinople before John, 'was completely persuaded by her even in matters of the church' (*Life of Olympias, Deaconess* 14) – for, amongst other considerations, he seems to have been fairly dependent on her financially. Albina and her daughter Melania the Younger similarly resisted all attempts at guidance from the upstart bishop of Hippo, when Augustine's congregation attempted to compel them and Pinianus to remain there. They took little notice of his and Bishop Alypius' contention that Pinianus' vow, albeit made under duress, should be regarded as binding on them to stay, and in their letters to him did not hesitate to take what, from the wounded and defensive tone of Augustine's replies was a very strong line, even to the extent of vilifying him to others in the locality (Augustine *Let.* 124, 125, 126)

This top-lofty self-confidence is manifestly one of the advantages of their possessive attitude towards the church: they evidently considered themselves comparable in terms of a God-given authority to any mere appointed functionary. The only men of God these women readily accorded respect as being more overtly directed by God than they (and they evidently thought little of men like Jovinus, Evagrius, Theodosius and Augustine in this respect) were the great hermits and coenobites of the deserts: who themselves operated from outside the church hierarchy. These were, seemingly, the only clerics seriously able to withstand their high-handedness, and indeed, their openhandedness – and manifestly perplexed them by so doing. The standard-bearers of a Christianity truer to its original conception, and the very folk that these women were more concerned to impress, these men of the desert distinguished themselves by most sturdily and most successfully evading the gilded cage of aristocratic adoption; while mainstream clerics tended swiftly to knuckle the forehead when faced with the sway and resources of a woman of the standing of Melania or Paula. In vain, however, did the Melanias try to buy coenobitic approval. Abba Pambo, a noted 'Old Man' was manifestly unimpressed by

Melania the Elder and her obvious pride in the extent of her alms, as she later used to relate:

> I remained standing in front of him, expecting to be honoured or praised by him because of my gift, but receiving no reply, I said to him: "So that you may know, Sir, how much is there, it amounts to three hundred pounds [of silver]." But without even looking up, he answered me: ". . . If you had given it to me, you were right to tell me; but if it was given to God, who did not despise the widow's two obols, then be silent."
>
> (*LH* 10)

He compounded the lesson by leaving her a basket on his death as 'I have nothing else to leave you' (*ibid.*).

Her granddaughter fared even more gallingly with Abba Hephestion, whom she visited in his remote cell in the Egyptian desert. The story is a fascinating one: and illuminating about a chasm between their cultures which Melania the Younger's apparent enthusiasm and devotion to notionally the same ends quite failed to bridge. In an echo of her grandmother, Melania begged him to receive a little gold from her hands. 'Being told brusquely that he could do nothing with it', she looked around his cell and saw that indeed he possessed nothing but his mat, a basket of dry biscuits and a little basket of salt; amazed and 'profoundly moved by the imponderable, heavenly richness of the saint' (Gerontius *Life of Melania the Younger* 38), she then attempted to rectify his blessed state by hiding some gold in his salt before hastening away. Hephestion quickly discovered this and was not a little annoyed; many of the desert Fathers fled from gold as from poison, believing, not unnaturally, that worry over valuables was destructive of their contemplative peace of mind:

> the man of God ran after them, holding out the gold and shouting "What am I supposed to do with this?" The blessed Melania said to him, "Give it to those in need." But he insisted that he could neither keep it nor distribute it, for the good reason that the area was a desert and he would be unable to find there anyone in need. . .
>
> (Gerontius *Life of Melania the Younger* 38)

– the only others residing in that wilderness being of the same attitude. Being quite unable to persuade Melania of this, or get her to take back her gold, he made his point still more eloquently by throwing it in the river.[8]

However, by Palladius' account, Melania's actions reveal an inability to comprehend the lesson implicit in this response; in this Melania the Younger proved herself not quite as apt a pupil in this respect as her grandmother (who used to tell the story of her stand-off by Pambo to her own discomfort). This does not seem to have been an isolated incident, nor did Hephestion's rebuke, if reliable, check her penchant for overbearing almsgiving: Palladius says it was her regular practice to surreptitiously leave deposits of money 'using spiritual subterfuge' in the cells of 'many other holy anchorites and pious virgins who did not wish to accept anything' for 'she considered indeed that it was as much a spiritual profit and a very great benefit for the soul, as to succour the saints by this means' (*LH* 61) – regardless of their wishes. Small wonder that Augustine and his fellow-bishops Alypius and Aurelius were so anxious to persuade her and Pinianus that their fortunes were better off being used to endow churches and monasteries rather than in being proffered to ungrateful hermits and the poor. Even if Christ did say 'what you do for the least of them, you have also done for me', the bishops' advice was 'if you give money to the poor, it is gone again tomorrow. If you give revenue to a monastery, you will endow it permanently' (Gerontius *Life of Melania the Younger* 20).

However, the corollary of their unconscious retention of world-based arrogance was that these women could and would mobilise equally formidable and irresistible powers in defence of the clergy – particularly those they regarded as 'their' clergy, just as the monastic foundations were 'their' foundations. In the insecure world of the time, the life of a cleric was particularly hazardous, since as well as the dangers of an autocratic state and a variety of marauding hordes, not least their own peasantry, they were also liable to be hauled neck and crop into a church squabble and have to flee even a safe environment. Thus Pambo, Paphnutius, Isidore and companions might have cocked a properly unimpressed snook at Melania the Elder's materialistic preoccupations when she first appeared, but they soon had need of her material resources when the prefect of Alexandria banished them and various others to Palestine and she 'followed them and ministered to them from her own money' and 'servants being forbidden them . . . wearing the dress of a young slave she brought them in the evenings what they required' (*LH* 46). Just so hosts of clergy from Constantinople and its environs were dependent on Olympias for their subsistence:

She did more to maintain the blessed Nectarius – so much so that he even took her advice in ecclesiastical affairs – and I need not mention Amphilocius, Optimus, Gregory, Peter the brother of Basil, and Epiphanius, Bishop of Cyprus, those saints to whom she actually made gifts of land and money. When Optimus was dying in Constantinople, she closed his eyes with her own hands. Besides these, she generously provided everything they required for the wretched Antiochus, Acacius and Severianus; and, to put it briefly, for every priest who visited the city, and a host of ascetics and virgins

(Palladius *Dialogue* 61)

– earning herself a rebuke from Chrysostom for being too rash in her charity:

I applaud your intentions; but would would have you know that those who aspire to the perfection of virtue ought to distribute their wealth with prudence. You, however, have been bestowing wealth on the wealthy, which is as useless as if you had thrown it into the sea.

(Sozomen *EH* 8.9)

This may be uncharitably seen as John keeping a jealous eye on the goose that laid the golden eggs; the same openhandedness to him evidently did not count as imprudence. Olympias donated to John for his church '10,000 pounds of gold, 20,000 of silver together with all the land she had in the provinces of Thrace, Galatia, Cappadocia Prima and Bithynia' (*Life of Olympias, Deaconess* 5). The anonymous *Life of Olympias, Deaconess* also states that she gave him all the rest of her property, 'including her stake in the public bread supply' (*ibid.* 7) – but as with some of Jerome's claims of absolute largesse, this should not be taken too literally, since she was manifestly still well able to provide for his subsequent personal needs after he was banished 'and those with him in his exile' (*ibid.* 8) after falling into dispute with the Empress and a powerful faction in the Byzantine church. Even Theophilus the bishop of Alexandria, who had been in the main responsible for John's deposition, and incurred her subsequent enmity afterwards, had had recourse to Olympias' charity: 'How often do you suppose he kissed Olympias' knees when he hoped to get money from her, the woman who he now reviles; while she threw herself upon the ground in vexation and shed tears at such things being done by a bishop' (Palladius *Dialogue* 56).

Nor was financial support all Chrysostom received from Olympias while he was in exile. She kept him informed about and in contact with his allies and acted as his right arm. From his letters reporting the gist of what she said (hers in their actual form, typically, do not survive), we know that she was his contact with various priests and bishops both still in office and in exile; she was charged with transmitting letters and messages to them and quizzing them about affairs with which John was still embroiled, for instance over Bishop Maruthas' mission to Persia; she was entrusted with the delicate task of attempting to prevent a priest hostile to John being sent as bishop to the Goths to replace the man John had consecrated, who had died; she kept him posted about the attempt to make the bishop of Ephesus resign; she was, in fact, one of John's main instruments and sources of intelligence while he was in exile (John Chrysostom *Letters to Olympias* 4 and 9).

For this is the other side to the dynamic leadership exercised by pious aristocratic women in this twilight period of the Roman empire: armed with their moral righteousness, they would sally unconcernedly into battle with formidable authorities fortified by the knowledge that when they took up the cudgels for a foray into the men's preserve of public affairs, because of their 'special' motivation, they would likely receive support and approbation, not vilification, for their unwomanly behaviour. To be 'unwomanly' was no longer a reproach for such females; it was the patristic authors' highest accolade. It was accorded, for instance, to Olympias, who though a 'modest woman', seems to have had little difficulty in outfacing the authorities. Besides the above activities, she was also summoned as a witness and then tried by the prefect of Constantinople in connection with the fire in the cathedral, fairly evidently simply on the grounds of being a known troublemaker and focus for discontent. On this occasion she went on the offensive, asserting 'my past life ought to avert all suspicion from me' and insisting that if the prefect had any real proof 'you ought to appear as our accuser instead of sitting as our judge' (Sozomen *EH* 8.24). Her obduracy triumphed in this and the prefect 'adopted another tone' and tried by persuasion at least to prevent her and her ladies from seceding from communion with the bishop:

> All [the ladies] deferred to the advice of the prefect with the exception of Olympias, who said to him, "It is not just that, after having been publicly calumniated, without anything being

proved against me, I should be obliged to clear myself of charges totally unconnected with the original question. Let me take counsel concerning the original accusation that has been preferred against me; for, even if you resort to unlawful compulsion, I will not hold communion with those from whom I ought to secede, not consent to anything that is contrary to the principles of piety." The prefect, finding that he could not prevail upon her to hold communion with Arsacius, dismissed her so that she could consult with the advocates.

(Sozomen *EH* 8.24)

Palladius links Olympias with Melania the Elder in his narrative, in his statement of their manliness in defence of the Truth; and in this, indeed, they show the same tendencies. Melania, summoned to account for tending to the Nitrian priests exiled by the prefect of Alexandria, makes a redoubtable figure.

The consular of Palestine came to know of it and wishing to line his pockets, thought he could intimidate her. So, having arrested her, he threw her into prison, not knowing that she was a lady. But she said to him: "For my part, I am So-and-so's daughter and So-and-so's wife, though I am still Christ's slave. So do not despise the poorness of my clothing; for if I wish to I am able to elevate myself, and you cannot terrify me like this or take any of my goods. And I have told you this in case you should be accused in the courts because of your ignorance. For in dealing with undiscerning people, one must be as bold as a hawk."

(*LH* 46)

She too won the day resoundingly: the judge, 'recognising the situation', made hasty and advisable reparation and 'both gave her an apology and his respect, and ordered that she should be allowed to succour the saints unhindered' (*ibid.*). Her relative, Paulinus of Nola, is a perhaps more accurate witness to her attitude on a similar, or possibly the same, occasion; and enlarges on the case against her, that she not only aided prohibited priests, but acted as an underground railroad for those fleeing the temporal authorities, hiding and assisting them: 'the defender and companion of all those who stood firm for the faith, she gave refuge to fugitives or accompanied those arrested' and 'she hid those who were particularly victimised by the heretics' until 'she was ordered to be dragged before them for holding the state law in contempt and to suffer the same fate in store for her hidden protegés unless she agreed to give them up' (Paulinus of Nola *Let.* 29.11). She was undismayed by this, says Paulinus: 'Though she had not anticipated arrest, she swiftly went to the judge's tribunal, outpacing her would-be escort. His respect for the woman troubled him, and his surprise at her audacity in her faith caused him to give up his heretical fury' (*ibid.*) – having achieved which result Melania reportedly went away and fed 5,000 more monks who were in hiding for three days.

Melania the Younger, her granddaughter, similarly showed a talent for throwing her weight around in influential company. When in 436 her uncle Volusianus (her mother's brother) invited her to the imperial court in Constantinople for the wedding of the Western Emperor Valentinian III to Eudoxia, daughter of the Eastern Emperor Theodosius II, she accepted in the first instance with the plan of converting her pagan uncle, according to Gerontius. Peter Brown suggests she may have had more pragmatic motives, such as assisting with a political marriage (Brown 1961:8); just as Volusianus may have had more pragmatic reasons than her inspirational presence for his ultimate conquest, such as fear of forcible conversion by Theodosius. Melania's conversion of her procrastinating uncle is an example *par excellence* of pious bullying by a strong-minded woman of faith. When he is represented as begging her not to involve the Emperor, saying

> do not take away from me the gift of free will with which God has favoured us since the beginning of time. I am quite ready, in fact I do wish, to be washed free from the stain of my innumerable wrongdoings. But if I do this under the Emperor's orders it will be as if I had been driven to it by compulsion and I will lose the benefits of making my own resolution in this matter
>
> (*Life of Melania the Younger* 53)

it may have been true, as she evidently suspected, that he was just dragging his feet and attempting to put off a little further the inevitable. Equally, his reasons as given are a very cogent and reasonable plea for Christian free-will and self-determination in this most all-important decision of his conversion; a delicate matter over which 'the holy woman', his niece, did not hesitate to ride rough-shod. Displaying the same inability to see an opposing viewpoint we have seen in her relations with Augustine and Abba Hephaestion, 'she was unable to resign herself to silence' and called in the Imperial thought-police, in the person of Proclus, the Patriarch of Constantinople. Her uncle's baptism swiftly followed; not content with this, Melania presided over his deathbed; 'she sat by the bedside of her uncle all night, encouraging him', and talking to him of God; and 'had him make communion in the holy mysteries three times' before allowing him to die at dawn – most thoroughly Christianised.

Nor did Melania hesitate to throw herself into the thick of the religious strife of that troubled city, gathering about her a circle of women from the court 'and other persons of great brilliance and culture' (*ibid*. 56), whom she instructed in orthodox theology, against the heresy of Nestorius, enlisting the support of Lausus, chamberlain to Theodosius (a notably pious man, he was also the dedicatee of Palladius' *Lausiac History*) and at some stage winning the friendship of the Empress Eudocia. Subsequent to this, when Eudocia fulfilled her vow to go to the Holy Land on pilgrimage after her daughter's wedding, Melania was the obvious person to act as her guide, journeying to Sidon to meet the Empress and conducting her back to and around Jerusalem, including showing her around Melania's own foundations – now in need of another cash injection to support her new *martyrium* where a community of monks could chant perpetual praises – before escorting her back to Caesarea. Melania was exercising a kind of state-sponsored asceticism that still had its connections with the secular world; manifesting in this more influence than her cousin Paula the Younger, who though her social equal and of equivalent status in religion, was not attested as being involved in the imperial visit, though she was back in evidence in Melania's deathbed scene. Melania may have rebuked Paula's pride, but her own pretensions to worldly status were considerably more evident (*Life of Melania the Younger* 53–7).

This was a visible altering of the accepted status quo in terms of women's 'place' in the scheme of things, for both church and society. Women in this position, portrayed as 'servants' and 'slaves' were pursuing service of a kind that scarcely merits the name; they were, in fact, displaying their aptitude for fulfilling a public and social role of maximum visibility. And in taking up this unprecedentedly autocratic style they all seem to have achieved a kind of legitimacy in the eyes of their chroniclers because they assumed definable positions arguing legitimate authority; all the accounts of them were written with hindsight of their official ministries as foundresses and heads of established communities. In fact, they all manifested exactly these talents for authoritativeness as much prior to attaining their 'rank', when they had no more status than any of the pious sightseers we have seen being so imperious: such as the tribune's wife Aristaenete we have seen dragging Abba Hilarion out of his isolation, and the arrogant 'senatorial virgin' to whom Arsenius gave such a reprimand for insisting on seeing him after being given his refusal (see p. 29 and 152). But the greater arrogance of the Melanias and their type was sanctified in retrospect by their subsequent ecclesiastical rank; there can be little doubt that being, in the final analysis, under vows, and in a position to represent church *auctoritas* obtained support for the kind of enterprises that otherwise would have been difficult to carry off or reconcile with ecclesiastical approval.

THE 'OTHER HALF': NON-ARISTOCRATIC FEMALE MINISTRIES

Communities and community headship

This brings us necessarily to a look at the other side of the coin; the consideration and comparison of women who exercised leading roles in communities, but of a non-creative and rather less dynamic kind, and who were concomitantly less high-profile; women who were neither owners of extensive property, nor sisters, aunts, nieces or mothers-in-law of famed ecclesiastics, but who still, from relatively humble backgrounds and with nothing but themselves and their own deeds to attract attention, made it into the sources as worthy of note. Unsurprisingly, a number of them are from the desert-based sources, who are fascinated with the ability of the little man – and woman – to create sweetness in the wilderness. Knowing little about how such women as are mentioned in these attained their positions, or the qualifications deemed suitable for leadership if one did not preempt the question by founding the establishment oneself, we can yet gain valuable insight into female ecclesiastical 'employment' as provided by conventual life at this time by examining the functions and concerns of these more typical monastic women; less likely to be interrupted by miraculous events, literary controversies or royal visitations.

High amongst these rank Amma (mother) Theodora and Amma Syncletica; as 'everyday' female monastics they are unparalleled in our sources for having what purports to be their own words – the teaching of women – preserved by men. This must be entered into with reservations, for their testimony comes from the *Apophth-*

thegmata Patrum, the *Sayings of the Fathers*, the product of 'an essentially fluid and changing tradition' (Ward 1975a:xiv) which were passed on through many hands and memories with accretions and wrong attributions, being regarded primarily for their value in spiritual edification rather than as a verifiable historic witness to the sayings of a given person. However, for us it is more than significant that even under these unreliable conditions, the teaching of three women was deemed to be edifying, and worthy of representation and collection under their own names; appended as persons of note with the implicit expectation that the monks of the time would recognise their renown. The third is Amma Sarah, who as a female solitary, living as a hermit, was even more *sui generis* in the sources and will be considered in a separate context. Theodora and Syncletica were at least familiar and identifiable as possessing a role as abbesses of convents of nuns; it may be significant that in this position they seem to have been the confidantes and advisors of monks, whereas Sarah, taking on a spiritual task regarded in the desert as being much heavier – and very rare in women – for all that her sayings were preserved, evidently attracted a certain amount of hostile attention from some men.

While we know nothing schematic about the history or origins of these women, a certain amount of background may be gleaned from their teachings. It is possible that Theodora may be identified with the woman of the same name known to Palladius, 'the wife of a tribune who reached such a depth of poverty that she became a recipient of alms, and finally died in the monastery of Hesychias near the sea' (*LH* 41). That background would certainly fit the Theodora of the *Sayings*, who was a woman of education and the product of a well-to-do environment. Her sayings reflect a wider world than is displayed by many of the abbas, numbers of whom originated from the illiterate Egyptian and Palestinian peasantry, in whose company the indulgences displayed by Abba Arsenius 'the Roman' were noted as standing out, and whose sayings were more concerned with everyday exigencies of nourishment, work and the struggle with the passions. In the sayings attributed to Theodora, we find a scriptural question to Olympias' *bête noir*, the combative Archbishop Theophilus of Alexandria (*Alph.* Theodora 1); a discussion of the difference in the teaching of a Christian and a Manichaean on the body (Theodora 4) and references to 'sitting at a table where there are many courses' (*ibid.* 8). Theodora's position seems to have been that of a widely accessible and broad-ranging teacher and sage. A number of questions were put to her by 'an old man' (the generic term in these sources for the desert-dwelling monastic), many of whom she evidently counselled; monks figure largely in the instructional tales she told. Her subject matter included analyses of the ascetic life, theological insights on the body, resurrection and humility, and pronouncements on the rationale for teaching and the qualities of mind necessary in a teacher: patience, humility, a lack of desire for domination and vainglory – above all, 'he must be tested' (*ibid*. 5).

If Theodora seems to be presiding over a well-bred desert symposium of mixed company, Syncletica speaks to us from a more homely and secluded community, and her sayings are derived from her shrewd, down-to-earth observations upon it. 'She uses the imagery of the laundry, the infirmary and the dinner table to express her ideas' (Ward 1985:64) in analysing the trials and temptations of the ascetic life for the benefit of her nuns and in addition uses images taken from seafaring and agricultural husbandry. As distinct from Theodora's lofty considerations, there is a more direct and pithy commonsense in Syncletica's pronouncements such as 'do not gorge on bread and you will not crave wine' (*Alph*. Syncletica, 4) and 'when you must fast, do not imagine to yourself that you are ill' (*ibid*. 9) and a trenchant pronouncement on the greed of merchants, turned to an uplifting metaphor for the proper Christian greed for commerce with God (*ibid*. 10). An ascetic herself, she yet shows a blunt realism about extremist observances: 'Obedience is preferable to asceticism. The one teaches pride and the other humility' (*ibid*. 16) and

> There are many who are living out in the wilderness but behaving as though they were still in the town; their efforts are wasted. For it is possible to be a solitary in mind and spirit while living in the midst of a throng of people; or to live as a solitary while pressed about as though by an unruly crowd by one's own thoughts.
>
> (*Alph*. Syncletica 19)

She counsels on disputes and grievances in the tone of one who has settled many such amongst the sisters; on temptation, negligence and moderation as a veteran who has seen many forms of error and and indulgence. Syncletica also, like Theodora, had opinions on teaching, and the necessary qualifications for it, which are of a piece with this pragmatism: while Theodora's priorities are suitable qualities of mind, Syncletica considered 'it is not safe for someone to teach if he has not first had the discipline of the practical life' (*ibid*. 12), since while words might lead to salvation, evil behaviour certainly led to downfall.

A few other ammas of this stratum we do know about, although not from the honour of their teachings being preserved. Palladius, being concerned, as he says, to fairly represent the case of women also, since many there were in the desert 'to whom God has apportioned labours equal to those of men', carefully presents some exemplary personalities amongst his generalities about the communities of women; some of the things he says about them are more revealing about the state of community life when it was not so exemplary. He is inadvertently enlightening on what he finds most notable about the convent of the 'great' Amma Talis, for instance: she was

> an old woman who had spent eighty years in asceticism, as she and the neighbours told me. With her dwelt sixty young women who loved her so greatly that there was not even a key fixed on the outer wall of the convent, as in other convents, but they were kept in by love of her.
>
> (*LH* 59)

This was evidently an impressive feat in the head of a convent and worth highlighting.

Egeria also gives testimony of another abbess at work, in her *Pilgrimage*; indeed, this woman is extremely rare amongst those that Egeria met in that she writes of her by name rather than by function, and with flattering attention: this is 'my very dear friend, the holy deaconess Marthana, to whose life everyone in the East bears witness' who governed the monastic cells of 'holy monastics or apotactites, both men and women' at, significantly, the *martyrium* of St Thecla, near Seleucia (*Egeria* 23.3). Egeria is writing to assure her sisters of the particular devotion that is paid to St Thecla still, and of someone who, half a world away, 'is carrying on the living tradition of an ecclesiastical woman with authority and responsibility as are they' (Wilson-Kastner *et al.* 1981:76). Possibly, Marthana is specially marked out because she is the only person in the journal that Egeria considered a friend and a colleague and an ecclesiastical equal. From our point of view she is particularly worthy of note as being the person of authority not merely over other women, but over a mixed community; but with no sign of a parallel male head superior. If true (and Egeria is usually punctilious in noting and honouring every passing cleric), it would make Marthana highly unusual (though we know also of a highly regarded female leader of a mixed Monophysite community (Harvey 1990:124)). Not one of the dynamic aristocratic women who set up or presided over monastic foundations of men and women conjoined did not have a male figurehead for their men's foundations.

In this connection we should consider another variety of dedicated life which has great relevance to the question of whether monastic life gave women legitimate authority; the non-community holy women, those living in seclusion as hermits and solitaries, either in the wilderness proper, or within their own homes. Accepting Michael Whitby's analysis of the 'anti-social holy man',[9] who was seen as fulfilling a ministry even though remote, truculent and misanthropic, it is plain that the same tendencies were shown and expectations raised of the anchoresses and housebound solitary nuns; those who lived individually a pattern of the lifestyle of, and fulfilled the functions of, a monastic life, while not living in a community or a foundation as such. Those staying close to points of habitation sometimes remained at large within the community, but more often retired to live in seclusion within their own households, being thus neither a conventual as such, nor an anchoress, but occupying a curious half-way position between the two; this was one of the earliest forms of leading a consecrated life before state sanction of the church made it less hazardous to start banding together for mutual support. Some of these 'household communities' indeed lived in small domestic or familial groups, but were not constituted as an attempt at community life, open to outsiders and ultimately accorded a rule and a head; they owed more to the example of the solitaries than to what was to become conventual community life.

Besides those household communities we have already encountered, such as those run by Marcella and Marcellina (see p. 92), there are numerous instances in our sources of women who 'cultivated solitude and would meet no one' but who 'practised virtue ardently and scrupulously', 'in seclusion', 'in her house' (*LH* and *Apoph.*, *passim*). Palladius chronicles any number of them in the *Lausiac History*, some of them by name – Piamoun, Magna, Juliana for example – besides a host of anonymous women referred to just as 'a holy virgin' who hid fugitive clerics (*LH* 63, 64), hid themselves (*ibid.* 28, 37, 60), gave inspiration (*ibid.* 34) or material benefits (*ibid.* 61, 67) or sometimes prophecy (*ibid.* 31) to their community, or displayed unbecoming spiritual pride (*ibid.* 37), or avarice (*ibid.* 6), or fell from grace (*ibid.* 28, 70), or sometimes recovered from a fall through penitence (*ibid.* 69). We know more about the observances of the Roman women practising this kind of life such as Marcella's circle, whose regime was detailed to some degree by Jerome. But we can take them as a reasonable example, since the *humiliores* had acted as a model for them in the first place; since, as previously stated, the aristocratic women though most publicised were not at all in the forefront of the movement to adopt these lifestyles, but followed the impulse for asceticism already in existence and percolating through from the lower levels of society. It is therefore reasonable to infer that, just so they would have adopted and adapted the practices of the classes whom Palladius attests to have been leading this life early enough to influence Anthony and for one of them to have given sanctuary to Origen (*LH* 64).

These household nuns seem to have lived in a fairly severe regime: all traces of creature comforts were banished, putting aside fair clothing and cosmetics for coarse, squalid dress, shunning bathing, and sleeping on hard mats on the floor, combined with stringent and continuous fasts (Jerome *Let.* 24). The seclusion was broken only by secret visits, often made at night, to martyrs' tombs or basilicas for worship, though in some cases even this was denied; as in the virgin noted above (see p. 77) who had not appeared in public for 25 years and was taken to task by Abba Serapion for being isolated through spiritual pride; or Amma Taor, who for 30 years refused to make any change of clothing or shoes – to the end that it would be impossible for her to appear abroad even if she had a reason to do so (*LH* 59); or the nun who lived next door to Palladius who 'was a neighbour of mine, but I did not see her face, for she never came out, so they say, from the day she renounced the world' (*ibid.* 60). Some more conspicuously failed in the standards: such as the household nun that Palladius refers to simply as 'The rich virgin', who, 'having fallen away from her aspirations after heaven', clung to her wealth and thought to keep it for her family rather than helping the poor and needy or the church, and whose re-education Macarius of Alexandria took in hand (*ibid.* 54); and the household virgins who 'fell', victims to carnal urgings and sinned, with their serving-man, or with another cleric (*ibid.* 28, 69, 70; *Anon. Apoph.* 132).

But of humbler women who achieved this standard and status, quietly and unsung, there were many examples, often noticed by only a line in passing, to let us know that it was possible for such as these, not even known by name like as not: that such-and-such had shut herself up in her house, living alone, or with 'her mother', eating only every other day or never going out. Palladius gives us one slightly more active example of her genre, however, whose name is known: Magna, who demonstrates alternatively the kind of useful activity that could be found by a woman so motivated, in her own community and of more use, probably, than the majority of secluded conventuals, for all it necessitated her going abroad. She was one of the women who had no choice in the matter of a husband but was forced into marriage all unwilling by her mother; in the style of Ammonas, she is related to have 'wheedled [her husband] and put him off' in the bridal chamber so that she 'remained inviolate'; and after his death not long after, she

> gave herself wholly to God, attending in a most serious spirit to her own house, living a most ascetic and continent life, having her conversation such that the very bishops revered her for the excellence of her religion. While she provided for the needs, primary and secondary, of hospitals, the poor and bishops on tour, she ceased not to work in secret with her own hands and by means of her most faithful servants, and at nights she did not leave the church.
>
> (*LH* 67)

In this instance, it is probably significant that Magna is a widow – or rather, another virgin-widow like Olympias – at all events, she is *sui iuris* and evidently used to handling her own property; and she bent herself, her devotion and her manifestly respectable resources to the assistance of her local community. But we have seen Piamoun (see p. 70) as an enclosed household virgin serving her community equally materially and yet without material resources, by supernatural means, through prophecy of natural disasters and prayerful protection. In this, Magna and Piamoun in their different ways are conspicuously of more overt, practical service than Marcella, or the virgin Serapion rebuked, or Palladius' neighbour, who held themselves aloof from their surroundings, devoting themselves rather to the necessities of the next life: but there is no suggestion that Magna and Piamoun were lacking in attention to that end through being more actively involved in service to their community – rather the reverse in the case of Magna, whom 'the very bishops revered for the excellence of her religion' (*ibid.*).

The anchoresses

There was, then, an ambivalence as to the proper end for a consecrated female; contemplative or active, Mary or Martha – Asella or

Paula. Nor was this just a problem for the women: it was the counterpart of the current debate in the male devotional circles over proper priorities. This was the source of divergence amongst ecclesiastics widely; many were the snide comments made in the more austere writings to the effect that it was difficult to listen to secular speech and live for God alone, which may be taken as a dig at urban bishops and clergy, compelled to do just that. This was a dilemma felt very deeply by some of sensitive conscience such as Evagrius and Arsenius, who consequently abandoned the haunts of men and the active practice of their urban ministry as being the source of temptation (*Alph.* Arsenius and Evagrius). But while a life amongst men was still accepted as necessary by the generality of clergy, although sneered at by the desert dwellers, the debate raged most fiercely within monastic circles as to whether one could be a true monk while maintaining connections with temporal life: whether the fittest way to serve God was to assist his other creatures on earth, or to secede entirely and attempt the perfection of one of them in oneself.

On this topic we find even writers from similar backgrounds and world views showing great ambivalence. The monastics responsible for the Anonymous Collection of the *Sayings of the Fathers* relate the tale of three friends, two of them active in the community, healing religious divisions and visiting the sick respectively, the last a contemplative 'in prayer and stillness in the desert'. In this story, the judgement handed down is that the third brother is living the best monastic life: the first two are related to have found their labours ultimately impossible and disheartening, and gone together to the third brother, who instructed them that 'for those who live among men, disturbances prevent them from seeing their faults. But when a man is still, especially in the desert, then he sees his failings' (*Anon. Apoph.* 134). But in the same anonymous collection, we subsequently find, offered as equally edifying, the completely contradictory standpoint:

A brother questioned an old man, saying, "Here are two brothers. One of them leads a solitary life for six days a week, giving himself much pain, and the other serves the sick. Whose work does God accept with greater favour?" The old man said, "Even if the one who withdraws from the world were to hang himself up by the nostrils, he could not equal the one who serves the sick."

(*Anon. Apoph.* 380 – trans. Ward)

192

It is in this context that the divergence between the women who were active in the community and those who withdrew to look into their own centre should be understood; they met with equally conflicting advice, those following the former way drawing the censure of the rigorists such as Jerome and Chrysostom that they went abroad too readily, and ministered in the community as a cover for an imperfect life, those of the latter way incurring such criticisms as that of Serapion to the anonymous virgin (see p. 77), and the Abba above that such solitude led to a completely self-oriented worship and a tendency to spiritual pride.

Many women, however, did absorb this ideal of complete isolation before God and became as noted proponents as the men of the most extreme tendency of eremitism, the way of the Solitary: we must here examine the ministry of the anchoresses. That this was actually a popular life-choice for devout women in the Eastern empire is indicated by the many examples we have of these, both those identified with known histories and the many brief passing references to individuals, named or anonymous. And yet, frequency of occurrence is no indicator of the ease of the path: on the contrary, their evidence is presented in such a way that it is clear that this was for women an odd and difficult choice and the female solitary a *res miranda*.

In the first instance, the numbers of them who were taken for males, and who deliberately fostered this idea about themselves argues a great need to hide their sex if embarking on this lifestyle. An instance of this is the case of the harlot-turned-hermit, Pelagia. She was an actress and courtesan of great note in Antioch who was 'rescued' from her immense fame and wealth by Nonnus, the monk-bishop of Edessa who had originated from the famous ascetic monastery of Tabennisi, and who was in town for a conference called by the bishop of Antioch. In the great penance imposed on her by Nonnus after her conversion, immediately following her baptism she fled secretly in male attire borrowed from Nonnus, 'went to Jerusalem and built a cell for herslf on the Mount of Olives' and achieved no small fame in the locality as 'a certain brother Pelagius, a monk and a eunuch, who has lived there for some years shut up in solitude' and 'performed many marvels'. When James the Deacon, the writer of her life, was sent there years afterwards at the instance of Nonnus, who was privy to the secret all along, he failed to recognise her when he saw her first, for the beauty so famed in Antioch, 'loveliness so great that all the world of men could never weary of it', had been transformed by the rigour of her life; 'how could I know her again, so wasted and haggard as she was with fasting? Her eyes seemed to have had sunk into great holes in her face.' James then discovered her death a few days after and alerted the monks from the nearby monasteries. The first reaction of her neighbours and colleagues in Christ to her true status is illuminating:

> They carried out the holy little body as if it had been jewels or precious metal they were carrying. When the fathers began anointing the body with myrrh, they discovered it was a woman. They would have hidden this marvellous thing, but they could not because of the people pressing round, who shouted aloud, "Glory to you, Lord Jesus Christ, who has such treasures hidden away on earth, women as well as men." So it became known to all the people.
>
> (*Life of Pelagia the Harlot* 15)

Though unusual in the detail it gives us, the story of Pelagia's eremitism represents a pattern of its kind in the desert sources: of the female solitary disguised as a man, whom the monks come upon just in time to bury and discover the truth, the tale usually purporting to be told by eyewitnesses or by the monks involved. Bessarion and his disciple Doulas, as told by Doulas, while on their way to visit John of Lycopolis, came upon a cave in which they found 'a brother sitting and making a plait of palm-leaves; and he would not look at us or acknowledge us or speak to us'. Returning by the same route, they determined to visit again and see if the anchorite would be moved to speech:

> When we entered, we found him lying dead. The old man said to me, "Come, brother, let us take up the body; God has sent us here for this purpose, that we may bury him." When we lifted up the body, we found that it was a woman. Marvelling greatly, the old man said, "See how the women wage war against the devil in the desert while we live shamefully in the towns." And having glorified God . . . we went on our way.
>
> (*Alph.* Bessarion 4; *PJ* 20.1)

The anonymous *Sayings* impassively record another example. Except for this one divergence of being told of a female, this tale is in itself typical in all respects of the experience of the desert monk; hence suggestive of the similarities between the male and female experience of suffering in extreme *ascesis*:

Some seculars visited an anchorite; when he saw them he received them joyfully, saying "God sent you so that you could bury me. For I have received my call; but for your benefit and that of others, I shall tell you of my life. Brothers, I am a virgin in body as in soul; but up until this very moment, I have been tempted almost beyond endurance by fornication. Indeed, as I am talking to you, I see the angels waiting to take my soul; meanwhile Satan is standing by and suggesting lustful thoughts to me." When he had finished speaking, he laid himself down and died. While making the body ready, the seculars found that he was in fact a woman.

(*Anon. Apoph.* 63)

Some of these women, indeed, carried out the deception so success-fully that a recurring problem amongst male monastics of the desert assumes a new piquancy in being applied to them: the accusation of having impregnated local maidens. A detailed history of one such case given in the Syrian *Lausiac History* concerns one Maria, who did not merely disguise her sex to be an anchorite, but successfully infiltrated a male community, with the help of her father who became a monk. When sent out to beg for the house, Mary (in her male guise renamed Maryana) became the victim of one of these almost formu-laic accusations by a girl in the locality of which we find so many examples in the tales of the desert Fathers (not all baseless by any means); who, left in trouble by a local man, told her father 'it was the monk who seduced me'. Her father and Maryana's community believed her and Maryana was refused admittance to the monastery when 'he' returned from 'his' wanderings. The upshot was that Maryana proved her fitness for inclusion into the austere brother-hood by displaying the extremes of self-abasement proper to the desert-dweller being tested by God: she took on herself unresisting the burden of guilt and opprobrium, accepted the charge, and, ultimately, the baby as her own, and did penance at the door of the monastery for four years until deemed worthy of re-admittance. In this, she manifested an entirely proper ascetic attitude: we have tales of other desert monastics gladly accepting the blame and doing extravagant penance for crimes they had not committed, merely rejoicing in the chance of waging a still doughtier struggle for the faith. Maryana's 'sin' was more preposterous, but that would make her all the fitter for the life by her unhesitating acceptance of it and the responsibility, since in the desert mentality the chance to struggle was seen as a privilege accorded those who were stronger in the faith. So her actions were consistent, she even after her re-admittance declining to prove her colleagues wrong but persisting for the rest of her life in penance for her 'crime': in formulaic fashion, they discovered the mistake and her true sex only after her death, to general astonishment and edification and the remorse of the accuser (Syriac *LH* 2.26).

The most obvious reason for the switch is, of course, the risk. Being lone in an already hostile environment carried hazards that were accepted as part of the testing of the soul; doing so as a female would guarantee extra unwanted attention. Abba Patermuthius, before he was converted to *ascesis* had been a bandit and the story was told of how he had attempted a robbery upon an anchoress (*HM* 10.3). Abba Paphnutius was directed by heavenly insight to seek out another former brigand of reformed life; amongst other incidences of piety, 'once in his days as a brigand, he rescued a nun who was about to be raped by a gang of robbers and at night led her back to her village' (*ibid.* 14.4). The many church councils promulgating edicts to decide the status of nuns and anchoresses who had been raped indicate the commonplace nature of the problem amongst those consecrated women who retained their skirts, even those living in comparative safety in community life. To present oneself as a sitting target by being an evidently female solitary must have required a more than ordinarily firm resolution in the life. We have evidence of a probably reasonably common solution in the case of the anchoress whom Patermuthius attempted to rob; she lived in a hermitage alone, but near a community of priests with a church who looked after her (*ibid.* 10.3). The anchoresses' vulnerability to rape and pillage, however, did not by much distinguish them from their male colleagues who witnessed, or suspected each other of, similar assaults on boys, and who told cheerful homilies about assisting robbers to denude themselves of their own few possessions.[10]

But if not alone in this, the female proponents of the solitary life certainly had a problem that their male colleagues did not have that added greater moment to the need to disguise their sex: namely, a truculent attitude towards female solitaries from those who could have assisted, their own male colleagues in the life. That Bessarion's attitude of edified admiration that a woman could achieve where his brethren were failing was not typical we have seen in the attitude of the monks attempting to cover up the embarrassing fact of Pelagia's femaleness; it is reinforced by the experiences related of Amma Sarah, the anchoress who achieved the accolade of her own place in the Alphabetical collection of the *Apopththegmata*. Sarah's life was a model one by the standards of desert monastics, according to the *Sayings*. 'It was said about her that she lived beside a river for sixty years and she never lifted her eyes to look at it' (*Alph.* Sarah 3); and on being visited by monks and offering them fruit for refreshment, she complimented them when they took the bad fruit and left the good on being 'true monks of Scetis' according to the best precepts of self-discipline and the conquest of the fleshly will (Sarah 8). Despite this exemplary attitude, and a prolonged struggle against sexual temptation on a par with those fought by male monastics (and related in exactly the same style), Sarah had to add to her trials hostility from her male colleagues:

> On one occasion, two old men who were anchorites from the district of Pelusium came to visit Amma Sarah. As they walked, one said to the other, "Let us humble this old woman." So they said to her, "Be careful that you don't puff yourself up with pride, saying to yourself, 'Look how men who are anchorites come to visit me, a woman.'" But Amma Sarah said to them, "I am a woman in sex, but not in spirit."
>
> (*Alph.* Sarah 4; *PJ* 10.73)

The weary tone of another of her sayings indicated that male uncharitableness was something she frequently endured: 'If I asked God that all men should approve of my conduct, I should find myself a penitent at the door of each one; rather shall I pray that my heart be pure towards all' (*Alph.* Sarah 5). In addition, 'She also said to the monks: "It is I that am a man and you that are women"' (*ibid.* 9). The self-deprecating willingness to learn from a fellow-fighter who happened to be female that we find in Bessarion and James the Deacon is little in evidence here; perhaps Bessarion and James were the exception and the attitude of some of the monks around Sarah and those who tried to re-disguise Pelagia was more the kind of attitude women attempting to become solitaries could expect – in which case their decision to stay in male attire, or simply as invisible as possible becomes even more cogent. Benedicta Ward says of Sarah's example, 'Sarah was accepted but it is clear that to achieve this she had in effect to become a man' (Ward 1985:65). In fact, this is far from clear: the significant thing about Sarah is that she precisely did *not* 'become a man' as did all those 'brothers' who turned out to have been women all along; she was clearly identifiable as a woman being a solitary, which was why she was *not* readily accepted, but given rigorous testing. Ward also regards the option to don male attire as symbolic of the transcendence of gender that went with the liberation of *anachoreisis*, thus by implication a liberation in itself as well as a protection from the attention of marauders; I think it is probable that Pelagia and the others who achieved anonymity by means of this route more simply found it a device of liberation from unwanted notice as much from their colleagues as from bandits.

In Pelagia's case, however, this may have been an additional necessity because of her former fame, or infamy; not for her the comfort of Sarah's self-knowledge of the blamelessness of her life. Nor was she alone in this; not a few women came to the extreme of the anchoress's life out of a particular need for its greater hardships and rewards. There are many tales left us of exemplary penitents who were reformed courtesans performing their expiation for having led so many other souls along the path to damnation. Their stories in fact become somewhat formulaic in character: the woman famed in beauty and notorious in morals leading many souls to doom until brought by the perseverances of a charismatic holy man to a cognisance of their own likely end, whereon they adopt the most extravagant penances which are the wonder of all beholders. The story of Pelagia and Nonnus follows this pattern; Pelagia actively sought out her conversion at the hands of the one man who felt disposed to offer her help, the other bishops turning their heads at the very sight of her – and by inference drawing aside the hem of their garments. Once converted by Nonnus, to general consternation she simply disappeared the night after her baptism, until she was discovered in death disguised as a male anchorite, as related above. The implication is that Nonnus had given her her choice in working out her own expiation with his loving advice and help. Abba Serapion converted an unnamed courtesan in the *Sayings* in similar fashion, and like Nonnus, left her to work out the details of her salvation, conducting her to a convent of virgins and saying to the sister in charge: 'Take in this sister; do not put her under any restraint or rule as you do the other sisters, but allow her to have what she wants and to go where she pleases' (*Alph*. Serapion 1). The penitent woman herself then asked for gradually harsher regimes to be given to her – eating only every second day, then every fourth day, until at her own request she was enclosed completely in a cell and given only a little food and work through the window. However, the more famous story of another prostitute-turned-solitary, Thaïs, presents a harsher picture of what the penitential female might expect at the hands of an austere desert abba. As a prostitute she was sought out by the stern Abba Paphnutius who, having convinced her of the danger to the souls of herself and others by her lifestyle, also led her to a monastery of virgins. Here the similarities end. Papnutius is depicted as putting her into a small cell, the door of which he then proceeded to seal up with lead to leave only a small opening for food and water. This action seems to have allowed little room for the desert Fathers avowed tenet that each believer should only perform such observations as he felt up to, and lays itelf open to the interpretation that he was more concerned that if her resolve were to weaken she should not in any case be able to backtrack and ruin the effect of his notable conversion. Thaïs' prior awareness of and consent to this procedure is depicted as at best dubious:

> When Thaïs realised that the door was sealed with lead, she said to him, 'Father, where do you want me to urinate?' and he replied, 'In the cell, as you deserve.' Then she asked how she should pray to God, and he said to her, 'You are not worthy to name God or to take his divine name upon your lips, or to lift up your hands to heaven, for your lips are full of sin and your hands are stained with iniquity; only stand facing towards the east and repeat often only this: "You who have made me, have mercy upon me".'
>
> (*Life of St Thaïs the Harlot* 3 – trans. Ward)

Seemingly faced with little or no choice, Thaïs spent three years thus; after which it is not surprising to learn that she was judged worthy of such a glorious reception in heaven that the monk who had a vision of it first assumed that it must have been prepared for the great Anthony himself before being told it was for 'the harlot Thaïs (*ibid.* 3). Paphnutius promptly went to unseal Thaïs, who by this time did not wish for release but 'begged to be allowed to be left and shut up in there'; again, she was given no choice but was 'taken out' (*ibid.*). She died fifteen days after her enforced release from her enforced incarceration.

Marginally less formulaic, and accordingly more informative are those reformed harlots who the sources reveal had not altogether turned to their harlotry of their own volition, but whose evil life may actually be laid at the door of the 'old men' who convert them away from it again; earning for themselves the plaudits of Christian opinion, and for their penitents a lifetime of tears by so doing. One such 'prostitute' Paësia, converted to the status of penitent by Abba John the Dwarf, had commenced her story as a devoutly Christian orphan heiress of charitable disposition: like Paula, her charities outstripped her means and she was reduced to a condition of poverty where selling her body became a necessity when 'her means were exhausted until she was in need' as a direct result of her decision 'to turn her house into a hospice for the fathers of Scetis' (*Alph*. John the Dwarf 40). But she is presented as reaping her reward eventually: once the 'deeply grieved' Abba John the Dwarf had brought her back to her correct order of priorities and led her with him in penitence out into the desert, where she promptly died, he observed her to go straight to heaven with 'the angels bearing away her soul'. This was deemed to be not bad going: 'One single hour of repentance has gained more for her than that of many who do penance continually, but without ever displaying such ardour' (*ibid*.). Maria 'the Harlot', niece of Abba Abraham, similarly has her place in this genre; she only turned to her harlotry after she had been seduced almost under the nose of her awesomely ascetic uncle and had fled rather than face telling him (cf. pp. 73–5); she too won free of her years of degradation by such perfect penitence that ultimately she gained not only the assurance of salvation but the power of healing while on earth.

This extraordinary power of penitence demonstrated by these women hitherto steeped in the squalor of complete subjection to bodily sin, penitence that was able to put them on a par with ascetics possessed of lifelong freedom from the flesh, was of great fascination to the Fathers; these are only some of the stories told of 'polluted' women arriving at a greater state of grace than lifelong ascetics. But some of the thinking behind this seeming contradiction can be seen addressed on a more theoretical level by Paulinus of Nola, in a letter to Sulpicius Severus in which he addressed the question of female modesty. This led him on to a discussion of the archetype of penitent harlots, Mary of Magdala, who washed Christ's feet with her hair, along with ointment and tears. She, who has been both immodest and impure originally, has her status not just restored but actually elevated by her humility and repentance, says Paulinus, achieving remission of sins and the glory of being in the Gospel; and not only this, but she is by virtue of this 'worthy to pre-figure the Church that is to be called forth from the Gentiles, bearing within her all the signs of the mystery of salvation' (Paulinus of Nola *Let*. 23.31 ff.) – this for a woman who has proved all too evidently her own subjection to sin through carnality. But through her humbleness and willing subjection to the Lord's judgement she attains glory; 'she anticipated us in taking onto her hands and mouth the living, life-giving Bread itself' and is preferred to the Pharisee, that man without sin, for 'she tasted and felt Christ's body and fasted while he feasted': in sum, 'she deserved to symbolise the Church' (*ibid.*). This may represent a metaphor of what might be attained by the devoted woman, however sinful: a consciousness of sin and subjection properly displayed in conjunction with devotion to the immolatory ideal as the means to achieve more than ordinary standing when returned to the body of the Church.

As an addendum and an illuminating sidelight to the category of penitential female monastics should be considered the maid-turned-anchoress Alexandra; she was not a harlot, in fact, and so is proof that not only the great sinners in the flesh, but more ordinary women followed the logic of patristic theology in matters of this kind. She judged herself by these same criteria of being a sinful, because fleshly, woman and, obeying patristic logic, regarded the cause for tempta-tion in others as a sin in oneself, and imposed a harsh penance on herself because of it. She 'left the city and shut herself up in a tomb, receiving the necessities of life through an opening, and seeing neither men nor women face to face for ten years' and lived out her life 'waiting for my end with cheerful hope' and filling the time spinning flax, praying and meditating 'on the holy patriarchs and prophets and apostles and martyrs' (*LH* 5). When Melania the Elder, who visited her, asked her the reason for her lifestyle,

> she called out to me through the opening: "A man was disturbed in his mind because of me and so that I should not afflict or dishonour him, I chose to go into the tomb alive, rather than cause a soul made in the image of God to lapse."
>
> (*LH* 5.)

These women accepted their place in the scheme of things according to the patristic outlook; in abasing themselves and doing extravagant penance for indulging in sexual licence (or in Alexandria's case, merely provoking another's sexual fantasy), they are fulfilling the male monastic association of the feminine with the body and the sexual, and demonstrating the supplicatory relationship with God that many of the clerics of the time felt most appropriate from women. It is worthwhile remembering Sarah's difficulties in this context. Though a fighter against the temptation of sexual urges, like the men, she had no such shameful history to relate, it seems – and the monastic writers are keen to tell us of inspirational figures converted from such lifestyles – so that in her ministry she was preaching from a position of strength. This is barely discernible from the confrontational nature of her contacts with the monks: perhaps they were more at ease with more sinful women who were hence constrained to express the abjection felt to be proper to female worship. Sarah was fighting her nature from on a level with the men near her; and seems to have endured their uncomprehending resentment as a consequence.

PLEBEIAN *DYNAMEIS*: SHIFTING FROM BELOW

Something that emerges from studies of these non-élite, uncelebrated holy women is how they too, in their more limited orbit, show some of the same tendencies towards confronting and confounding clerics as did the élite females from whom it could be more expected. Women we often do not even have names for – 'a certain virgin', 'a certain widow', or just 'a nun' demonstrate that they too have imbibed the idea that being female need not deter them from showing themselves to be in the right over unwary clerics if they feel they have adequate cause and are in a position to edify. Just as Albina took Augustine to task and Melania scolded Jovinus as one fighter to another, so Sarah challenged Paphnutius when she found him to be lacking in discernment: '[Sarah] sent someone to say to Abba Paphnutius "Have you really done the work of God by letting your brother be despised?"' and Paphnutius was just as stung as Augustine: 'Abba Paphnutius said "Paphnutius is here with the intention of doing the work of God and he has nothing to do with anyone else!"' (*Alph.* Paphnutius 6). A passionate squabble in the same vein over dignity and precedence between male and female monastics, in Egypt in the early fifth century, can be seen in a portion of an extremely hostile letter that exists from Abba Shenoute of Athribe to Amma Tachom, the head of a convent attached to his. Tachom has defied him or set up her authority in opposition to his, apparently resisting the imposition of a priest that Shenoute had sent to her convent and whom she took exception to; and Shenoute takes a strong line with her.

> I come to you vengefully, since the sound of your folly fills the village where you are, not because I am lord over you, but for the love of God... If you do not know what [message]

is proper to send us – namely, "forgive me" ... then you do not understand anything. And if your "father" is not the one we sent in accordance with order and the rules of God, then you yourself are not a "mother" ... If you are not a wise mother, what will those who call you "mother" do to become wise without you?

(*CSCO* 42.21–22; trans. Timbie in Kraemer 1988:125)

This is rather reminiscent of the nuns to whom Augustine wrote, who were agitating against their superior, with whom they could not get on and riotously demanding their own choice of superiors. Tachom, evidently a force to be reckoned with since Shenoute says he has heard of her over a long time in the surrounding district, has made no bones about shunning Shenoute's nominee, refusing point-blank even to meet with him: Shenoute warns darkly 'If you say of the one whom we sent "we are not his" though he is your brother in the flesh, then you have separated yourself from us' (*ibid.*). These are two career monastics in full battle array over authority and the right to self-determination; it would be good to know the outcome of this dispute. The tone is directly comparable with that of the contretemps between Sarah and Paphnutius above, Sarah's incident distinguished only in the fact of it being the female to take the lead in rebuking the male cleric (though we can infer that Tachom did not deal gently with Shenoute from the tenor of his reply). Sarah, further, felt herself able to comment on the fitness of male visitors to qualify as true monks of Scetis, and to take on the two 'old men' by virtue of her confidence in her own way of life, as examined above. An anonymous amma similarly scores off an 'old man'; to the tacit applause of other 'old men', since they included it in the *Sayings*: 'A monk met some nuns on the road, and at the sight of them turned aside. Their superior said to him, "If you had been a perfect monk, you would not have looked close enough to discover that we were women"' (*PJ* 4.62).

Further, as a counterpoint to all the stories of clinging womenfolk importuning their monastic relatives to see them, we have also stories of female consecrated relatives who decline to compromise their dedication by seeing male relatives, even if also consecrated, judging it imprudent:

A brother went to visit his sister, who lay ill in her convent. She was greatly devout; and she was unwilling even to see a man, or to cause her brother temptation by his coming for her sake into the company of women, so she sent him only a message, saying "Go, my brother and pray for me; for by Christ's grace, I will see you again in the kingdom of heaven."

(*PJ* 4.61)

Further offsetting the tales of monks tempted by wanton women and succumbing or resisting, are a group of tales of women rebuking or holding off monks who (sometimes in their first meeting with women in years) had solicited them: one such brother when sent out of his *coenobium* on an errand chanced across a washerwoman, and, immediately 'overcome', propositioned her; to be told

> It is easy enough to think of, but I could cause you great suffering ... After performing the act you would be attacked by your conscience and you would either give yourself up to despair, or if not, you would still have to go through immense labours to reach again the point at which you are now: therefore, before you subject yourself to that pain, go on your way in peace.
>
> (*Anon.* 49)

This fairly sophisticated, if somewhat optimistic, appraisal did succeed in appealing to his conditioning and, much struck, he thanked her and went back to his monastery marvelling, and concluding it would be best never to leave his enclosure again. Another monk was sent on errands to a devout secular who, as so often in these tales, had an attractive daughter by whom he was tempted; in the reverse of the usual pattern in these tales, of false accusations by village girls, she realised this and 'kept herself from appearing to him' till, arriving on one occasion when her father was absent, he approached her, confessing rather pathetically that he had never been with a woman 'which is just why I want to find out what it is like'. She bade him to 'make an effort and pray to God', but 'he did not want to pray'; finally, as a last resort, she told him 'I am in the middle of my menstrual period; noone should come close enough even to smell me because of the odour.' This had the desired effect, and as he recoiled from her in disgust and came to his senses and wept, she drove the lesson home by urging him to think how he would have faced his monastery and her father had he given way to his impulse: 'So I urge you to be wise from now on; and not to want to destroy all the fruits of your hard work just for a little weak pleasure.' He gave thanks for her 'wisdom and self-restraint' – and told the story on for edification to another monk, the narrator of the tale (*Anon.* 52).

Even prostitutes are shown having their share in rebuking erring holy men. Thaïs, when Paphnutius first approached her in the guise of a client had a smart answer ready when he asked 'Let us go within to a more private room if there is one'; She said 'There is one; but if you fear intrusion, noone ever comes into this room – except for God, of course, for no place can be private from the presence of the divine.' But in the case of this unusual client, far from being a rebuke, this was just the kind of answer to assure him that she was ripe for his harsh conversion measures. In the *Life of Saint Ephraim*, a prostitute is represented catching out a desert monk and pointing out to him the moral in a story that is reminiscent of the above rebuke of the amma to the monk. Having gone into the city of Edessa, Ephraim very properly sent up a prayer that as he entered the city he would meet someone with whom to discuss scriptural difficulties. He was much chagrined, then, to first espy walking towards him a woman who was evidently a prostitute – 'what could such a woman know of the Bible?' – only to learn from her unholy lips God's rebuke to his lack of faith.

> The woman walked towards him gazing fixedly at him. Much astonished he said to her, though not impatiently, "Why do you look at me in such a way?" The woman replied referring to the story in Genesis of the creation of man and woman, "It is natural for me to look towards you, since I was formed out of you; but, you should have no cause to look towards me, for you were formed from earth – so it is on that earth that your eyes should be fixed."
>
> (*Life of Saint Ephraim, PL* 73.2321)

THE DEACONESSES

We should lastly consider the ministry of the deaconesses. These women were holding what seems to be the only official position on offer to women of the later period within the church structure; but their condition, though frequently attested and widely used, was still subject to dispute and ambiguity in the eyes of the church hierarchy and so they are rather an anomalous addendum than the primary figures one might have thought in a consideration of Christian female ministry. These women 'took the veil' to exercise authority not by turning their back on the world and all its works, but the reverse; they were by some authorities accorded clerical rank (*ragma*) and dignity (*axioma*) in certain restricted areas (mainly to do with ministering to their own sex) within the church setup. The deaconesses further distinguish themselves by being a category which seems to have included recruits from the ranks of both *honesti* and *humiliores*. Their position (unlike the others we have examined) having at least some sort of job-description and that mainly concerned with moral qualities, in theory any woman upright enough qualified; and we can find as deaconesses notable women from the top drawer of society and socially undistinguished women seemingly drawn from the body of the congregation.

The word has its origins in the New Testament usage of 'diakonos' (as used of Phoebe – Rom. 16:1), simply meaning 'servant' or 'helper' and only gradually acquiring precise ministerial functions, the nature of which varied from period to period and differed in Eastern and Western observance. Fr. Daniélou, in his seminal examination of early female ministries,[11] considers that the constitution of the actual office of deaconess was the church's attempt in the third century to turn the ministry of women into an institution to combat the temptation of greater pay-offs offered to women in the heretical sects, by giving them a 'ministerium' of sorts and entitling them to be listed as ecclesiastical dignitaries; and that once so constituted, they effectively went on to absorb most of the functions and privileges of the existing order of widows, which (though still an active and separate entity in the later period) declined in importance and activeness in our sources from the third century on (see pp. 90ff.).

By the time of the *Apostolic Canons*, the role of the deaconesses was a reasonably distinguished one: they are mentioned after the deacons in the order of church dignitaries and sit to the left of the bishop during the liturgy, parallel to the deacons who sit on his right, and they make their communion first after the deacons. Depending on the location of their church, they might be actually ordained, with the laying on of hands; but this was an Eastern tendency which met with resistance in the West. Where the councils of Nicaea in 325 and Chalcedon in 451 talk in terms of 'ordination' ('Women may not be ordained [*cheirotoneisthai*] under the age of forty', *Council of Chalcedon*, Canon 15), the Council of Orange in 441 stated 'deaconesses should not be in any way ordained'. To qualify for the elevation to near-clerical status, women were carefully scrutinised to ascertain that they fulfilled certain requirements: they must be of irreproachable life, known good character and works, possibly only once-married, and once elevated to the dignity of deaconess, vowed to chastity in the same way as a nun; 'if she takes the veil and keeps the ministry, then gives herself in marriage, to the insult of God's grace, she should be anathematised along with him who married her' (*Apostolic Church Order* 1.23.17). There was also, as seen above, some kind of age qualification: a law of 390 stipulates sixty years of age (*CT* 16.2.27), but church canons evidently diverged from this, as seen above in the Council of Chalcedon's stipulation of an age of forty; and in any case, such a restriction might or might not be rigorously applied, at the discretion of the bishop.

Olympias, for instance, shows the aristocratic facility for circum-navigating regulations again in this: 'notwithstanding her youth, Nectarius had her ordained deaconess' (Sozomen *EH* 8.9) – she seems to have been only thirty (Clark 1979:123). Nectarius, it is worth pointing out, was financially beholden to Olympias; it is a moot point whether such notable piety as Olympias displayed would have been deemed adequate for premature elevation in a woman of lesser background and means.

Their tasks were specifically 'the service of women': in ministry to their own sex, their authority was parallel with that of deacons. This would comprise pastoral and liturgical duties. The pastoral side included sick visiting: 'For there are houses where you [the bishop] cannot send the deacon to the women's quarters because of the unbelievers: there you will send the deaconesses' (*Teaching of the Apostles* 16.134) and 'where Christian women live in the households of unbelievers it is necessary that it should be the deaconess who goes there and visits women who are sick' (*ibid.* 16.135). They instructed and prepared candidates for baptism and catechism, and assisted at the ceremonies:

> In many other matters besides it is necessary to employ the deaconess. First of all, when women descend into the water for baptism, it is necessary that those who thus descend should be anointed with the oil of unction by the deaconess. When no women, and above all, no deaconesses are available, then it is inevitable that he who performs the baptism should anoint her who is baptised. . .
>
> (*Teaching of the Apostles* 12.134)

– the minister would normally only anoint the head, the deaconess having the task of anointing the body of a woman candidate. Then 'When she who is baptised comes out of the water, the deaconess shall receive her, instruct her, and tend to her, in order that the unbreakable seal of baptism may be impressed on her with purity and holiness' (ibid. 15.135). Further, in all matters they should be the intermediary between women and the clergy: 'No woman should approach the deacon or the bishop unaccompanied by the deaconess' (Apostolic Constitutions 2.26.6). Their duties in the congregation were often those of a mere functionary: 'The doorkeepers should stand at the entries for men, the deaconesses at those for women, as the officials responsible for the orderliness of their movements' (ibid. 2.57.10) and if any woman, rich or poor, is without a place, the deaconess must find her one (2.58.7).

We have many samples of how this would work in practice. When Pelagia, the harlot-penitent of Antioch examined above was received into the church by Nonnus, the deaconess Romana figures largely in her preparation from first to last. When Pelagia first expressed her desire for baptism and repentance, Nonnus' first act was to send James, his deacon, to the Bishop of Antioch 'to ask him to send back one of his deaconesses with me ... And he sent with me the lady Romana, the chief of the deaconesses' (Life 8). She fulfilled duties almost exactly as prescribed by the Teaching of the Apostles. She was present at every stage: at Pelagia's baptism, 'the holy lady Romana was her godmother, and she received her and took her to the place of the catechumens' (ibid.) and subsequently took complete charge of the new convert. Pelagia was tempted by the devil 'two days later when [she] was asleep in her room with her godmother the holy Romana' (ibid. 10); and when she wished to communicate with her other godparent 'she sent word to the holy bishop Nonnus through the lady Romana' (ibid. 11). When Pelagia subsequently disappeared, Romana is attested as being distraught with grief – perhaps at the possibility of her own seeming dereliction of duty – until comforted by Nonnus, who had assisted with her disappearance.

More evidence is gained from the Life of Macrina. At the death of his sister, Gregory tells of the rather officious bustling of 'a lady called Lampadion, the leader of the group of sisters, a deaconess in rank' who 'declared she knew Macrina's wishes about burial exactly' (Gregory of Nyssa Life of Macrina 990) and dismissed with great finality his mild suggestion that to put finer clothing on Macrina's body as a last respectful office before burial would not go amiss. She took charge of the body and the preparations for burial, and the behaviour of the sisters at the ceremony. Sozomen also tells us of 'a deaconess of the Macedonian sect', one Eusebia, who was the keeper of the martyrium of the Forty Martyrs in Constantinople (EH 9.2);

Marthana, to whom Egeria accorded such respect also combined the offices of deaconess, keeper to a *martyrium* and head of a community (*Egeria* 23.3, see p. 188). Olympias' greater authoritativeness as a deaconess was to a large degree idiosyncratic as a result of being also a wealthy aristocrat and head of community; nonetheless, being a deaconess was evidently an official legitimation of some value, as bugled in the proud title of her *Life*, the *Life of Olympias, the Deaconess*. The teaching and ministry she displayed, while rooted in personal *dignitas* and influence were justified and validated by her clerical dignity, the church of Constantinople setting the official seal on the actual situation in making her 'leader of the women' as deaconess of the cathedral. It is by virtue of this clerical dignity that she is seen to be 'engaging in much catechizing of unbelieving women' (*Life of Olympias, the Deaconess* 15) and converting her household servants, among all her more typically ascetic personal observances. Indeed, Constantinople seems to have been well provided for as regards deaconesses, since the *Life* also notes that John Chrysostom (whose own aunt was 'the deaconess Sabiniana' whom Palladius had met at Antioch – *LH* 41) as Patriarch 'also ordained as deaconesses of the holy church [Olympias'] three relatives Elisanthia, Martyria and Palladia' and Palladius notes in connection with her also 'Pentadia and Procle, the deaconesses' (*Dialogue* 35). We have nothing of these ladies but their names: though their office gave them respect, Olympias' greater fame was from her greater consequence on every level – it is difficult to resist the conclusion that for her holding the office of deaconess was merely the icing on the cake.

Increasing numbers of deaconesses in the later period appear combining the office with headship of a community. We have noted Marthana and Lampadion in this respect; and it seems to be Olympias' preeminent function in fact, since the enclosed quality of her life and her observation of *ascesis* are always stressed over the public service to the church that the *Apostolic Canons* and *Apostolic Constitutions* lead us to expect of the deaconesses. Once deaconess, she built a monastery south of the cathedral and had constructed 'a path from the monastery up to the narthex of the holy church' (*Life of Olympias, the Deaconess* 6); but though her community thus had a lien on the church, 'no one from outside was permitted to come in to them, the only exception being the most holy patriarch John' (*ibid.* 8). Palladius also has a passing reference to 'the deaconess in charge of a sisterhood' in a convent; into whose charge a cleric gives a virgin whom he has been unjustly accused of seducing, to support her until she gives birth (*LH* 70). In this instance, the deaconess was combining enclosure with service to the church in the community. Further, when Justa, the pious virgin portrayed in the highly suspect *Martyrdom of St Cyprian*, is honoured by Cyprian, the former magician turned bishop, for her part in his conversion, 'honouring her with the deaconship and changing her name from Justa to Justina, the blameless, he made her the mother of all the tender girls who were handmaids of the great God' (Wilson-Kastner 1981:156) – an evidently normal linking, illustrative of what was increasingly expected of deaconesses. One Nicarete, also from Chrysostom's circle, apparently 'would not accept the office of deaconess nor of instructress of the virgins consecrated to the service of the church, because she thought herself unworthy, although the honour was pressed upon her by John' (Sozomen *EH*. 8.23). Manifestly the two go together, as with Olympias and her relatives. What is also evident is the honorific quality that was attached to it; the implication is almost that John wished Nicarete to have the signal honour as a compliment to her life. In this her attitude is very reminiscent of all the clerics we read of who were brought, supremely reluctant, to clerical honours as a kind of honorific rather than as a vocation, and some of whom once consecrated, like Gregory of Nyssa, felt unable to perform the expected duties and retreated again to obscurity. There is something of this in the way also Egeria notes Marthana's 'fame' throughout the world; and Palladius asserts Sabiniana similarly to have been 'venerable' – though presumably being the aunt of John Chrysostom might have been a help in that respect.

There seems to be not a little kudos attached to the dignity: although it is difficult to tell exactly how much was due to the office and how much to personal fame when our most eminent examples were celebrated in their own right – and indeed their personal illustriousness may have swamped that of the office, as with Olympias. However, even this *dignitas* in this rare example of an office for women was relatively short-lived; never really achieving respectability in the West on its own terms (none of the 'Roman' dynamic holy women undertake it), by the fifth century the deaconesses in the East, ordained though they were, were mostly combining the honour with community responsibilities, thus of necessity limiting their administration of authority within the generality of the church. The logical outcome, then, was that their ministry and chief privileges were in the Middle Ages completely subsumed within rules only to be exercised within the cloister: these later developments inheriting the mantle of the female Orders which saw some of the pre-eminent women of the fourth and fifth centuries exercise so much power, but which also defined and crystallised the limitations of this power. Ultimately, personal *auctoritas* was all-important in exercising any kind of *dynameis* within the church; and to assume heavenly precedence was ultimately to forfeit this. For the ideals posited for them were that, as the shining example as head, they should be 'least remarkable' in speech, gait and demeanour, and precisely because they were 'masters of many' they should be 'servants of all': and, most importantly, servants of the church. In any case, such authority as some of these astonishing women displayed rarely outlived the individual: their more modest successors were inevitably put under the yoke by the official, male proponents of the male church hierarchy.

9

CONCLUSION
Holy 'women': the *imago dei* revisited

THE MILLSTONE OF THE FEMALE LEGACY

In the fourth century, the church, only newly legitimated with
Constantine, held out new promise: and women were not behindhand in seeking out established roles. In this process, women
devotees of higher secular status were forging the way, and their
importance in the eyes of the world and the church necessitated a
reconsideration of the rhetoric addressed to the female condition.
One of the primary disadvantages under which women laboured was
that 'because you destroyed God's image, man', women 'deserve to
be judged by men' (Tertullian *On Female Dress* 1.2). Man's judgement on their integral nature was indissolubly linked to the body,
backed by traditional philosophical thinking as by apostolic teaching, and this association was advanced as their historical destiny
following Eve's sin and since at the outset women had tempted the
fallen angels to lust: 'those angels who rushed from heaven on the
daughters of men; so that this shame also attaches to women'
(temptation, as we have seen, being the responsibility of the tempting
party), and 'were thus enslaved' (*ibid.*). But if sufficiently pious,
women were exhorted that they had the potentiality to attain 'that
self-same angelic nature as a reward, the self-same sex as men'(*ibid.*);
as written by men, the reward for being a virtuous female was seen
as negation of her original abject nature.

To attain this quasi-masculine state, 'women must seek wisdom
like men' said early church teachers (Clement of Alexandria *Miscellanies* 8.1275); adopting and adapting from neo-Platonist advice,
such as Porphyry's to his wife: 'Do not consider yourself a woman:
I am not attached to you as a woman. Flee all that is effeminate in
the soul as if you had taken a man's body' (Porphyry *Letter to*

Marcella 33). Some believed such a condition could best be imposed externally, for instance by one's spiritual advisor: Sisinnius the Cappadocian, having collected together a mixed community, bore the responsibility for having curbed the masculine lusts and the feminine elements of the men and women in it 'by his grave manner of life' and 'by self-discipline' 'so that the words of scripture were fulfilled: "in Christ Jesus there is neither man nor woman" (*LH* 49). This was also the path that Hierakas tried, rather less successfully, to follow in Egypt, according to Athanasius (see p. 44). Other believers used their own capacities to de-sex themselves, inducing writers to reassess their potential in rather less didactic and more respectful terms. For Augustine, who knew so many, the church is 'the strong woman' to the extent that 'it would not be decent for us to speak of another woman' (Augustine *Sermon* 37.1–2): for some of the women of his acquaintance were taking note of and obeying the command to rid themselves of the 'nature' which equated with their sex, at their own impulse and according to their own lights.

In fact, we have example after example of women applauded for this capacity; the striking thing about the reports of pious women of the fourth to fifth centuries is how uniformly their virtue is judged in the context of their sex rather than set in a background of Christian achievements of their area or age in general. When women scored points for Christianity, their achievements were accounted as note-worthy not for the common Christian edification in the spectacle of fellow-believers striking a blow for the faith, but (in tones reminis-cent of Dr Johnson's aphorism about the dog on its hind legs[1]), for being more simply startling as women doing such a thing. When fourth century church writers considered the virtuous woman they would invariably refer to her sex, only to set her apart from it. What is more unexpected is quite how many writers were eager to report this phenomenon of the woman achieving virtue; and with what similarity of style they write of them, specifically in very gender-directed terminology, their virtue being directly and proportionately linked with a perceived ability to cast off the qualities and trappings of their tainted gender. There was a connection at something like visceral level for the Christian writers of the ancient world between virtue and masculinity: in both Latin and Greek, the very name of virtue – *virtus, andreia* – derives from words for maleness – *vir, andros*. So the property of virtue pertains to being like a man: in which case the writers all accord the virtuous women they note the

213

ultimate compliment of being 'manly' – 'women more like men than nature would seem to allow' (Palladius *LH*, Introduction 5).

VIRTUE BY STRUGGLE: ESCAPING THE FEMININE VIA THE MASCULINE

There were more ways than one to reach this plateau above 'nature'. Some women reached the goal by 'masculine' means: i.e. by direct action, by 'fighting'. Those writers who took a positive line about women's capacities often stressed that the nature became equal because so often the work was: witness the pugnacious words of Palladius who said he intended to record what he knew of many such examples, 'certain women with many qualities to whom God apportioned labours equal to those of men, lest any should pretend that women are too feeble to practise virtue perfectly' (*LH* 41). The examples of these 'God-inspired matrons, who with masculine and perfect mind have successfully accomplished the struggles of virtuous asceticism' (*LH*, Introduction 1) were many. Such a one was Melania the Elder: 'What a woman she is, if one can call so manly a Christian a woman!' was her relative Paulinus of Nola's opinion (*Let.* 29.6); 'a soldier for Christ . . . though of the weaker sex' (*ibid.*) she 'lowered herself to practise humility, so that as a strong member of a weaker sex, she could censure indolent men' (*ibid.* 7) and 'Melania, a perfect woman in Christ, yet retaining unaffected the courage of her manly spirit' (*ibid..* 45.3). For Palladius, most strikingly, she was *'He anthrôpos tou deou'* – 'the female man of God'.[2] And of Olympias similarly, 'not a woman but an *anthrôpos*, a manly creature: a man in everything but body' (Palladius *Dialogue* 56). Thus also it was said of Macrina: 'It was a woman who provided us with our subject; if indeed she should be termed woman, for I do not know if it is appropriate to describe her by her sex who so surpassed her sex' (*Life of Macrina* 960). And Nonna: 'displaying in female form the spirit of a man' (Gregory of Nazianzus *Concerning Himself* 116); 'a woman in body, yes, but in character she eclipsed any man' (*On His Own Life* 51) And Melania the Younger, who performed 'manly deeds' (*Life of Melania the Younger*, prologue) and was received by the Fathers of Nitria 'like a man': since 'she had surpassed the limits of her sex and taken on a mentality that was manly, or rather angelic' (*ibid.* 39).

Some were accorded this status for specific manly qualities: in the case of Paula 'her endurance [in *ascesis*] was scarcely credible in a woman' who was 'forgetful of sex and weakness' (Jerome *Let.* 108.14). Monica was manly in reaching the mark of philosophy, according to Augustine: 'we, forgetful completely of her sex, believed some great man was seated with us' (*On the Good Life* 2.10) – though she reached it by 'feminine' means – through her innate qualities of faith, intuition and sound common sense, while the men around her had to struggle for the goal by cold reason. In this, she was like the unlettered old men of the desert whom the learned 'Roman' Arsenius considered had taught him his ABC of the true way (*PJ* 15.7). These examples were all pronounced on by men: but women also acknowledged this as a goal and might adjudge themselves worthy of it. Sarah is after all reported as saying of herself: 'According to nature I am a woman, but not according to my thoughts' (*Alph.* Sarah 4).

The 'manliness' of women also affected the men around them. This might be by cooperation: the de-sexing effect could be worked out in conjunction with a good enough man, by sharing a vocation, or refusing to share a bed, or both. So, according to Paulinus of Nola, Bassula and her son-in-law Severus were 'animated by a single vocation and faith which brings you together into a perfect man and empties you of your sex' (Paulinus of Nola *Let.* 31). Paulinus himself was believed to have had in his wife Therasia, 'a wife who does not bring her husband to effeminacy but by union with him is brought herself to share the strength of his nature' (Augustine *Let.* 27). Writing to his friends Aper and Amanda, Paulinus echoed the compliment made to his own wife, saying that Amanda 'does not bring her husband to effeminacy' (Paulinus of Nola *Let.* 44.3). Jerome similarly praised the married woman Theodora, 'once [Lucinius'] wife, now a sister; once a woman, now a man; once an inferior, now an equal' (Jerome *Let.* 71.3), whose husband 'resolved to treat you even on earth as a sister, or, indeed, I may say, as a brother, for difference on sex, while essential to marriage, is not so to a continent tie' (*Let.* 75.2).

More contentiously, adopting this ideal might culminate in pious women representing the masculine to their menfolk in confrontation. The masculine in patristic terminology by inference being the virtuous, if the woman was more virtuous, therefore she was more manly than the men – and might throw this in their teeth. Artemia was placed in this position over Rusticus: 'Souls are of no sex; therefore I may fairly call your soul the daughter of hers', Jerome says to him stingingly (*Let.* 122.4). Mary of Egypt, veteran harlot and archetypal penitent, for her natural and inherent gifts of faith and taking no account of her sex or her past was by the 'perfect monk' Zossimus allotted the masculine role of teaching him:

> It is plain above all that grace is given to you since you called me by name and recognised me as a priest, though you have never seen me before. Since grace is recognised not by office, but by gifts of the spirit, bless me, for God's sake, and pray for me out of the kindness of your heart.
>
> (*Life of St Mary of Egypt* 10 – trans. Ward)

Gorgonia by this means was portrayed by her brother as being able to reverse the natural order of things so completely that by virtue of her sustained and devoutly-practised faith in the face of an 'un-perfected' man, in Gregory's account she represented the *imago dei* to her unpromising husband rather than the man to her: 'her nobility consisted in the preservation of the image and the perfect likeness of the Archetype' (Gregory of Nazianzus *Or.* 8.6).

VIRTUE BY SUBMISSION: WORKING THROUGH THE FEMININE

Some women, however, were not in a position to exercise the option for positive action. For a woman to embark on the struggle as a 'soldier of Christ' presupposed a fortunate enough background to endow her with the repute of being of 'good life': seen again, customarily, in sexual terms, i.e. to have 'known only one man' and dealt faithfully with him and her children. Many women could not exercise their own options in these matters. Concubines and *probrosae* would have been at a great disadvantage over these sort of requirements; many women came to the ideal late in life with varied histories of which to repent. These women could not escape their tie to the sexual by directly denying it in a masculine display of virtue: so they became instead even more 'female', in the abject meekness of their worship. They proved new things about femininity by accepting with complete passivity its innate subjection and being submissive to the harshest of its burdens; then turning these to advantage. They wept so sorely that the male monks envied them their tears, signifying as they did the capacity for the complete negation of self the males seemed unable to attain; and they became 'pregnant with the Holy Spirit' (Paulinus of Nola *Let.* 23.24 on Mary of Magdala), a wholly acceptable reversal of terminology. In so doing, these most feminine Christians are placed in a position from which the men can learn from them.

The idea is clearly stated in another tale from Palladius of an anonymous virgin who sinned and became pregnant. This is a rather dark tale, in which her powers of penitence are made manifest in praying for – and obtaining – the death of her baby, 'the fruit of my sin, which I cannot bear': after which one of the local priests received a vision from God that 'this one has pleased me more in her penitence than in her virginity' (*LH* 69). Paësia, another downfallen believer, had but one short hour of repentance permitted her, and yet this was undergone in such a perfect spirit that John the Dwarf heard the judgement of heaven on her that 'One single hour of repentance has gained more for her than that of many who do penance continually, but without ever showing such ardour' (*Alph*. John the Dwarf 40). These 'many', presumably, with less to repent of in the first place, and certainly without the chequered career with which these women were endowed would find it hard to be so genuinely subsumed with remorse; small wonder the monks so envied the women their tears – their 'legacy of Eve'. The idea was carried to extremes by Alexandra the maid-servant and Maryana, the girl-monk, who displayed total, accepting passivity in taking on sins which they had not committed. Many of the desert monks struggled towards and did not achieve this level of indifference to the opinion of men; we have stories in about equal numbers of monks justifying themselves against accusation or disproving accusations and monks accepting the infamy of a wrongful accusation – the latter stance probably being the more admired. Maryana is represented as achieving the ultimate in abjectness in having her infamy disproved only on death (most monks in this kind of tale were proved innocent in time to reap the benefits) while Alexandra devoted her life to the expiation of her potential guilt for a wrong that had not even happened.

PERCEPTIONS OF THE FIGHT AND ITS CONSEQUENCES

Those who did fight pursued the struggle in much the same terms as the men. The aristocratic women fought their overt campaigns in the same spirit and with seemingly as much vehemence as the most contentious of male clerics. The Melanias and Olympias defy temporal authorities and upbraid clerical opponents in terms entirely reminiscent of the doughtier battles of Ambrose and Jerome with just the same sort of opponents. Just so the women of the desert, on their level, fought the same battles as the men of the desert, against more nebulous opponents. The battle against lust, for instance was in the desert mentality accounted a great privilege as well as a severe trial, the sign of a stronger nature battling to a potentially greater reward – witness Abba Apollo's judgement on a monk succumbing that it was because 'you are not deemed worthy for the fight' (*PJ* 5.4). In this fight the women were not behindhand. Sarah 'battled against the demon of fornication for thirteen years' in an immaculately correct manner: 'she never once prayed for the struggle to end only asking "God, give me strength"' (*Alph*. Sarah 1). The same was recorded of the anonymous 'anchorite' who related to the seculars who had gone to visit him that he had been 'tempted almost beyond endurance by fornication' right up until the moment of his death, which they witnessed. Unsurprised by this confession in a brother, they set about burying him – and discovered the body was that of a woman (*Anon Apopth*. 63). Mary of Egypt, who by her own admission knew more than most about what she was missing, prayed to her namesake and mentor, the Virgin Mary, for release from 'thoughts that would drive me into prostitution again'; and more piquantly confessed that throughout her forty-seven years in the desert, her greatest temptations had been a craving for wine and 'a longing for the lewd songs which I used to sing' (*Life of St Mary of Egypt* 19).

These combative females also fought their fight *against* men, equally positively. Amma Sarah talked of the sheer futility of struggling constantly for male approval, which we have seen her notably short of: 'if I asked God that all men should approve of my conduct, I should find myself a penitent at the door of each one' (*Alph*. Sarah 5) – as effectively were the suppliants noted above. Their tales may be symptomatic of a monkish belief that all women should strive only in this self-abasing way; but Sarah knew of two ways to fight the battle, and regarded suppliance towards male colleagues as a waste of time – 'rather shall I pray that my heart may be pure towards all' (*ibid*.), as the real crux of the Christian life. And without tremor she confronted Paphnutius with not having done the will of God in 'letting a brother be reviled' (*Alph*. Paphnutius 6). Pelagia reached out and seized Nonnus by the conscience in directly confrontational terms, not at all in the abject manner proper in a woman of her station approaching a bishop for salvation:

> You will answer to God for my soul; you will be charged with all the evil of my sins, if you delay in baptising me and washing me out of my foul wickedness. May you have no place with the

saints in God's mansion unless you free me from my sin; if you
do not give me new birth as a bride to Christ and offer me up
to God, you will be like an apostate and an idol-worshipper

– at which 'all the bishops and clergy gathered there . . . were amazed,
saying in wonder that they had never seen such faith and such desire
for salvation' (*Life* 8).

But some women fought male clerics not by overtly fighting but
by applying the males' own logic to turn the tables, sometimes to
teach them, sometimes simply to wrongfoot them. Not all women
submitted to the male conclusions of the link between femaleness
and physicality. The school of thought that told women to avoid
being seen in order not to provide temptation could be countered by
the observation of the amma secure in her own self-awareness to the
monk sedulously avoiding seeing her nuns: 'if you had been a proper
monk you would not have even noticed we were women' (*PJ* 4.62).
Saint Ephraim similarly we have seen being edified by the response
of a woman and she not even a nun, when a harlot reinforced the
concept of the *imago dei* to his discomfiture so as to give him the
lesson from Scripture for which he had prayed: 'It is natural for me
to look towards you since I was formed out of you; but you, you
should have no cause to look towards me, for you were formed from
earth – it is on that earth that your eyes should be fixed' (*Life of
Ephraim* 2321). Nor was it only the women who thought that the anti-
female attitude could be overdone. John Cassian told a tale of Paul,
a monk who made a virtue of exaggeratedly avoiding women, to the
extent of actually running away from them; eventually he had a
stroke and had to end his days in a nunnery being cared for by them.
The illuminating point about this conclusion is that it was evidently
regarded by his colleagues in the light of a just lesson to his over-
scrupulosity (John Cassian *Coll*. 3.26).

CONCLUSION: 'FEMALE' SPIRITUALITY?

Women in the first century of legitimate Christianity were astonish-
ingly forceful and influential, so much so as to obtain from critical
male sources all the accolades noted above: well has it been said that

the enthusiasm with which they took to the ascetic life, their
repugnance for sexual relations within a marriage which had
been forced on them and the chance to be recognised in a way
of life in which they could be men's equals made the women

of the Empire one of the principal forces in the transformation of the ancient world.

(Rousselle 1988:193)

And yet it has also been said of this period that 'there was no concept of feminine spirituality as such and women who were able to compete with the men were rare' (Ward 1985:65). Which contains more truth?

Unquestionably, what women did altered society: they were powerful movers and shakers, not merely in the circles of power, but in the epicentres of social change; in community and familial life. And yet, despite all the examples of these powerful women related above; despite accolades such as 'man-woman of God' and 'soldier of Christ'; despite women being accounted worthy to be taken as models by men, not just their own sex; despite being in a position to teach holy men (and the men frankly admitting that it was so) either by direct instruction or by indirect inspiration from their tears and perfect repentance; despite the male monastics' conclusion that they could and should learn from the feminine example because ultimately all souls were feminine (i.e. supplicatory) before God: despite all these things, feminine spirituality as a concept had no currency in the eyes of the patristic writers of their period – indeed, to these guardians of the perceptions of the church it was almost a contradiction in terms. To the Fathers, women remained 'harlots or hearthkeepers' (Ward 1985:66); the constant re-iteration of the theme 'so holy was she that she was more man than woman' in fact only serves to reinforce this. The paradigm of patristic thought on women was that women were not holy; they were creatures of error, of superstition, of carnal disposition – the Devil's gateway. This being so, anyone holy enough to be an examplar of the faith could not *be* a woman: every one of the many who achieved fame through piety was held to 'surpass her sex' – never, be it noted, to elevate the expectations that might be held of her sex. The argument is self-fulfilling: however many of this kind of women there were, in being superior they were always excepted from their sex, never taken as representative; always regarded as a superior anomaly from their sex and in spite of it, and never as an example of their sex's capacity. The fathers could thus know of, and advertise, pious female activities without ever facing a contradiction in the central tenet of their belief on women: being holy, these women were in essential respects clearly, and self-evidently, male.

There is a desert tale that gives this sub-text more clearly than most: Macarius was presented with a young girl to heal whose flesh was all eaten away with disease and worms. He healed her without difficulty: 'but in such a way that no femininity showed in her form, no feminine parts were apparent so that in all her contact with men she never beguiled them with womanly deceits' (*HM* Macarius 21) – the perfect woman from the clerical viewpoint. Note how 'womanly parts' equate completely with 'womanly deceits'; Macarius 'cured' her from her womanly parts as from her disease. The mere possession of these disqualifies from the ultimate in piety. Whatever was said of women, they could not truly 'transcend gender differences' (Ward 1987:62) or 'constitute a "third sex"' (Clark 1983a:17): they could only disguise the sex they had, either actively, in assuming the outward habit and guise of a man, or by assuming inward 'male' habits of determination and courage in piety, to be written up as having disguised outwardly the real masculinity of their souls – being, therefore, evidently 'a man' despite all appearances. It was not thus necessary for their contemporaries to take them seriously in the context of church office: and after, because of this verdict, and their lack of purchase on the church in specifically 'female' (as opposed to quasi-male) terms, their enormous and unquestionable contribution to the spirituality of the age was persistently overlooked or underestimated. Saintly women of the later empire might indeed be able to change the disposition of the empire, but they could not change the dispositions of the church Fathers.

NOTES

2 PATRISTIC PERCEPTIONS

1 In addition, as pilgrimage literature it is something of a special case and as such it has already received extensive treatment (cf. particularly Wilkinson (1971) and Hunt (1982)). I felt that there was not room in this study for another detailed consideration of Egenia and her genre, though one or two useful points may be adduced for general consideration.
2 Jerome *Let.* 130.
3 See pp. 94ff.
4 See pp. 91ff.
5 See pp. 93ff.
6 Jerome *Let.* 127.7 and 9ff.; 107.9.
7 See pp. 172ff.
8 Gorce, *Vie de Ste Melanie*, n. 3 on sec. 23 and n. 1 on sec. 26.
9 Though a collection of letters including some purporting to be from Macrina was known to a fourteenth century scribe, who from them judged Macrina a *theosophos* – and elected not to copy them. MS Vaticanus Graecus 578.11 (f. 189), cited in Momigliano (1985), p. 456.
10 Palladius *LH* 56 ff.; *Dialogues* 35, 55; Sozomen *EH* 8.9; 8.24.
11 *LH* 46 ff.; Jerome *Let.* 39.5; *Chronici Canones* 329; Paulinus of Nola *Let.* 29.
12 Augustine *Conf.* 6.2; *Let.* 36.
13 John Chrysostom *Letter to a Young Widow* 2; *On the Priesthood* 1.5.
14 *De Ordine* 1.10.31; *De Beata Vita* 3.19.
15 Jerome *Let.* 77.

3 MODELS FOR PIETY IN A SOCIAL CONTEXT

1 Cf. *Life of Thaïs the Harlot*, *Life of Saint Pelagia the Harlot* and *Alphabetical Collection of the Apophthegmata Patrum*, John the Dwarf 40; *LH* 5.
2 For instance *Anon. Apoph.* 13, 176, 178.
3 Gregory of Nyssa *Life of Macrina* 962 – significantly, it was Emmelia

who named Macrina also Thecla as a secret name, for her dream that she was bearing 'a new Thecla'.

4 Pelagius in *PL* 30.15–45. 'Pelagius never doubted for a moment that perfection was obligatory; his God was, above all, a God who demanded unquestioning obedience. He had made men to execute his commands; and he condemned to hellfire anyone who failed to perform a single one of them.' So Peter Brown (1961) *Augustine of Hippo*, p. 342.

5 Ambrose *On Virginity* 1.24, 34; John Chrysostom *On Virginity* 1.2; Gregory of Nyssa *On Virginity* 8; Jerome *Let.* 48; *Against Jovinian, passim.*

6 Jerome *Let.* 49.2 – 'I quite recognise the kindness and forethought which have induced you to withdraw from circulation some copies of my work against Jovinian. Your diligence, however, has been of no avail, for several people coming from the city have repeatedly read aloud to me passages which they have come across in Rome.'

7 Cf. M. K. Hopkins (1965) 'The age of Roman girls at marriage', *Population Studies* 18, pp. 309ff; Brent D. Shaw (1987a) 'The age of Roman girls at marriage: some reconsiderations', *JRS*, 30–46; *CJ* 5.4.24 (530); 'Justinian said that his ruling would do away with much dispute, but that is the only indication of doubt about these ages which survives. They became canon law. *D.* 23.1.9' – Hopkins, *op. cit.* p. 313.

8 Oribasius in the fourth century citing Rufus *Coll. Med., lib. incert.* 18 (ed. J Raeder (1933) Leipzig, 6.2.2 pp. 107–8).

9 *Anth. Pal.* 7.568; 7.604; cf *CIL* 9.1.817 also, an epitaph to a 12-year-old girl 'ripe for marriage'. Cited in Hopkins *op. cit.* p. 317.

10 On this particularly Jane Gardner (1986) *Women in Roman Law and Society* p.41; Beryl Rawson (1991) *Marriage, Divorce and Children in Ancient Rome*, Chapter 2.

11 'The mode is a measure of central tendency; it indicates the category which contains the largest number.' Hopkins, *op. cit.* p. 309.

12 R. Saller (1987) 'Men's age at marriage and its consequences in the Roman family', *CPh* 82, 21–34.

13 Collected by A. G. Harkness (1896) 'Age at marriage and at death in the Roman Empire' in *TAPbA* 27. He rejected them out of hand as 'manifestly incorrect'.

14 But that this occurrence cannot be attributable only to ignorance or coercion in marital arrangements of the time (though they cannot have helped): I am indebted to Gillian Clark for the information (from an area in which I lack personal experience) that this is a phenomenon continuing into modern times and midwives nowadays relate that 'quite a lot of women announce in mid-labour that they will go home now and have the baby another time'.

4 'EUNUCHS FOR THE LOVE OF HEAVEN'

1 Basil of Ancyra *On Virginity* (fragmentary) *PG* 30.669–810.
2 cf. Peter Brown (1961) 'Aspects of the Christianisation of the Roman Aristocracy', *JRS* 51 p. 10.

3 cf. e.g. *Alph*. Ammonas 8, Theodore of Eleutheropolis 3.
4 These sections from Benedicta Ward's translation (1987):92–101.
5 Gregory of Nyssa *On Virginity* 23; Basil of Caesarea *Let*. 55; Gregory of Nazianzus *Epigrammata* 10–20; See Pierre de Labriolle (1921) 'Le "Mariage Spirituel" dans l'Antiquité Chrétienne', *Revue Historique* 137, p. 222 for a list of councils condemning the practice; John Chrysostom *Contra eos qui apud se habent subintroductas virgines* (*Against those men who cohabit with virgins*) and *Quod regulares feminae viris cohabitare non debeant* (*That women under vows should not cohabit with men*); cf. also Elizabeth Clark (1977) 'John Chrysostom and Subintroductae', *Church History* 46, pp. 171–85; *Apoph. Alph*. Cassian 26 (amongst others).
6 John Chrysostom *That women under vows etc*. 5–6; *Against those men etc*. 9, 11.

5 'THE CONTINENCE WHICH IS AWARE OF ITS OWN RIGHT'

1 John Chrysostom, *Letter to a Young Widow*; Augustine *On the Good of Widowhood*; Ambrose, *On Widows*.
2 A. Harnack (1985) *Sources of the Apostolic Canons* London, 20.
3 Fr J. Daniélou (1961) *The Ministry of Women in the Early Church*.
4 Cf. Jerome *Let*. 51, 52, 59 127.7.
5 Reports on the exact length of her 'short' marriage differ; its duration is given variously as 'a few days' (*LH* 56), 'less than a year' (*Life of Olympias, Deaconess* 2) or 'twenty months' (Palladius *Dialogue* 60).

6 MARRIED SANCTITY I: 'THE BED UNDEFILED'

1 A subject which has been covered in ample detail elsewhere; see particularly Veyne (1987), Rawson (1991), Treggiari (1991).
2 Cf. also Cicero's tale (*de Orat*. 1.40.183) of a man whose extreme informality in this respect amounted to bigamy; though under Roman law, marrying a second wife might betoken *de facto* divorce of the first with no further notification.
3 Though the satirists and moralists were responsible for propagating an idea of women initiating divorce – by implication for immoral motives – that is not borne out by evidence of any significant number of actual instances where divorce was decided by the wife: Susan Treggiari, p. 44, in Rawson (1991) *Marriage, Divorce and Children* – 'Divorce by men is material neither for ethics nor for satire.'
4 By Paul Veyne (1987) in *A History of Private Life* p. 36; Saller and Bradley (in Rawson, 1991) take issue with this. For an assessment of the arguments for and against this view of marriage and a summary of current scholarship on the subject, cf. Suzanne Dixon's 'The sentimental ideal of the Roman family' in Rawson (1991).
5 Cf. Callistratus *D*. 49.14.2.7. Ignorance of the law could, however, be an

advantage; it could excuse female defendants – but not male. cf. Jane Gardner (1986) *Women in Roman Law and Society* p. 126.

6 Galen cited in an Arabic anthology; from R. Walzer (1949) *Galen on Jews and Christians* p. 15.

7 Attested in Veyne (1987) *A History of a Private Life*, p. 40.

8 In fact, wives were well advised to put up with the philandering, having no recourse and given the hazards of seeking consolation. 'A wife could not prosecute her husband since in the eyes of the law he had committed no offence against their marriage [only against the other woman's] and women could prosecute in criminal courts only for offences against themselves. She could perhaps get her *pater* or someone else to prosecute him, but only if the 'other woman' was married and then only if the latter's husband failed to prosecute within the statutory time-limit.' Jane Gardner (1986) *op. cit.* pp. 127–8.

9 Cf. Augustine *Sermons* 9.4.

10 Cf. Amy Richlin (1981) 'Approaches to the sources on adultery at Rome' in *Reflections on Women in Antiquity* ed. Helen Foley, p. 397.

11 The legal condition of transferring herself absolutely from *patria potestas* into the power of her husband – so rare in our period as to be negligible.

12 For more detailed examinations of the issues encapsulated here, Jane Gardner (1986); Beryl Rawson (1991); Suzanne Dixon (1988) *The Roman Mother*; Susan Treggiari (1991) *Roman Marriage*.

13 Cf. Augustine *On the Good of Marriage* 1, 31; Augustine *On the Sermon on the Mount* 1.15.41 – later revised, *Retract.* 1.19.5.

7 MARRIED SANCTITY II

1 Jane Gardner (1986) *Women in Roman Law and Society*, pp. 146ff. Cf. also Chs 4–6 in Rawson (1991) *Marriage, Divorce and Children in Ancient Rome* for a more detailed consideration of parent and child relations from various viewpoints.

2 This and following excerpts from R. S. Pine-Coffin's elegant Penguin translation.

3 Gregory of Nazianzus *Or.* 27.1; 34.10; 43.11; *Carmina ad Seleucum* 1.61, echoing Basil of Caesarea's *Address to young men on the right use of Greek literature*.

4 Louis MacNeice, *Autumn Journal*, Canto XIII – 'Which things being so, as we said when we studied the Classics . . .'.

5 There are passing and inconsistent references in the Greek version of the *Life of Melania the Younger* and in some versions of Palladius to 'other children' or another child, possibly a boy, possibly dead by this time. For the arguments for and against their existence, cf. Clark (1984): p. 90.

6 Although he reveals himself to have been less than completely free from blame for having been 'economical with the truth' in this incident: 'For I am aware that I passed over some things which seemed to me irrelevant but what I did say I know was nothing but the truth' – 126.6.

8 'NOT BY OFFICE BUT BY GIFTS OF THE SPIRIT'

1 Eva Cantarella (1987) *Pandora's Daughters* (trans. Maureen B. Fant), Ch. 10 *passim*.

2 On these areas see especially Susan Treggiari (1975, 1976, 1979); Jane Gardner (1986) Ch. 11; Gillian Clark (1993) Ch. 2.

3 Jerome *Let*. 127.8; 'I had the joy of seeing Rome turned into another Jerusalem. Monastic establishments became numerous'.

4 *Acts of Paul and Thecla* in *The Ante-Nicene Fathers* ed. Roberts and Donaldson.

5 cf. F. X. Murphy, 'Melania the Elder: a biographical note' in *Traditio* vol. V (1947), pp. 59–77.

6 Rufinus seems to have developed a school where he taught; Jerome ridicules his poor Latin and his pusillanimous teaching style (Jerome *Let*. 125). Jerome, besides his plentiful writings, worked for the preservation and dissemination of existing texts and tended a scriptorum for copying manuscripts; Rufinus criticises his extravagance in this respect and his readiness to pay more for the production of pagan classical authors (Jerome *Apology Against Rufinus* 2.8).

7 Paulinus *Natalicia* 21.60; Palladius, *LH* 54–6 & 61; Gerontius *op. cit.* 22–30; 40–49; 54–56; Jerome *Let*. 127.5; *Life of Olympias, Deaconess* 6, 15.

8 Not, as Rosemary Ruether writes, that 'faced with his determination to return the gold *Melania* finally threw it into the river' ('Mothers of the Church', p. 90 in *Women of Spirit* ed. Ruether and McLaughlin (1979)); quite apart from endowing Melania with a disregard for the power of money which she showed no signs of for all her ostentatious personal degradations, this is not the sense of the Greek text, which is quite clear that 'ho hagios' (Hephestion) did the throwing, not 'he makaria' (Melania).

9 Michael Whitby, 'Maro the Dendrite: an anti-social holy man?' in eds. Whitby, Hardie, Whitby (1987) *Homo Viator*, pp. 309–17.

10 Cf. *Alph*. John the Persian 1; *PJ* 16.13; *Anon. Apoph*. 360.

11 Fr. Jean Daniélou, S.J., *The Ministry of Women in the Early Church* (1961).

9 CONCLUSION

1 'A woman's preaching is like a dog's walking on his hinder legs. It is not well done; but you are surprised to find it done at all.' (James Boswell, *Life* vol. 1).

2 The translation of W.K. Lowther Clarke, with which I am in complete agreement; Herbert Moore, commenting on the same expression in the *Dialogue*, used of Olympias, also notes that 'anthropos' with the feminine article is a 'most unusual expression'. So unusual, I feel, as to be very deliberate: the intention is not merely to indicate a 'female human being', but actively to convey androgyny of sexual status, such as idea being highlighted in the surrounding text.

BIBLIOGRAPHY

PRIMARY SOURCES

Acts of the Christian Martyrs, ed. and trans. H. Musurillo, Oxford: Clarendon Press, 1972.

Acts of Paul and Thecla, ed. and trans. F. Conybeare in *The Ante-Nicene Fathers*, ed. Roberts and Donaldson, vol. 8, pp. 487 ff. 1894.

Ambrose *On the Institutions of Virgins PL* 16.319–347.

—— *Letters PL* 16.913–1342. Trans. H. Walford in *A Library of Fathers*, Oxford: Parker & Co., 1881.

—— *On Widows PL* 16.247–275. Trans. in *A Select Library of Nicene and Post-Nicene Fathers*, Oxford: 1896.

—— *On Virginity PL* 16.197–243. Trans. in *A Select Library of Nicene and Post-Nicene Fathers*, Oxford: 1896.

Ammianus Marcellinus, *The Histories*; trans John Rolfe, *Loeb Classical Library*, London and Harvard : 1937.

Apophthegmata Patrum, Sayings of the Fathers. PG 65.72–440; *PL* 73.851–1062.

—— *Anonymous Apophthegmata: MS Coislin 126* ed. F. Nau, 'Histoire des solitaires égyptiens (MS Coislin 126, fol. 158f.)', *Revue de l'Orient Chrétien* (1908).

—— *The Sayings of the Desert Fathers: the Alphabetical Collection*, trans. Benedicta Ward, SLG, Oxford: Mowbrays, 1975.

—— *The Verba Seniorum of Pelagius the Deacon and John the Subdeacon*; from *Vitae Patrum* V and VI, Rosweyde, Antwerp 1628. Partially trans. Helen Waddell in *The Desert Fathers*, London: Constable & Co., 1936.

—— *The Wisdom of the Desert Fathers: Apophthegmata Patrum from the Anonymous Series*, trans. Benedicta Ward, SLG. Oxford: SLG Press, 1975.

—— *The World of the Desert Fathers: Stories and Sayings from the Anonymous Series of the Apophthegmata Patrum*, trans. Columba Stewart, OSB. Oxford: SLG Press, 1986.

Apostolic Constitutions: s.v. Didascalia.

Augustine: *Confessions, PL* 32.659–868. Trans. R. S. Pine-Coffin. Harmondsworth: Penguin, 1961.

227

—— *De Beata Vita* (On the Good Life). *PL* 32.959–976. Trans. R. A. Brown, Catholic University of America Patristic Studies vol. 72 (Diss. 1944).

—— *De Bono Conjugali* (On the Good of Marriage). *PL* 40.373–396. Trans. Salmond, Haddan *et al.* in *A Select Library of Nicene and Post-Nicene Fathers* vol. 3. Buffalo: 1887.

—— *De Bono Viduitatis* (On the Good of Widowhood). *PL* 40.429–451. Trans. Salmond, Haddan *et al.* in *A Select Library of Nicene and Post-Nicene Fathers*, vol. 3. Buffalo: 1887.

—— *De Conjugiis Adulterinis* (On Adulterous Marriage). *PL* 40.451–486.

—— *De Continentia* (On Continence). *PL* 40.349–372. Trans Salmond, Haddan *et al.* in *A Select Library of Nicene and Post-Nicene Fathers* vol. 3. Buffalo: 1887

—— *De Fide et Operibus* (On Faith and Works) *PL* 40. 197–230.

—— *De Nuptiis et Concupiscentis* (On Marriage and Concupiscence). *PL* 44.413–475. Trans. in The Anti-Pelagian Writings vol. 2. Edinburgh: 1874.

—— *De Ordine PL* 32.977–868.

—— *De Sermone in Montibus* (On the Sermon on the Mount). *PL* 34.1229–1320. Trans. W. Findlay and S. D F. Salmond in *The Works of Aurelius Augustine* vol. 8. Edinburgh: 1873.

—— *De Virginitate* (On Virginity). *PL* 40.395–428. Trans Salmond, Haddan *et al.* in *A Select Library of Nicene and Post-Nicene Fathers* vol. 3. Buffalo: 1887.

—— *Letters. PL* 33. Trans. J. G. Cunningham in *The Works of Aurelius Augustine*, vol. 6, 13. Edinburgh: T. & T. Clark, 1872.

—— *Sermones* (Sermons) *PL* 38, 39.

—— *Soliloquia* (Soliloquy) *PL* 32.869–905.

Ausonius: *Parentalia.* Trans. Hugh G. Eveyn White, *Loeb Classical Library*, London and New York: 1919–21.

Basil of Ancyra: *De Virginitate* (On Virginity). *PG* 30.669–810.

Basil of Caesarea: *Address to Young Men on the Right Use of Greek Literature.* Trans. F. M. Padelford in *Yale Studies in English*, New York: 1902.

—— *Letters.* Trans R. J. Deferrari, *Loeb Classical Library.* Cambridge: Harvard University Press, 1961–62.

—— *Moralia. PG* 31–8.

Clement of Alexandria: *Paedagogus* (The Instructor). *PG* 8.247–684. Trans. William Wilson in *The Ante-Nicene Christian Library*, vol. 4. Edinburgh: T. & T. Clark, 1867.

—— *Stromata* (Miscellanies). *PG* 8.685.-1382. Trans. William Wilson in *The Ante-Nicene Christian Library*, vol. 4, 12. Edinburgh: T. & T. Clark, 1867.

Codex Justinianus (Justinian Code), s.v. Justinian.

Didascalia et Constitutiones Apostolorum (The Teaching of the Apostles and The Apostolic Constitutions). Ed. F. X. Funk. Paderborn: 1905. Trans. R. H. Connolly, Oxford: Clarendon Press, 1929.

Digest, s.v. Justinian.

Egeria: *Peregrinatio* (Pilgrimage). Trans. John Wilkinson in *Egeria's Travels*. London: SPCK, 1971.

Epiphanius: *Panarion* (Medicine Box Against All Heresies). *PG* 42.743.

Eudocia: *Martyrdom of St Cyprian* Trans. G. Ronald Kastner in Patricia

Wilson-Kastner *et al.* eds, *Lost Traditions: Women Writers of the Early Church*. University Press of America, 1981.

Galen: *On the Natural Faculties* Trans. A. J. Brock, *Loeb Classical Library*. London: Heinemann, 1916.

Gerontius: *Vita Melaniae Iunioris* (Life of Melania the Younger), s.v. Vita.

Gregory of Nazianzus: *Orations. PG* 35.395–1252. Trans. C. G. Browne and J. E. Swallow in *A Select Library of Nicene and Post-Nicene Fathers*, 2nd Series, vol. 7. Oxford, 1894.

—— *Poemata de Vita Sua* (On His Own Life). *PG* 37.1029–1166. Trans. Denis M. Meehan in *Fathers of the Church* vol. 75. Washington: Catholic University of America Press, 1987.

—— *Poemata de Rebus Suis* (Concerning Himself). *PG* 37.969–1018. Trans. Denis M. Meehan in *Fathers of the Church* vol. 75. Washington: Catholic University of America Press, 1987.

Gregory of Nyssa: *De Virginitate* (On Virginity). *PG* 45.317–416. Ed. and trans. M. Aubineau, *SC* 119, 1966. English trans. in V. W. Callaghan, *Gregory of Nyssa: Ascetical Works. Fathers of the Church* 58. New York, 1967.

—— *Vita Macrinae* (Life of Macrina), s.v. Vita.

Historia Monachorum in Aegypto (A History of the Monks in Egypt). *PL* 21.387–462. Trans. Norman Russell, *The Lives of the Desert Fathers*. Oxford: Mowbray, 1981.

Jerome: *Against Helvidius: The Perpetual Virginity of Blessed Mary*. Trans. W. H. Fremantle in *A Select Library of Nicene and Post-Nicene Fathers*, 2nd Series, vol. 6. Michigan: Eerdmans, 1983.

—— *Adversus Jovinianum* (Against Jovinian). *PL* 23.221–352. Trans. W. H. Fremantle in *A Select Library of Nicene and Post-Nicene Fathers*, 2nd Series, vol. 6. Michigan: Eerdmans, 1983.

—— *Apologia adversus libros Rufini* (Apology Against Rufinus). *PL* 23.415–518.

—— *Commentary on Ephesians. PL* 26.468–588. Trans. W. H. Fremantle in *A Select Library of Nicene and Post-Nicene Fathers*, 2nd Series, vol. 6. Michigan: Eerdmans, 1983.

—— *Commentary on Galatians. PL* 26. 331–467. Trans. W. H. Fremantle in *A Select Library of Nicene and Post-Nicene Fathers*, 2nd Series, vol. 6. Michigan: Eerdmans, 1983.

—— *Commentary on Philemon PL* 26.635–656. Trans. W. H. Fremantle in *A Select Library of Nicene and Post-Nicene Fathers*, 2nd Series, vol. 6. Michigan: Eerdmans, 1983.

—— *Translatio Homiliarum Origenis in Lucam, ad Paulam et Eustochium* (Translation of Origen on St Luke). *PL* 26.229–332.

—— *Letters. PL* 22.325–1197. Trans. W. H. Fremantle in *A Select Library of Nicene and Post-Nicene Fathers*, 2nd Series, vol. 6. Michigan: Eerdmans, 1983.

—— *Vita Sancti Hilarionis* (Life of Saint Hilarion), s.v. Vita.

John Cassian: *Collationes* (Conferences). Ed. and trans. E. Pichery, SC 42, 54, 64.

—— *Institutiones* (Institutions). Ed. and trans. J.-C. Guy, SC 109.

John Chrysostom: *Ad eandem de non iterando conjugio* (Against Remarriage). *PG* 48.609–620. Trans. Sally Rieger Shore, *Studies in Women and Religion*, vol. 9. Lewiston: Edwin Mellen Press, 1983.

—— *Contra eos qui apud se habent subintroductas virgines* (Against those men who cohabit with virgins). *PG* 47.495–514.

—— *De Inanu Gloria* (On Vainglory) SC 188, ed. A. M. Malingrey

—— *De SS. Bernice et Prosdoce* (On Saints Bernice and Prosdoce) *PG* 50.629–640.

—— *De Virginitate* (On Virginity). *PG* 48.533–596. SC 125, ed. H. Musurillo and B. Grillet. Trans. Sally Rieger Shore, *Studies in Women and Religion*, vol. 9. Lewiston: Edwin Mellen Press, 1983.

—— *Homiliae in Epist. ad Corinthios* (Homily on Corinthians). *PG* 61.11–382. Trans. Chambers in *A Select Library of Nicene and Post-Nicene Fathers*, 1st Series, vol. 12. New York, 1889.

—— *Homiliae in Epist. ad Ephesios* (Homily on Ephesians). *PG* 62.4–176.

—— *Homiliae in Epist. ad Thess.* (Homily on Thessalonians) *PG* 11.467–500. Trans. John A. Broadus in *A Select Library of Nicene and Post-Nicene Fathers*, 1st Series, vol. 9. New York, 1894.

—— *Ad Viduam Juniorem* (Letter to a Young Widow). *PG* 48.599–610. Trans. W. R. W. Stephens in *A Select Library of Nicene and Post-Nicene Fathers*, 1st Series, vol. 9. New York, 1894.

—— *Letters to Olympias*. SC 13, ed. A. M. Malingrey. Paris, 1947.

—— *De Sacerdotio* (On the Priesthood). *PG* 48.624–625. Trans. Revd. T. Allen Moxon. London: SPCK, 1907.

—— *Quales Uxores Ducendae* (What sort of women ought to be taken as wives). *PG* 51.225–42.

—— *Quod regulares feminae cohabitare none debeant* (That women under vows should not cohabit with men). *PG* 47.513–532.

Justinian: *Digest, Institutes, Codex Justinianus* in *Corpus Iuris Civilis*, ed. Th. Mommsen and P. Krueger. Berlin: Wiedmann, 1954. *Digest* trans. A. Watson. Philadelphia: University of Pennsylvania Press, 1985.

Lactantius: *The Works of Lactantius*. Ed. and trans. W. Fletcher in *An Ante-Nicene Christian Library*, vols. 21, 22. Edinburgh, 1871.

Macrobius: *Saturnalia*. Trans. P. V. Davies. New York and London: Columbia University Press, 1969.

Methodius: *Symposium*. SC 95, ed. H. Musurillo, trans. V. H. Debidor.

Optatus: *Against Donatists*. Trans. Revd. O. R. Vassall-Phillips. London: Longmans, 1917.

Oribasius: *Collectionum Medicarum Reliquiae* (Medical Collections). *Colléction Médicale incl. Libri Incerti* ed. and trans. U. Bussemaker and C. Daremberg. Paris, 1851.

Origen: *In Exodum* (On Exodus). *PG* 12.281–396.

—— *In Leviticum* (On Leviticus) *PG* 395–572.

Palladius: *Dialogus de vita Johannis Chrysostomi* (Dialogue). *PG* 47.3–82. Trans. H. Moore, New York: SPCK, 1921.

—— *Historica Lausiaca* (Lausiac History). ed. Dom C. Butler, in 2 vols. Cambridge: Cambridge University Press 1896–1904. Trans. W. K. Lowther Clarke, New York: SPCK, 1918.

Paulinus of Milan: *Vita Beati Ambrosii*, s.v. Vita.

Paulinus of Nola: *Letters*. Ed. Wilhelm von Hartel, CSEL 29. Leipzig: G. Freytag, 1894. Trans. and annotated by P. G. Walsh in *Ancient Christian Writers*, vols. 35, 36. New York: Newman Press, 1966.

—— *Natalicia*. Trans. and annotated by P. G. Walsh in *Ancient Christian Writers*, vol. 40. New York: Newman Press, 1975.

Pelagius: *Epistula ad Demetriades* (Letter to Demetrias). *PL* 30. 16–487.

Plutarch: *Lycurgus and Numa* in *Lives*, vol. 1. Ed. Bernadotte Perrin, Loeb Classical Library, London and New York, 1914.

—— *Praecepta Conjugalia* (Marital Advice) in *Moralia* vol. 2. Ed. F. C. Babbitt, *Loeb Classical Library*, Cambridge: Harvard University Press, 1969.

Possidius: *Vita Augustini*, s.v. Vita.

Socrates Scholasticus: *Ecclesiastical History*. Trans. in A. C. Zenos, ed. *A Library of Nicene and Post-Nicene Fathers*, 2nd Series, vol. 2. Michigan: Eerdmans, 1979.

Soranus: *Gynaecia* (Gynaecology). Ed. J. Ilberg, Leipzig: Teubner, 1927. Trans O. Temkin, *Soranus' Gynaecology*, Baltimore: Johns Hopkins University Press, 1956.

Sozomen: *Ecclesiastica Historia* (Ecclesiastical History). Ed. J. Bidez, GCS 50; Berlin: Akademie Verlag, 1960. Trans. E. Walford, London: Bohn's Ecclesiastical Library, 1855.

Tertullian: *Ad Martyras* (To the Martyrs). *PL* 1.619–628. Ed. and trans. S. Thelwall in *Ante-Nicene Christian Library*, vol. 11. Edinburgh: T. & T. Clark, 1869.

—— *Ad Uxorem* (Exhortation to his Wife). *PL* 1.1273. Ed. and trans. S. Thelwall in *Ante-Nicene Christian Library*, vol. 11. Edinburgh: T. & T. Clark, 1869.

—— *Adversus Praxean* (Against Praxeas). *PL* 2.153–196. Trans. Peter Holmes *in Ante-Nicene Christian Library*, vol. 15. Edinburgh: T. & T. Clark, 1870.

—— *De Cultu Feminarum* (On Female Dress). *PL* 1.1303–1334. Ed. and trans. S. Thelwall in *Ante-Nicene Christian Library*, vol. 11. Edinburgh: T. & T. Clark, 1869.

—— *De Exhortatione Castitatis* (An Exhortation to Chastity). *PL* 2.913–930. Ed. and trans. S. Thelwall in *Ante-Nicene Christian Library*, vol. 18. Edinburgh: T. & T. Clark, 1870.

—— *De Monogamia* (On Monogamy). *PL* 2.929–954. Ed. and trans. S. Thelwall in *Ante-Nicene Christian Library*, vol. 18. Edinburgh: T. & T. Clark, 1870.

—— *De Virginibus Velandis* (On the Veiling of Virgins). *PL* 2.887–914. Ed. and trans. S. Thelwall in *Ante-Nicene Christian Library*, vol. 18. Edinburgh: T. & T. Clark, 1870.

Vita Antonii (Life of St Anthony – Athanasius). *PG* 26.835–976. Trans. E. A. Wallis Budge in *Stories of the Holy Fathers*, London: Oxford University Press, 1934.

Vita Beati Ambrosii (Life of the Blessed Ambrose – Paulinus of Milan). Trans. John A. Lacy in *Early Christian Biographies*, Fathers of the Church, vol. 15. Catholic University of America Press, 1952.

Vita Augustini (Life of Augustine – Possidius). *PL* 32.33–66. Trans. Sr. Mary M. Muller and R. J. Deferrari in *Early Christian Biographies*, Fathers of the Church, vol. 15. Catholic University of America Press, 1952.

Vita Sancti Hilarionis (Life of Saint Hilarion – Jerome). *PL* 23.29–54. Trans. W. H. Fremantle in *A Select Library of Nicene and Post-Nicene Fathers*, 2nd Series, vol. 6. Michigan: Eerdmans, 1983.

Vita Malchi Monachi Captivi (Life of Malchus, the Captive Monk – Jerome). Trans. W. H. Fremantle in *A Select Library of Nicene and Post-Nicene Fathers*, 2nd Series, vol. 6. Michigan: Eerdmans, 1983.

Vita Mariae Aegyptiacae. (Life of St Mary of Egypt). *PL* 73.671–690. Ed. and trans. Benedicta Ward in *Harlots of the Desert: a Study of Repentance in Early Monastic Sources*. London: Mowbray, 1987

Vita Macrinae (Life of Macrina – Gregory of Nyssa). *PG* 46.962–998. Trans. W. K. Lowther Clarke. London: SPCK, 1916.

Vita Mariae Meretricis (Life of Maria the Harlot – Ephraim). *PL* 73.651–660. Ed. and trans. Benedicta Ward in *Harlots of the Desert: a Study of Repentance in Early Monastic Sources*. London: Mowbray, 1987.

Vita Melaniae Iunioris (Life of Melania the Younger – Gerontius). SC 90, ed. D. Gorce. Trans. Elizabeth A. Clark, *Studies in Women and Religion*, vol. 14. Lewiston: Edwin Mellen Press, 1984.

Vita Sanctae Olympiadis Diaconissae (Life of Olympias, Deaconess – Anon.). *Anal. Boll.* 15 (1896) 409–423. Trans. Ross S. Kraemer in *Maenads, Martyrs, Matrons and Monastics: A Sourcebook on Women's Religions in the Greco-Roman World*. Philadelphia: Fortress Press, 1988.

Vita Sanctae Pelagiae Meretricis (Life of Saint Pelagia the Harlot). *PL* 73.663–72. Ed. and trans. Benedicta Ward in *Harlots of the Desert: a Study of Repentance in Early Monastic Sources*. London: Mowbray, 1987.

Vita Thaisis Meretricis (Life of Thais the Harlot). *PL* 73.661–62. Ed. and trans. Benedicta Ward in *Harlots of the Desert: a Study of Repentance in Early Monastic Sources*. London: Mowbray, 1987.

SECONDARY SOURCES

Achelis, Hans (1902), *Virgines Subintroductae: Ein Beitrag zum VII Kapitel des I Korintherbriefs*. Leipzig: J. C. Hinrichs.

—— (1926), 'Agapetae', *Encyclopedia of Religion and Ethics*, Hastings, James, ed. New York: 1.177.

Bailey, Derrick Sherwin (1959), *The Man–Woman Relation in Christian Thought*. London: Longmans.

Balsdon, J. V. P. (1962, revised 1974), *Roman Women: their History and Habits*. London: Bodley Head.

Barnes, T. D. (1971), *Tertullian: A Historical and Literary Study*. Oxford: Clarendon Press.

Bonner, G. (1963), *St. Augustine of Hippo – Life and Controversies*. Library of History and Doctrine, London: SCM Press.

Bremmer, J. (1989), 'Why did early Christianity attract upper-class women?' In Bastiensen, A. A. R. *et al*. eds. *Fructus Centesimus: Mélanges offerts à Gérard J. M. Bartelink*, Steenbrugge, in Abbatia S. Petri: 117–34.

Brock, Sebastian P. and Harvey, Susan A. eds. (1987), *Holy Women of The Syrian Orient*. California: University of California Press.

Brown, Peter (1961), 'Aspects of the Christianisation of the Roman Aristocracy'. *JRS* 51:1–11; also in Brown (1961) *Religion and Society* (q.v.) 183–207.

—— (1967), *Augustine of Hippo*. London: Faber & Faber.

—— (1970), 'The Patrons of Pelagius: the Roman aristocracy between East and West'. *JTS* 21:56–72; also in Brown (1961) *Religion and Society* (q.v.) 208–26.

—— (1971) 'The rise and function of the holy man in late antiquity'. *JRS* 61.

—— (1977), *Religion and Society in the Age of Saint Augustine*. London: Faber & Faber.

—— (1981), *The Cult of the Saints*. Chicago: University of Chicago Press.

—— (1987), 'Late Antiquity' in Paul Veyne ed. (1987) (q.v.) *A History of Private Life* 1:235–313.

—— (1988), *The Body in Society: Men, Women and Sexual Renunciation in Early Christianity*. New York: Columbia University Press.

Budge, E. A. Wallis (1934). *Stories of the Holy Fathers*. London: Oxford University Press.

Cameron, Averil and Kuhrt, Amélie, eds (1983), *Images of Women in Late Antiquity*. Detroit: Wayne State University Press.

Cameron, Averil (1980), 'Neither Man nor Woman'. *Greece and Rome* 27:60–68.

—— (1989) 'Virginity as Metaphor' in Cameron. A., ed. *History as Text* London: Duckworth, 181–205.

Cantarella, Eva (1987), *Pandora's Daughters: the Role and Status of Women in Greek and Roman Antiquity* (trans. from the Italian by Maureen B. Fant with an introduction by Mary Lefkowitz). Baltimore and London: Johns Hopkins University Press.

Church, F. F. (1975), 'Sex and Salvation in Tertullian'. *Harvard Theological Review* 68:83–101.

Clark, Elizabeth A. (1977), 'John Chrysostom and the Subintroductae'. *Church History* 46:171–85.

—— (1979), *Jerome Chrysostom and Friends: Essays and Translations*. New York: Edwin Mellen Press.

—— (1983a), *Women in the Early Church*. Delaware: Michael Glazier.

—— (1983b), Introduction in *John Chrysostom: On Virginity, Against Remarriage*, trans. Sally Rieger Shore (q.v.), *Studies in Women and Religion*, 9; Lewiston, Edwin Mellen Press, vii–xvii.

—— (1984) *The Life of Melania the Younger*. Lewiston, *Studies in Women and Religion*, vol. 14: Edwin Mellen Press.

—— (1986) *Ascetic Piety and Women's Faith*. New York: Edwin Mellen Press.

Clark, Gillian (1993), *Women in Late Antiquity: Pagan and Christian Lifestyles*. Oxford: Clarendon Press

Courcelle, P. (1968), *Récherches sur les Confessions de S. Augustin*. Paris: de Boccard.

Coyle, J. Kevin (1982), 'In Praise of Monica: a note on the Ostia experience of Confessions IX'. *Augustinian Studies* 13:87–96.

Craik, Elizabeth M., ed. (1984), *Marriage and Property*. Aberdeen: Aberdeen University Press.

Daniélou, Fr. Jean, S.J. (1961), *The Ministry of Women in the Early Church* (trans. Glyn Simon). Leighton Buzzard: Faith Press.

Dixon, Suzanne (1988), *The Roman Mother*. London: Croom Helm.

Dudden, F. Homes, (1935), *The Life and Times of St. Ambrose*. Oxford: Clarendon Press.

Ferrari, Leo Charles (1979), 'The Dreams of Monica in Augustine's Confessions'. *Augustinian Studies*, 10:3–18.

Fiorenza, Elizabeth Schüssler, (1979), 'Women in the early Christian movement'. In Christ, Carol P., ed. *Womanspirit Rising*. San Francisco: Harper & Row.

Foley, Helene P., ed. (1981), *Reflections of Women in Antiquity*. New York: Gordon & Breach.

Gardner, Jane (1986), *Women in Roman Law and Society*. London and Sidney: Croom Helm.

—— and Thomas Wiedemann (1991), *The Roman Household: A Sourcebook*. London: Routledge.

Gould, G. (1990), 'Women in the writings of the Fathers: language, belief and reality'. In W. J. Sheils, W. J. and Woods, D., eds. *Women and the Church*, Studies in Church History, 27. Oxford: Blackwell, 1–13.

Harnack, A. (1895) *Sources of the Apostolic Canons*. London.

Harries, Jill D. (1984), '"Treasures in heaven': property and inheritance among senators of late Rome'. In Craik, E. M., ed. (q.v.) 54–70.

Harvey, Susan A. (1990), *Aseticism and Society in Crisis: John of Ephesus and the Lives of the Eastern Saints*. Berkeley: University of California Press.

Holum, Kenneth G. (1982), *Theodosian Empresses: Women and Imperial Dominion in Late Antiquity*. Berkeley and Los Angeles: University of California Press, 1982.

Hopkins, M. K. (1965), 'The age of Roman girls at marriage'. *Population Studies* 18:309–27.

—— (1966), 'On the probable age structure of the Roman population'. *Population Studies* 20:245–64.

Humbert, M. (1972), *Le Remariage à Rome: Étude d'histoire juridique et sociale*. Milan: Giuffré.

Hunt, E. D. (1972), 'St Silvia of Aquitaine: the role of a Theodosian pilgrim in the society of East and West'. *JTS* 23:351–73.

—— (1973), 'Palladius of Helenopolis: A party and its supporters in the church of the fourth century'. *JTS* 24:456–80.

—— (1982), *Holy Land Pilgrimage in the Later Roman Empire AD 312–460*. Oxford: Oxford University Press 1982.

Hunter, D. G. (1987), 'Resistance to the virginal ideal in late fourth century Rome: the case of Jovinian'. *Theological Studies* 48:45–64.

Jones, A. H. M. (1959), 'Were ancient heresies national or social movements in disguise?' *JTS* 10:280–98.

—— (1963), 'The social background of the struggle between paganism and Christianity'. In Momigliano, A. ed. (1963) (q.v.), 17–37.

—— (1964), *The Later Roman Empire*. Oxford: Basil Blackwell.

Kelly, W.N.D. (1975), *Jerome: His Life, Writings and Controversies*. London: Duckworth.

Klawiter, Frederick C. (1980), 'The role of martyrdom and persecution in developing the priestly authority of women in early Christianity: A Case-study of Montanism'. *Church History* 49:251–61.

Kraemer, Ross Shepard (1988), *Maenads, Martyrs, Matrons, Monastics: A Sourcebook on Women's Religions in the Greco-Roman World*. Philadelphia: Fortress Press.

—— (1992), *Her Share of the Blessings: Women's Religions Among Pagans, Jews and Christians in the Greco-Roman World*. Oxford: Oxford University Press.

Labriolle, Pierre de (1921), 'Le "Mariage Spirituel" dans l'antiquité Chrétienne', *Revue Historique* 137:204–25.

Lane Fox, Robin (1988), *Pagans and Christians*. Harmondsworth: Penguin.

Lefkowitz, Mary (1976), 'The motivations for St Perpetua's martyrdom'. *JAAR* 44:417–421; also in Lefkowitz (1981) *Heroines and Hysterics* (q.v.)

—— (1981), *Heroines and Hysterics*. London: Duckworth.

—— and Fant, Maureen B. (1982), *Women's Life in Greece and Rome: A Sourcebook*. London: Duckworth.

Loveren, A. E. D. van (1982), 'Once again: "The monk and the martyr": St Antony and St Macrina'. *Studia Patristica* vol. 17, pt 1:528–38. Oxford: Pergamon.

MacDonald, D. Ronald (1983), *The Legend and the Apostle: the Battle for Paul in Story and Canon*. Philadelphia: Westminster Press.

McNamara, Jo Ann (1979), 'Wives and widows in early Christian theology'. *International Journal of Women's Studies* 2:575–92.

—— (1985), *A New Song: Celibate Women in the First Three Christian Centuries*. New York: Harrington Park Press.

Meeks, Wayne (1974), 'The Image of the Androgyne: some uses of a symbol in earliest Christianity'. *History of Religions* 13:165–208.

Momigliano, Arnaldo, ed. (1963), *The Conflict Between Paganism and Christianity in the Fourth Century*. Oxford: Clarendon Press.

—— (1985), 'The Life of St Macrina by Gregory of Nyssa'. In Eadie, John W. and Ober, Josiah, eds, *The Craft of the Ancient Historian: Essays in Honour of Chester G. Starr*. University Press of America: 443–58.

Murphy, Francis X. (1947), 'Melania the Elder: a biographical note'. *Traditio* 5:52–77.

Musurillo, H. (1956) 'The problem of ascetical fasting in the Greek patristic writers'. *Traditio* 12:1–64.

—— (1972) *Acts of the Christian Martyrs*. Oxford: Clarendon Press.

O'Meara, John J. (1980), *The Young Augustine*. London: Longmans.

Pomeroy, Sarah B. (1973), 'A selected bibiography on women in antiquity'. *Arethusa* 6:123–57.

—— (1975), *Goddesses, Whores, Wives and Slaves: Women in Classical Antiquity*. New York: Schocken Books.

—— (1976), 'The relationship of the married woman to her blood relations in Rome'. *Ancient Society* 7:215–27.

Rawson, Beryl, ed. (1991), *Marriage, Divorce and Children in Ancient Rome*. Oxford: Oxford University Press.

Richlin, Amy (1981), 'Approaches to the sources on adultery at Rome'. In Foley, H., ed. 1981:379–404.

Rousseau, Philip (1978), *Ascetics, Authority and the Church in the Age of Jerome and Cassian*. Oxford: Oxford University Press.

Rousselle, Aline (1988), *Porneia: On Desire and the Body in Antiquity* (trans. Felicia Pheasant). Oxford: Basil Blackwell.

Ruether, Rosemary (1969), *Gregory of Nazianzus: Rhetor and Philosopher*. Oxford: Clarendon Press.

—— and Eleanor McLaughlin (1979), *Women of Spirit: Female Leadership in the Jewish and Christian Traditions*. New York: Simon and Schuster.

Saller, R. (1987), 'Men's age at marriage and its consequences in the Roman family'. *CPh* 82:21–34.

—— and Garnsey, P. (1987), *The Roman Empire: Economy, Society and Culture*. California: Berkeley.

Salzmann, M. R. (1989), 'Aristocratic women: conductors of Christianity in the fourth century'. *Helios* 16/2:207–20.

Shaw, Brent D. (1987a), 'The age of Roman girls at marriage: some reconsiderations'. *JRS* 77:30–46.

—— (1987b), 'The family in late antiquity: the experience of Augustine'. *Past and Present* 115:3–51.

Shore, Sally Rieger, (1983), *John Chrysostom: On Virginity, Against Remarriage*. Studies in Women and Religion, 9. Lewiston, Edwin Mellen Press.

Treggiari, Susan (1975), 'Jobs in the Houshold of Livia'. *PBSR* 43:48–77.

—— (1976), 'Jobs for women'. *AJAH* 1:76–104.

—— (1979), 'Lower class women in the Roman economy'. *Florilegium* 1:65–86.

—— (1981), 'Concubinae'. *PBSR* 49:59–81.

—— (1991), *Roman Marriage: Iusti Coniuges from the Time of Cicero to the Time of Ulpian*. Oxford: Clarendon Press.

Veyne, Paul, ed. (1987), *A History of Private Life* vol. 1, From Pagan Rome to Byzantium (trans. Arthur Goldhammer). Cambridge, Mass.: Belknap Press of Harvard University Press.

Walzer, Richard (1949), *Galen on Jews and Christians*. Oxford: Oxford University Press.

Ward, Benedicta (1975a), *The Sayings of the Desert Fathers: The Alphabetical Collection*. Oxford: Mowbrays.

—— (1975b), *The Wisdom of the Desert Fathers: Apophthegmata Patrum from the Anonymous Series*. Oxford: SLG Press.

—— (1985), 'Apophthegmata Matrum'. *Studia Patristica* vol. 16, pt. 2:63–6.

—— (1987), *Harlots of the Desert: A Study of Repentance in Early Monastic Sources*. London: Mowbray.

Wilson-Kastner, Patricia *et al.* (1981), *Lost Traditions: Women Writers of the Early Church*. University Press of America.

BIBLIOGRAPHY

Wilkinson, John (1971), *Egeria's Travels*. London: SPCK.
Whitby, Michael (1987), 'Maro the Dendrite: an anti-social holy man?' In Whitby, Michael, Hardie, Philip, Whitby, Mary, eds *Homo Viator: Classical Essays for John Bramble*. Bristol: Classical Press, 309–17.
Yarbrough, Anne (1976), 'Christianisation in the fourth century: the example of Roman women'. *Church History* 45:149–65.

INDEX

238

INDEX

Ausonius 129, 160
Avita 50, 66, 97, 127, 153

Bacchic rites 115
Basil of Ancyra 22, 61–2, 97
Basil of Caesarea (– the Great) 18,
    22–3, 64, 69, 112–13, 134, 138–9,
    144, 168
Bassula 175, 215
Benedict (St) 175
Benenatus (priest) 63–4
Benigna 83
Bessarion (Abba) 194, 197
Blesilla (daughter of Paula) 20, 54,
    58, 67, 86, 94, 114, 123, 135, 171
Bona Dea 160
Boniface (Count of Africa) 133, 154
Bosporia 144
Brutus 105

Callixtus (pope) 106
Carterius 138
celibacy 28, 33, 38–43, 48, 55, 101,
    104, 121–2, 126–7
Celsus (son of Paulinus of
    Nola) 123
children: difficulties
    concerning 34, 41,
    87, 125–6, 134, 172
Cicero 102, 137, 139
circumcellions 43
Clement of Alexandria 22, 32, 39,
    89, 104
Clementinus 95
coenobitism 8, 165
commerce 159–60, 162
concubines 52, 105–7, 154–5, 216
contemplative ideal 65, 191–2
conversion of men by
    women 116, 183–4
councils, church 78, 206–7
Cybele 55
Cyprian (bishop) 210

deaconesses 89, 91, 188, 205–210
Demetrias 17, 19, 22, 42–3, 50, 52,
    58, 60, 61, 65, 66, 68–70, 84, 98,
    123, 151
demonic possession 77

diakonos, Phoebe referred to
    as 26, 206
Didascalia Apostolorum (Teaching
    of the Apostles) 90
Dido 85
disorderly women 43–4, 86, 88
Donatus 9
Donatism 11, 43, 76
Doulas (monk) 194

Ecdicia 38, 42, 128–133, 149–50, 155
education 136–140
Egeria 13, 165–6, 209–10
Elias (Abba) 73
Elisanthia 173, 209
Elpidius 95
emancipation 157–8, 161–2
Emmelia (mother of Gregory of
    Nyssa and Macrina) 18, 40,
    67, 98, 113–14, 144, 165
Epictetus 107–8
Epiphanius 9, 43, 93, 154, 164, 170
Ephraim 74–5, 205, 219
Eucharisticos the Secular 127
Eudocia (empress) 13–14, 172, 184
Eudoxia (empress) 183
eunuchs 62, 97
Eunomia 50, 66, 97–8, 153
Eusebia (deaconess) 208
Eustathius of Sebaste (heretic) 44
Eustochium (Julia Eustochia) 15,
    20, 50, 52–4, 58, 63, 66–7, 69, 79,
    96, 98, 114, 123, 126, 140, 148; at
    Bethlehem convent, 169, 171–5
Evagrius Ponticus 176, 192
Eve 63, 117, 122, 142, 155, 212
Evodius 90
exposure of infants, 48

Fabiola 20, 32, 107, 119
family pressures on ascetic
    women 35–7, 49–50,
    79–80, 119–20, 145–6
fasting 65, 93–4, 141, 170–1,
    187, 190
Felicia (nun) 76
femininity 43, 68, 80, 120–1, 127,
    213–5
fornication 122, 131, 195, 218

239